BEING A ROMAN CITIZEN

Jane F. Gardner

London and New York

First published 1993
by Routledge
11 New Fetter Lane, London EC4P 4EE

Simultaneously published in the USA and Canada
by Routledge
29 West 35th Street, New York, NY 10001

© 1993 Jane F. Gardner

Phototypeset in 10 on 12 point Garamond by Intype, London

Printed in Great Britain by T.J. Press (Padstow) Ltd, Padstow, Cornwall

British Library Cataloguing in Publication Data

Gardner, Jane F.
Being a Roman Citizen
I. Title
323.60937

Library of Congress Cataloging in Publication Data

Gardner, Jane F.
Being a Roman citizen / Jane F. Gardner
p.   cm.
Includes bibliographical references and index.
1. Citizenship – Rome.   2. Capacity and disability (Roman law).
3. Roman law – Popular works.   4. Romans – Social life and customs.
5. Rome – Social life and customs.   I. Title
KJA2930.G37   1993
340.5'9—dc20   92–29382
ISBN 0–415–00154–4

CONTENTS

PREFACE

This book has been a long time gestating. It proved rather more difficult to write than I had anticipated, since I soon discovered that few writings by lawyers on Roman law attempted the kind of analysis in which I was interested, and then only over a limited area and in insufficient depth, while historians, if they discussed Roman law at all, on the whole were content not to go beyond straightforward description of certain central areas. Richard Stoneman of Routledge has shown remarkable patience and forbearance as deadlines came and went, and for this I am grateful to him. I am grateful also to numerous others who have helped in a variety of ways, by discussion, bibliographical help, sending offprints, access to their unpublished work, and so on. I am sure I shall omit to mention some, and ask their forgiveness in advance; but thanks especially to Antti Arjava, Keith Bate, Keith Bradley, John Crook, Catharine Edwards, Andrew Fear, Andrew Lewis, Fergus Millar, Philippe Moreau, Hanne Sigismund Nielsen, John Richardson, Boudewijn Sirks, Susan Treggiari, Paul Weaver and Thomas Wiedemann. My use of what I learned from them may occasionally surprise, but I hope will not offend them.

Reading, June 1992

ABBREVIATIONS

For periodicals I have followed the conventions of *L'Année Philologique*, with the following exceptions (*AP* version in brackets):

RHDFE	*Revue historique de droit français et étranger* (*RD*)
ZSS	*Zeitschrift der Savigny-Stiftung für Rechtsgeschichte, romanistische Abteilung* (*ZRG*)

Other abbreviations (excluding those for classical authors):

AE	*Année Epigraphique*
ANRW	*Aufstieg und Niedergang der römischen Welt*, ed. Temporini.
CIL	*Corpus Inscriptionum Latinarum*
CJ	*Codex Justinianus*
C.Th.	*Codex Theodosianus*
D.	*Digest*
Eph. Epigr.	*Ephemeris Epigraphica*
FIRA	*Fontes Iuris Romani Ante-Iustiniani*, ed. Riccobono, Baviera, Arangio Ruiz.
Frag. Dosith.	*Fragmentum Dositheanum*
Gaius	Gaius' *Institutes*
ILS	*Inscriptiones Latinae Selectae*, ed. H. Dessau.
Inst.	Justinian's *Institutes*
Paul Sent.	Julius Paulus' *Sententiae*
RE	Pauly-Wissowa, *Real-Encyclopädie*
Tab. Herc.	*The Herculaneum Tablets*, ed. Arangio Ruiz and Pugliese Carratelli in *PdP* between 1946 and 1955.
TP	*Tabulae Pompeianae* from Murecine, Pompeii.
Ulp. Reg.	The Rules of Ulpian.

1

THE DISABILITIES OF ROMAN CITIZENS

What was a Roman citizen? Answers to the question can follow a number of different lines of approach. One which is currently very influential is via the examination of the characteristics of Roman society and life in 'Roman' communities; the emphasis is not so much on citizenship as on 'Romanness'. The definition of 'Roman' can be constructed, for example, by reference to the foreign, Hellenic model, cultural and also institutional, which the Romans both infiltrated and dominated, and at the same time absorbed and assimilated. It is possible therefore to study the subject from two angles, i.e. the 'Hellenisation' of the Romans, or the 'Romanisation' of their Eastern empire and its neighbours.

Another approach is to concentrate on Roman citizenship as a political phenomenon, usually with particular regard to the citizen in relation to the state and its authorities. This can follow two paths. So, for example, the emphasis of Sherwin-White (1973) is on the historical process of extension of the Roman citizenship, and his study is primarily concerned with the admission of communities or individuals from outside to share in Roman political life.

The actual workings of political institutions themselves, and the participation required of the individual citizen, can also be the object of study. Nicolet (1980) considers the adult male citizen only, and in three main areas of his participation in the public life of the state at Rome in the Republic: military, financial and fiscal, and comitial (i.e. electoral and legislative). He discusses the differences between individual citizens specifically in relation to these functions, and only briefly and generally.

This approach, obviously, is not one which can be continued in quite the same terms into the imperial period, after the decay

1

of the comitia. Its place, however, can be and is being fruitfully taken by study of the workings of local governmental institutions. The importance of the epigraphic evidence from Spain of the adoption or imposition of Roman institutions in the provinces has long been recognised, for the light this sheds on the character of Roman citizenship itself, and the publication of the recent find from Irni (Gonzalez 1986) has provided additional material. For the late empire, Jones (1964) provided the basis for much later work on the changes in the relationship between the state and the individual, especially as mediated through local institutions.

However, those political rights and duties of citizens in which studies like the ones mentioned above are interested, rights some of which changed or even disappeared over the course of time, belonged at any given period only to a portion of those individuals entitled to be called Roman citizens. Some citizens never had them, others acquired or lost them in the course of a single lifetime. The second half of Sherwin-White's book is concerned almost exclusively with the admission of outsiders to Roman citizenship, and, as he observes (1973: 267), by the middle of the second century AD the political content of the citizenship to which they were admitted, as far as concerns public duties or public honours, had been whittled down. 'There should be left, as the core and heart of citizenship, the social status which it conferred, the *iura privata* affecting the family and its uniform subjection to Roman law, and so forth.'

It is this 'core and heart' which I think deserves closer investigation. What was it like to be a private Roman citizen? What were these *iura privata*, private rights? This takes us into the realm of civil law, and it is with the legal capacity and disabilities of Roman citizens that this book will be concerned.

At once, however, one runs headlong into the difficulty that there is no single answer that will apply to all citizens. On the other hand, although there are striking differences between the legal capacities of various groups of citizens, it is not immediately obvious whether there is any clear-cut principle of division that will account for all of these differentiations between citizens.[1] This does not, of course, necessarily mean that there is no such principle, merely that it is not explicitly set out in the legal sources. This could be because it is in the main implicit, since its origins lie in a period earlier than our first documentary evidence.

Nor is it clear whether Roman citizens can be separated neatly, on any particular principle, into distinct groups with distinctly different rights. The problem presents itself immediately when one turns to legal sources for definitions of legal status. The distinctions drawn in the first book of Gaius' *Institutes* appear fundamental, but we soon find complications. Although he appears to set up certain basic principles of categorisation, each presented in the form of polar oppositions, these cannot be straightforwardly applied, since from the start more than one category level is involved. However, one can perhaps discern, among his bases of distinction, birth and 'power'; to these we may add gender, since (virtually) everyone is either male or female.[2]

By 'power', I mean whether one is subject to the power (*potestas*) of another person or not, and by 'birth', whether a citizen was freeborn or not. On birth, Gaius says (*Inst.* 1.9–11):

> The principal distinction in the law of persons is this, that all men are either free or slaves. Next, of free men some are *ingenui* (freeborn), others *libertini* (freed). The freeborn are those born free (*liberi*); the freed are those manumitted, from lawful slavery.

Already, however, we are running into complexities, for Gaius goes on to tell us that not all freedmen are Roman citizens. Some are Latins, who can become Roman citizens, others are *dediticii*, who cannot. Nor (though this is not germane to Gaius' exposition) are his definitions of *ingenui* and *libertini* sufficiently precise. Some Roman citizens were in fact born free, but not as citizens, and these included not only free foreigners granted citizenship, but also freed slaves. The latter were not accounted as *ingenui*, though they may in fact have been born free. Roman law takes no account of this, since as slaves they had no personal legal existence; the period of slavery produces a discontinuity and their original free birth is lost sight of.

Moreover, a second principle of division is presently introduced (1.48), which cuts across the first. Some persons are in a state of dependence, legally subject to the power, *potestas*, of others, and are *alieni iuris* (dependent on another), while others are legally independent (*sui iuris*). However, those legally dependent include both free and slave. Sons (and sons' children) and daughters of a living father count as freeborn but are in his *potestas*; the practical legal consequences of this for them (and for him) will be discussed in Chapter 3. His slaves are also in his *potestas*, but are not freeborn. So, some free persons are subject to legal controls to which slaves also are subject, and some free persons can have *potestas* over other free persons. Here, possibly, is yet another principle of division, namely gender, for women can hold *potestas*, but only over slaves, not over free persons. This difference between women and men, as holders of *potestas*, is very important, as we shall see in Chapter 4.

However, this apparent principle of division according to gender also cuts across the categories set up by the previous two, because, as we soon realise, some men and some women have no independent legal capacity, being *alieni iuris*, i.e. subject to power, while others, men *and* women, are independent, *sui iuris*. This distinction in turn has nothing to do with whether they are freeborn or freed; all freed slaves (of either sex) are *sui iuris*.

It becomes evident that a distinction based on liability to *potestas* is too simplistic; and if we turn our attention away for a moment from Gaius' exposition in what was, after all, meant only as a basic handbook of Roman civil law, back to the political aspects of citizenship, we realise that here being in *potestas* is not a relevant criterion. Women cannot vote or hold office, regardless of whether they are in power or not, and freedmen cannot hold office, yet men subject to *potestas* can do both. Nevertheless, they do not have the power of independent legal action that women *sui iuris* and freedmen have. Both the latter, however, also have less than complete legal capacity, compared with a freeborn Roman man who is not in someone's *potestas*. He is, technically, a *paterfamilias* (head of household, whether he has children or not), and can have *patria potestas*, and it might begin to look as if only a *paterfamilias* is 'really' a Roman citizen (until we remember that a male freedman is also a *paterfamilias* and can have *potestas* over others).

All of these other people are none the less Roman citizens, and our enquiries will be directed towards discovering, first, what the particular legal disabilities are under which each group labours, and second, whether and how these can be related to the peculiarly Roman institution of *patria potestas*. Third, the practical implications for the lives of each group will be investigated. These enquiries will have the effect of exposing some mistaken notions (not all of them previously recognised) about the *raison d'être* of the legal disabilities peculiar, respectively, to freedmen, children in power and women.

Also citizens are those people whose behaviour has lost them some of the legal rights enjoyed by other citizens. These are the *infames*, considered at length in Chapter 5. Curiously, though the diminution of their rights is connected with something in them which is regarded as morally blameworthy, the actual legal handicaps they suffer are suffered also by certain other people, such as women, irrespective of whether or not the latter have incurred any moral blame. More curiously still, physical as well as mental handicap carries consequences for an individual's personal control of his own life which go beyond practical physical inconveniences, and even impossibilities, and can affect others besides the sufferers themselves in ways that seem unexpected to us. The blind, deaf and dumb, as well as the insane, will be considered in Chapter 6.

Patria potestas is a relevant factor in all these chapters, although in different ways and to differing extent. So also, to some extent, is the requirement among the Romans that certain transactions be conducted personally, by individuals who are physically present. This has effects on the lives of people in all our groups, especially those considered in Chapters 3, 5 and 6. Ways are found of coping with the practical inconveniences this can cause, but it is not simply disposed of, other than in a few instances and in late law, which suggests that some value was attached to it by the Romans. The same is true of the three principles of categorisation, by birth, gender and dependence. Although their legally defined content and consequences for the individual change over time, they appear fundamental throughout the history of Roman society, and this, I shall be suggesting, is due to their derivation from a common central principle. A study of these changes may lead to a fuller understanding of the history of the Roman concept of citizenship. Recent writers (e.g. Alföldy 1985: 202 ff. and de Ste Croix 1981: 453 ff.) have drawn attention to the blurring in the late empire of the distinction, at the lower levels of society, between slave and free; even among the latter, however, to a considerable extent, and very evidently among the upper class, the basic structures of Roman family and property law remain unchanged.

As mentioned above, I anticipate that these investigations will have the effect of exposing the mistakenness of some assumptions – both ancient and modern – about the nature, and reasons for the persistence, of various legal disabilities to which certain groups of people are liable. We may question whether *patria potestas* was really felt to be a handicap, whether patrons were ideologically a 'master-class', and whether the reason for women having restricted legal capacity was that they were looked down on as emotionally unstable and intellectual weaklings. We may also achieve a clearer understanding of the differing significance of *infamia* in the technical–legal and lay uses of the term.

For this, it is particularly important to be quite clear as to what the actual practical effects of these disabilities were for the ordinary Roman's life. Roman law consists not only in rules, but also in cases, and it is that which makes it so valuable a source for the Roman social historian. Both aspects, however, must be considered. The rules taken alone give a false picture of the actual workings of the society, and of its attitudes; looking at the cases on their own runs the risk of misinterpretation or unjustified generalisation.[3] Together, however, they are of unequalled value for the insight they afford into the actual conduct and outlook of the Romans. That is why this is essentially a book about Roman law, meant for Roman historians.

2

BIRTH: THE FREEDMAN'S CONDITION

The fact has aroused comment, both in ancient and in modern times,[1] that, unlike the rest of the Greco-Roman world, the Romans normally gave slaves citizenship upon manumission. Not only that, but although the state through its magistrates had to be involved at some point for manumission to result in the creation of a new citizen, the initiative for manumission rested with an individual Roman, the slave's owner, and the rôle of the state's officers, for much of the history of the institution, appears to have amounted to little more than acquiescing in the owner's action, without imposing any restrictions or controls. The watershed is the reign of Augustus. Under the Republic, manumission without reference to a magistrate did not even confer juridical freedom; under the empire, from the reign of Augustus onwards, it did – but not citizenship. Under the Republic, owners were free to manumit any and as many slaves as they chose; the empire brought in restrictions on whom an owner might manumit. The reasons for these restrictions are not strictly 'political' in the Republican sense. The decay of the voting assemblies under the empire curtailed the individual citizen's opportunity for active participation in political life; the new restrictions are concerned more with social order and stability, and reveal a certain concern for the successful integration of the new citizen. Under the Republic, the state's officers do not appear to challenge the wish of an individual owner to have his slave admitted into the citizen body.

However, if one analyses the manumission procedures, it appears that what by the late Republic had become a formality originally had much more of the character of a decision authorised by the community.

CREATING A CITIZEN

(i) Of the three types of manumission, the state's involvement is most obviously political in manumission by entry in the census[2] of a slave whom his master had ordered to be free. 'In former times,' says Ulpian, 'those who on the instruction of their master presented themselves among Roman citizens at the lustral (i.e., notionally at least, five-yearly) census, were manumitted by census.' The master had to be willing to release his slave; equally, the state had to be willing to receive him.[3]

Though probably a method of considerable antiquity, this is unlikely ever to have been the commonest method of manumission in the Republic, since the census took place at best only every five years, and at Rome, and the whole process of the census could take up to eighteen months to complete. A legal commentator remarks:[4] 'There is great disagreement among legal experts as to whether everything takes effect at the time when the census is being made, or at the time when the review is formally concluded (*lustrum conditur*).' In the interim, although the individual might manage very well without exercising his political rights in Roman voting assemblies, or being liable to conscription,[5] lack of citizenship could have drawbacks in his private life. Indeed, he would probably not have juridical freedom, either, since the master's words alone could not confer that during the Republic. Manumission by census disappeared with the census itself, and probably before the census, since other more convenient methods were available.

A disputed question[6] is whether the censor declared that he was conferring citizenship on the former slave, or whether he employed the fiction that the person had always been a citizen. Since, under the Republic, the master's assertion of freedom alone did not make a slave free in law, but merely *de facto*,[7] the question seems inappropriate. It was up to the Roman state, in the person of the censors, to whom the state had delegated the power to draw up the citizen lists, to decide to grant them citizenship. The censors were acting on behalf of, and in virtue of, the authority voted to them by the Roman people.

(ii) In manumission *vindicta*, the common formal method of manumission during an owner's lifetime, the magistrate's presence is again necessary, but he is not the sole actor. The technical

reason for his presence was that the procedure took the form of
a collusive lawsuit, of the type known as *causa liberalis* (Buckland
1908: 716). A third party asserted that the slave was a free man,
and touched him with a rod (*vindicta*), so rejecting the owner's
claim to ownership; the owner offered no defence; the magistrate
then awarded the suit in favour of the plaintiff, and declared the
slave a free man.[8] The *causa liberalis* existed at least by the time
of the Twelve Tables, and was originally a *legis actio* (Gaius 4.14),
which meant that the decision took immediate effect.

By the time of the younger Pliny (and probably long before)
it is accepted that the lawsuit is a piece of make-believe. He writes
to his wife's grandfather (*Ep.* 7.16.4):

> Calestrius Tiro is about to set off to the province of Baetica
> as proconsul, going by way of Ticinum. I hope, or rather I
> am sure, that I will easily prevail upon him to make a detour
> on the way and visit you, if you want to manumit in proper
> form the slaves you recently manumitted before friends.

Gaius (*D.* 40.2.7) confirms that the venue need not even be a
court; manumissions are often performed when a magistrate is
visiting the baths, out driving, or at the games; he need not even
have his lictor present (Ulpian *D.* 40.2.8).

What is not immediately clear is why this piece of juristic play-
acting conferred citizenship as well as freedom. Watson (1975: 88
ff.) draws attention to the story in Livy 2.5, allegedly about the
first manumission *vindicta*. A slave, called in the story (for obvious
aetiological purposes) Vindicius, informed about a conspiracy to
restore the monarchy, and was rewarded with money, freedom,
and citizenship. 'The question to be answered [by the story]', says
Watson, 'is: why does a private act, *manumissio vindicta*, by an
owner have public consequences, namely citizenship, for the slave?
Answer: Because the first *manumissio vindicta* was at the wish of
the state which desired citizenship to be acquired by the manumitted slave.'

Livy (and Watson) do not specify the precise nature of what is
supposed to have happened on this (imaginary) occasion, but it
resembles a voting meeting, rather than a lawsuit. The traitors are
condemned and publicly executed before the consuls' tribunal.
Then, to enhance the effect of the execution as a deterrent, the
informer is granted his rewards – money from the treasury, freedom and citizenship – presumably by the consuls, alone or (more

likely) taking a vote in the assembly. However, as Watson points out, since the slave is said to have been freed *vindicta*, by touching with the rod, this should mean that he was freed by his master. Plutarch's version (*Publicola* 7.5) shows some awareness of the problem, since it talks of a decree being passed conferring citizenship upon Vindicius. We must apparently think of the manumission itself as having been performed by the slave's master – but acting on the wish of his fellow citizens.

All this is fiction, but the implied involvement of citizens other than the slave's owner in the decision perhaps gives a clue to an answer to the question. The ordinary *vindicta* procedure for manumission involves not just a Roman magistrate, but at least one other citizen as well, the *adsertor libertatis*, who claims on behalf of the slave (who has no power to act at law). The *adsertor*, like the slave's owner, would be a *pater*, a head of household. He, not the owner, asserts the slave's freedom, and the magistrate then pronounces in his favour. The whole charade could be viewed as a fossilised mini-assembly, with the *adsertor* symbolically asserting the people's will and so conferring freedom as well as citizenship on the erstwhile slave.[9]

(iii) The third mode of formal manumission was manumission by will (*testamento*). Making a will, in early Rome, was the exception, rather than the norm, and in fact required an actual assembly of the people. The *familia*, not only its property but its religious functions, was normally expected to pass automatically within the kin-group, to a man's children or, failing them, his agnates. Any variation from this procedure required the assent of the whole people, and for this purpose a special meeting, *comitia calata*, was summoned twice a year; in emergency, when battle was imminent, a similar procedure could be performed before the assembled army. These were not 'wills' in the ordinary sense; what the assembly did amounted to a specialised form of the adoption of a named heir by *adrogatio* (i.e. adoption of someone already a *pater* in his own right). To cover civilian emergencies, a more convenient and frequently available procedure developed, the *testamentum per aes et libram*, in which the legal procedure for transfer of ownership (*mancipatio*, formal sale) was used, with the heir as 'buyer' of the estate (*familiae emptor*).[10] Five other adult citizens, besides the testator and his heir, had to be present as witnesses, plus one to hold the scales used in the ceremony.

In its original form, this can scarcely have permitted of specific transactions such as manumissions; it was merely a prospective transfer of ownership of the entire estate. However, it was the ancestor of the classical will. Testators began to give specific instructions to the *familiae emptor* for disposal of the estate; the *familiae emptor* himself ceased to be identical with the heir and became merely a formal participant in the ceremony of *mancipatio*; even the ceremony, it has been suspected (see Chapter 6, p.166), came to be taken as performed, and merely written into the will (though witnesses were still required). This third form of primitive will, then, developed out of a procedure involving the full assembly of the Roman people, and itself required the participation of a total of seven other citizens, not to mention the praetor, to whom approach had to be made when the time came for the heir to seek implementation of the will.

So far, I have been talking about the *how*, and have argued that manumission, carrying with it citizenship, had to have, at least formally, the consent of the community. This is particularly clear in method (iii) in which the basic procedure originally used is *mancipatio*, which covers a variety of transactions by a head of household, not only will-making, but adoption, emancipation of children, and even buying and selling of certain types of property. What all of these have in common with each other, and with manumission *vindicta* and adoption by adrogation, is that they have a political dimension. They must interest the community at large, since they involve the very existence of the *familia*, which is the basic property and family unit recognised in the law of the Roman state. They put an end to an existing *familia* (adrogation), or start a new one (emancipation, manumission), or transfer one in entirety (testation), or transfer persons from one *familia* into another (ordinary adoption), all with consequences also for the *sacra*, the religious rights and obligations. There were some types of property whose full legal ownership could be transferred to a buyer only by *mancipatio* – namely, those basic for survival in an early agricultural community (Italian land and buildings on it, work animals, slaves) and so fundamental for the survival of a *familia*.

I have not yet tackled the much more difficult question of *why* the Roman community was willing, from the earliest times of which we have knowledge, to integrate freed slaves into the citizen body.

Sons, slaves and *mancipium*

A number of lines of approach may be followed. A status known to civil law was that of being *in mancipio* (civil bondage). In classical law, this is practically obsolete. It is found mostly as a transient and technical status arising during the processes of adoption or emancipation, and it could also arise with more substantial effect, for sons at least, through noxal surrender, i.e. when a father chose to surrender his son rather than pay the money penalty to which his son's wrongdoing rendered him liable.[11] In early Rome, however, it appears that it was used as an economic device; a father borrowing money from another person put his son into bondage to that person until the debt was paid off. If or when it was, the son was freed and returned into *potestas*[12].

Amirante (1981), noting the virtual identity in early Rome of the content of an owner's *potestas* over his slaves and that which he had as *pater* over his children, has argued that slavery and the status of being in bondage were originally identical; he goes further, and claims that a separate judicial category for 'slave' was not necessary. The distinction between 'free' and 'slave' within the *familia* was, he suggests, not originally one of civil law, but of *ius gentium* ('the law of all peoples, that is, the law which natural reason makes for all mankind', as contrasted with codes specific to particular peoples: Gaius 1.1).

Amirante's conclusions, although not the details of his argument, in the main correspond with those of de Martino (1974), although de Martino is concerned mainly with the supposed origins of slavery. De Martino starts from a similar premise. For him too, the only slaves in early Rome were citizens, namely debt-bondsmen and persons under punishment for delicts, such as theft, and slavery in early Rome was a very limited phenomenon. No comprehensive law of slavery was developed even by the Twelve Tables; therefore, he thinks, it is the wars of the fourth century which first link the notion of slave to that of prisoner of war, and manumission by census then appears, as part of a 'politics of unification' of Italy; de Martino assumes that the labour force is mainly made up of free men. Unfortunately, this reasoning is based on an *argumentum ex silentio* about the content of the Twelve Tables.

If there really was, as Amirante thinks, no juridical distinction between 'son' and 'slave', then the latter would naturally, like the former, become a citizen on release. Manumission *vindicta* and by will, at least, would then be neatly explicable as release from another's control ('ownership' perhaps begs the question) of persons in a sense *already* citizens; even census registration would admit of explanation along these lines.

There are, however, difficulties with theories based on these ideas. First, despite the resemblances between *potestas* over slaves and over sons, the differences between the two are considerable. There are also differences in the rules that apply to slaves and to sons in bondage.[13]

Sons have two ways out of *potestas*, slaves only one. Manumission alone frees a slave. The death of a *pater* automatically makes his children legally independent, but he may also 'emancipate' them during his lifetime. A son may, therefore, leave *potestas* entirely, by being emancipated by his *pater*, as slaves do when emancipated by their owners. If he is in bondage, however, he does not become free on release by his holder, like other slaves, but reverts to the *potestas* of his *pater*. Unlike slaves, sons not mancipated to others are released automatically at the father's death, and have rights of inheritance. Slaves, if not manumitted by the owner's will, simply pass into other ownership. Whether this is also true of bondsmen is unclear; the only text we have on the subject (Gaius 1.123) tells us that a legacy left to someone *in mancipio* by his holder is valid only if the bondsman is also freed by the will, but, as he emphasises (1.141), the status of bondage operative in his day was, except for noxal surrender, nominal and of momentary brevity (*dicis gratia uno momento*).

Most importantly, sons' marriages, whether they are in bondage or not, remain legally recognised (unlike those of slaves), and their children are free. The child of a slave belongs to the slave's owner; on the other hand, that born to a son in bondage[14] is in the *potestas* of the son's *pater*, not his holder. The power of the *pater* has not been entirely relinquished. Whether a son is in bondage or not, at his death or release his child does not remain in the power of the person who held its father (Gaius 1.135); a slave's does. So a conflict of *potestates* can arise, because of the preexisting legal status in the Roman community of the bondsman; a slave, however, is liable only to the *potestas* of his owner. 'The law of all peoples' (*ius gentium*) alone is insufficient to explain these distinctions.

Second, we cannot be sure that as sources of slaves warfare, or other means such as purchase or breeding, were not at least as old as the 'institution of giving sons in bondage. The supposed right, in early Rome, of a father to sell his son into slavery 'across the Tiber', if it existed, would surely indicate, first, that the condition of slavery was not identical to that of being in bondage and, second, that there existed in Rome also actual slaves, who were not the sons of other Romans, held in bondage, and were juridically distinct from them. When the Tiber marked the boundary of the primitive state, it was permissible for a father to sell his childen as slaves only to foreigners; he could not sell them in the same way within Rome.[15]

Are we to suppose, then, that the early Romans themselves used no slaves of external origin, only other Romans' sons in bondage? This does not seem plausible; and even if at one time all their slaves had been Romans in bondage, we should still have to explain why, later, slaves of non-Roman origin should have been admitted to citizenship on manumission.

War and slaves

Dumont (1987: 77 ff.) regards war as the basic source of slaves in the early Republic. The assimilation of the conquered, by slavery and subsequent manumission, accompanied by naturalisation of freedmen, was a response to Rome's problems of declining population; the connection with population level was made, he observes, by Philip V. Though he is writing mainly in the context of the wars of the late third century BC and later, he cites also Dio 56.7.6: king Servius is said to have given citizenship to manumitted slaves so that their offspring could add to the military manpower of Rome (a motive which reflects rather the concerns of government policy in Dio's own time).[16] There was, Dumont says, a constant passage, on a large scale, from slavery into citizenship. Imported slaves were necessary to supplement the inadequate manpower of the primitive community and ensure its survival. Their slave status was a temporary stage, a *propaideutikon* to liberty (and citizenship); the slave was a 'virtual' citizen. Unfortunately, there is no evidence to support such a theory. There is no justification for assuming that slavery at Rome was regarded as temporary, and manumission within a limited time a matter of course.[17] Manumission was for the individual owner to accord, or not, as he saw fit.

However, it is appropriate that Dumont directs attention to the shortage of manpower in early Rome, illustrated for us in the stories of the literary sources. In these accounts, this shortage of manpower explains the relative openness and accessibility of Roman citizenship to free outsiders, down at least to 338 BC.[18] Its extension also to ex-slaves needs further elucidation.

Neighbours as slaves

Sherwin-White (1973: 323–4) expresses his own view succinctly. The ethnic identity between archaic Romans and their earliest enemies, both being Latins, created institutions such as *postliminium* (resumption of rights on return to one's homeland) and exchange of citizenship by change of residence between different Latin communities. Freed slaves (i.e. Latin prisoners of war) therefore had the option of returning to their home territories and resuming citizenship there, or remaining at Rome and registering in the census as Roman citizens. This practice then spread to non-Latin freedmen from other Italian peoples.

How early the Romans and others had a formal right to change citizenship by changing domicile within the communities in their number is uncertain, but literary evidence provides support for belief in the willingness of the earliest Romans to admit free foreigners, not only from Latium but from Tyrrhenian central Italy, to the city and to citizenship. In the regnal period, this included two of the seven kings (Numa and Tarquinius Priscus), the Sabine king Titus Tatius and the supposed ancestor of the Claudian house, Attius Clausus.[19] On Sherwin-White's view, the freed slave did not automatically become a Roman citizen, unless he stayed in Rome; when he returned to his native state, he had the benefit *of postliminium*, that is, he recovered his original status there.[20]

BIRTH AND STATUS

It is assumed in Sherwin-White's account that originally the slaves manumitted were all prisoners of war. However, the possibility that there were in early Rome some *vernae* (homeborn slaves) should not too lightly be dismissed (see n. 16). Did free birth matter, then or later, in establishing either the political-legal capacity of the freedman, or his social acceptance?

15

Distinguishing freed and free

There are one or two pieces of evidence which indicate that in early Rome the distinction between born slaves and enslaved free men may have been of relatively little importance so far as their receiving membership of the citizen body was concerned. Gellius (*NA* 5.19.11–14) cites a jurist of the reign of Tiberius:

> Masurius Sabinus has written that freedmen (*libertinos*) can lawfully be adopted by freeborn men (*ab ingenuis*); but he says that it is not, nor should it be, permitted that men of freed status should by means of adoptions usurp the legal rights of freeborn men. Otherwise, he says, if this ancient regulation were to be preserved, even a slave could be given for adoption by his master through the praetor; and this he says many authorities on ancient law wrote was possible.

(One of these 'ancient authorities', according to Justinian's *Institutes* (1.11.12) was the elder Cato.)

According to Masurius, adoption had at one time removed the status distinction between freeborn and freed; he apparently believed that there had later been a change.[21]

We have no further direct evidence for such a change as this, but there are other indications that less importance had at one time been attached to the distinction between freeborn and freed than to certain other distinctions within the citizen body.[22]

The word *ingenuus* has two common meanings in classical Latin. In the technical sense it is used in distinction from 'freed' (*libertus/libertinus*), and as defined by Gaius in the second century AD it means 'born free'. The earliest text in which the two are explicitly contrasted is Plautus *Mil.* 784: *ingenuamne an libertam?* The other sense, found in Cicero and later writers,[23] indicates nobility of character, perhaps thought of as 'worthy of a free man', in contrast to 'servile'. It seems rather incongruous to find freed slaves who have it as a *cognomen* (and may have borne it as a slave name); e.g. *CIL* VI. 11995, *C. Antonio C. l. Ingenuo patronus l. bono*; 14516, *fecit Cassia Ingenua patrono*.

However, the use of *ingenuus* specifically of free birth may not be its original significance. Livy (10.8.10) gives a fanciful etymology for the word *patricios: qui patrem ciere possent, id est, ingenuos*, ('those who can name their father, that is, the *ingenui*'). The context, however, is not about freedmen, but a speech purporting to have been delivered in 300 BC on a proposal to admit plebeians to the priesthood. The etymology apart, Livy's definition equates *ingenuus* with *patricius*, and according to Festus 241, Cincius (presumably L. Cincius Alimentus, *floruit* c.210 BC) said in his book on the voting assemblies (*comitia*) that *patricii* was the term originally used for *ingenui*.

This may reflect the earlier usage of *in-genuus*, someone 'born inside' the exclusive circle of the Roman patriciate, rather than someone of free birth. The undifferentiated mass of outsiders, plebeians and ex-slaves alike, had no access to political office. Once this became open to plebeians, what mainly differentiated the potential magistrate from the rest was free birth rather than patrician birth, and *ingenuus* took on its more specific meaning 'freeborn', or, more accurately, 'not ex-slave'; thereafter, those becoming citizens from slavery (whether originally freeborn or not) continued to be denied access to the magistracies from which previously some other citizens had also been excluded on grounds of birth. When patricians monopolised government, it mattered less whether other citizens were Roman born, free immigrants or ex-slaves. The change is brought about by the success of the plebeian claim to access to office, rather than by any hardening of attitudes towards ex-slaves as such.[24] Thereafter, the possibilities are two: coming into the citizenship from freedom (Roman or some other nationality), or from slavery.

How early *ingenuus* acquired the specific meaning 'born free' is not clear. That is certainly how Gaius defines it, at a period when most slaves *were* born into slavery. His wording is careful (see n. 23): '*Ingenui* are those who are born free; *libertini* are those manumitted from lawful slavery' (the qualification is introduced because it was lawful for Romans to have as slaves foreigners, but not Roman citizens).

Gaius' definition is intended to be accurate and exhaustive. It does not quite succeed, since it does not take account, for example, of those who were born free, as foreigners, then enslaved, and ultimately manumitted. From the Roman point of view, though, the intervening period of slavery blots out any previous history as free men that the slaves may have had. As far as the Romans were concerned, ex-slaves originated as slaves. Freed slaves, even if free before enslavement, were excluded from office; free foreigners admitted to citizenship were not. So, in the late Republic, L. Cornelius Balbus, suffect consul in 40 BC, is an example of a free non-Roman (from Gades) enfranchised by Pompey, who achieved office.

Although the bipartite division is how Roman law distinguished between Roman citizens, more subtle distinctions could of course be, and were, made at a social level. Traces of such a distinction appear in a Herculanean inscription (*AE* 1978.119: Guadagno 1977) containing lists of the local *Augustales*. They are divided into three sections. First come the freeborn, who are clearly identified by filiation. Third are the freedmen, who are again clearly identified, this time by the designation, 'freedman of', with the names of their previous owners. Between comes a list of men with neither filiation nor freedman indication. These too are freedmen. This appears quite certain, since one of them is L. Venidius Ennychus who, as we know from Herculaneum Tablets 5 and 89, was a Junian Latin who achieved citizenship by *anniculi probatio* (Gaius 1.29) in AD 62. From the fragmentary tablets 83 and 84, it appears that Ennychus had some trouble with a man who challenged his right to stand for an unnamed office, probably that of Augustalis.[25] The inscription reassures us that he succeeded.

The probability is that all the men in the second group were of this status, i.e. former Junian Latins who had managed to become Roman citizens (I owe this suggestion to Paul Weaver). The social significance of the arrangement is hard to assess; the order of the inscription suggests that this group ranks above those described as freedmen, but below the freeborn. The principle of the division is fairly clear, however. The second and third groups both consist of freed slaves, but whereas the third had come directly from slave status by manumission (and so are correctly described 'freedman of'), the middle group achieved citizenship by one of the meritorious acts the law prescribed (Gaius 1.29–30), and not through their manumission. They had probably always been, and still were, in practice regarded as under obligations to their former owners in much the same way as ordinary freedmen to their patrons,[26] but the label 'freedman of' does not fit, since they were formerly Junian Latins, a status created under the early principate, which was essentially no more than a legal fiction to describe people not properly manumitted (Sirks 1983). On the other hand, they cannot be called 'son of', since they are neither freeborn Roman citizens nor enfranchised free foreigners.

The difference in the style of designation is necessary here in order to distinguish the middle group both from the freeborn

Romans and from those becoming citizens by manumission. This does not mean, however, that all names in this form on texts of all types have the same significance. We cannot, for example, be entirely confident about the status of a number of the individuals named, without indication of status, in the tablets from Murecine, discussed below.

Integration through a patron's *familia*

As mentioned above, there are many points of correspondence between the legal situation of the son (or, indeed, daughter) subject to *patria potestas* and the slave; as we shall see presently, there are also numerous correspondences between the legal obligations of freedmen to their *patroni*, ex-owners, and those of emancipated sons to fathers. An important factor, possibly the most important single factor, I suggest, in the willingness of the Romans to admit to their citizenship slaves freed by individual Romans was that the slave had been an integral part of a *familia*. All society's formal relationships with that *familia* had to be mediated through one person, its head. Each *familia*, however, was linked by blood relationships, either patrilineally or by affinities (in the Roman sense; *affines* were relations by marriage) with the general fabric of Roman society. Every freeborn citizen had more or less direct links to a number of *familiae*, and these links were part of the mechanism of social integration.

Each freed slave entered society entirely alone, without legal kin. However, certain obligations of *pietas* (an untranslatable word, but roughly 'proper dutifulness') towards the patron and certain other members of the *familia* were regarded as morally incumbent upon him (or her), just as upon an emancipated child. They gave the new citizen some points of attachment within the existing society. Similarly, those aspects of Augustan legislation which encouraged freed slaves to form marital relationships and establish a family increased the points of contact between the freed slave and the wider society.

The relationship to the patron and patron's family operated both as a means of social integration and of social control. The latter aspect, as well as the former, is briefly recognised in a recent discussion (Wallace-Hadrill 1989: 76):

The obligatory nature of this patronage obviously protects

the individual master; but it also has relevance for the relationship between the freedman and society at large. As a citizen, the ex-slave is a full member of Roman society; yet his membership is in some sense conditional, mediated through his patron who continues as a sort of sponsor.

This description brings out well the element of social control in the patron–freedman relationship, though to speak of conditional membership and sponsorship is perhaps misleading, in so far as it might suggest that a freedman's citizen status was revocable and in some sense dependent upon the continued approval and support of his patron. As we shall see presently, the evidence for the possibility of re-enslavement is by no means clear.

DISABILITIES OF FREEDMEN IN CIVIL LAW

With the exception of the ban placed by Augustus on marriage between senators and freed slaves, the latter had the same rights as any other citizen in civil law, except in relation to their patron and the patron's immediate family.[27] The legal restraints upon the freedman are usually summed up in modern writing under three headings: *operae*, inheritance and a cluster of banned or required activities that is usually, but misleadingly, referred to as *obsequium*[28] (another word hard to translate; roughly 'respectful compliance').

The requirement of *operae*

Operae, to which a whole title in the *Digest* (38.1) is devoted, were a specified number of days' work for the benefit of the patron, which might in certain circumstances be agreed as a part of the manumission deal. However, they constituted only a contractual obligation on the freedman, not an automatic one inherent in his condition. There is a comprehensive study by Waldstein (1986) on the subject. *Operae* were a way of recouping part of the slave's value; some manumitting owners exacted money payments instead – the law did not permit them to require both. They could, however, accept money in lieu of unperformed *operae*.

The evidence (*D.* 38.2.1.1, quoted below) on the edict issued by the praetor Rutilius in the late second century BC, which has occasioned a good deal of puzzlement, is most reasonably interpreted to mean that Rutilius would allow patrons to sue freedmen only to exact the fulfilment of specific contractual undertakings; *operae* and agreement to share acquisitions (*societas*, later declared illegal) are mentioned. More will be said about *operae* later.

Inheritance

The rights of the patron and patron's family to inherit from a freedman are set out in Gaius 3.39–73. The three main stages of historical development are conveniently summed up in 3.39–42.

(i) Under the Twelve Tables, if a freedman died intestate, leaving no *sui heredes* (automatic heirs, i.e. no children or wife *in manus*), the patron or his children (or grandchildren, etc. in the male line) would succeed.

(ii) Later, under the praetor's edict, this was modified to allow the patron to succeed on intestacy, against certain heirs, i.e. adopted children and wife *in manu*, and to take a half share even if there was a will.

(iii) Later still, under the *lex Papia Poppaea* (AD 9) the patron could claim a share, will or no will, even against natural (i.e. biological) children, and it took three children to exclude his claim entirely.

The provision in the Twelve Tables produced a situation in which a freedman's estate was treated as nearly as possible like that of a freeborn citizen. If he made a will, it was as valid as that of any other citizen. But by what right did the patron inherit on intestacy? The logic underlying the patron's right is clear, and is clearly signposted for us in *Digest* 37.12 *Si a parente quis manumissus sit* ('If someone is manumitted by a parent'), a title concerned with succession to emancipated children.[29]

Ulpian explains (*D.* 37.12.1) that the praetor's edict allowed a father to claim the inheritance of an emancipated son on the analogy of a freedman. Emancipation took a child out of the father's *familia* and so left the child with no agnates. If a father emancipated a child who was below the age of puberty (*impubes*; the best-known literary example is Regulus' son in Pliny *Ep.* 4.2), or an adult daughter, he became guardian, *tutor* – just as, in default of other arrangements, the nearest agnate did (but only until Claudius, for women) when a *pater* died. The same applied

21

to patron and freed children or women. A freedman had no agnates, since a slave had no legally recognised kindred. This accounts also for inheritance; the manumitting parent, or patron, is in the position of the nearest agnate. In both cases, that of the emancipated child and the freed slave, the *pater* was the nearest thing either had, in law, to an agnate, or indeed a relative of any sort.[30]

Stage two may be placed towards the end of the second century BC if that is what is referred to in *D*. 38.2.1.2: 'Later praetors (i.e. later than Rutilius, for whose edict, see below) promised possession of a fixed portion of the estate.'[31]

Gaius explains (3.40):

There appeared to be no cause for complaint if it was one of his natural children that he left as automatic heir; but if the heir was an adoptive son or wife in *manus*, it was manifestly unfair that no right should remain to the patron.

The timing is significant. By the late second century, a great deal of wealth had flowed into Roman society, and some Roman freedmen would have had the opportunity to amass substantial fortunes. Patrons no doubt became particularly aware of this 'unfairness' when they realised that they were missing out on inheritances worth having. Since freedmen, starting late, were at a disadvantage, specially if their wives also were freed, in trying to have legitimate children to succeed them (Treggiari 1969: 213–15), there is also the possibility that large numbers of freedmen themselves were resorting to the device of adopting sons, or of belatedly taking their wives into *manus*[32] (probably by a *coemptio*: Gaius 1.114), specifically in order to secure heirs of their own choice.

There appears to be no such interference with the wills of emancipated sons, presumably because their powers of independent acquisition of property had merely been granted earlier than they would, in the natural course of things, have acquired them anyway; at the father's death, each child in *potestas* became legally independent (*sui iuris*), head by right of his own *familia*. A freedman, however, got out of *potestas* only by grace of the patron, and it seemed 'unfair', in Gaius' word, that outsiders should have all the benefit of his success in life. A further mark of this difference between ex-slaves and emancipated sons was that the latter's brothers and sisters were not admitted to his estate against a will, although a patron's children had the same rights as the patron against a freedman's will (*D.* 37.12.1.5).

The third stage comes with the *lex Papia Poppaea*, i.e. in one of the periods of major change and development in the legal situation of the freedman. It is, however, part of much wider-ranging social legislation, and it is not easy to distinguish between intent and effect. It can be seen as a concession to the envy and greed of patrons, but other considerations probably predominated. As part of the legislation intended to encourage marriage and the production of children, it was no doubt meant to provide an incentive to freedmen to have heirs of their own to inherit from them. An incidental effect (though possibly only secondary, if present at all in the mind of the legislators) was that their very success in doing so would help to maintain the social stratification to which Augustan policy had given sharper definition. The more children a freedman had, the less each freeborn child could hope to inherit.[33]

By the late second century AD, legal actions (the *actio Fabiana* and *actio Calvisiana* (Buckland 1966: 597)) were available for the patron to bring claims against the estate of a freedman, testate or intestate, on the grounds that certain of the freedman's acts had defrauded the patron of some of the share that would otherwise have come to him. There could be no question, says Gaius (*D.* 37.12.2) of bringing these actions against the estate of an emancipated son, 'since it is unfair that *ingenui* should not be free to dispose of their own property'.[34]

The duty of *obsequium*

Obsequium is used in modern discussions as a conventional shorthand term to refer to a whole group of duties or prohibitions. It appears in the title of *Digest* 37.15; the word does not appear in the rest of the chapter. The content of the chapter includes both matters commonly grouped under this heading in modern accounts of patronal rights, and one or two references to the action for ingratitude (see below). In fact, a key word in 37.15 is *pietas*.

The content of *obsequium* (to continue to use the word for convenience) is in effect a series of rules, the chief of which are the following:

(i)   A freedman had to obtain the praetor's permission in order to summon to court his patron, or a patron's children or parents. If he did not get permission, and nevertheless tried to summon the patron to court, the latter could sue for a penalty of 10,000 HS; Gaius 4.46 gives us the formula.

(ii) A freedman was prohibited from bringing any action against a patron that brought discredit, or any criminal action (except for *maiestas*, which was of public concern: *D.* 48.4.7.2).

(iii) A freedman was required to support an indigent patron, in case of need (this one was reciprocal).

(iv) Paul adds (*D.* 22.5.4) that patrons and freedmen were not to be compelled to give evidence against each other in criminal cases.

Lambert (1934)[35] mistakenly thought that these rights a patron had over his freedman were grounded in some sort of patronal power, *potestas patronalis*, over the freedman, analogous to the power a *pater* had over his children. However, the whole point, as Gaius' comments on inheritance and guardianship, and the *Digest* headings, make clear is that the freedman is parallel not to the *filiusfamilias*, but to the emancipated child.

The above rules of *obsequium* and, in its earliest form, the rule about inheritance, are applied in the legal texts equally to freedmen and to emancipated children.[36] What both have in common is that they had been in the power of a *paterfamilias*, and that they had been taken out of *potestas* by the deliberate action of the *pater* (not, for the son, by his death). The inheritance rights are analogous, as we saw, to those of agnates. *Obsequium*, on the other hand, is grounded not in *potestas* (that, as we saw, had been ended) but in the moral, rather than legal, duty of *pietas*.

This factor of *pietas* is not always given sufficient weight. Duff (1958: 35 ff.) acknowledges it, but assumes that in attempted litigation, for example, the praetor would in practice virtually always take the patron's side. This is not proven. Can we assume that praetors would habitually ignore justice to please a patron, just because he was patron? Clout (*gratia*) was a strictly extra-legal factor which nevertheless did influence the legal process in general, and not just between freedman and patron (Kelly 1971). In the division of Roman society under the Empire into 'upper' and 'lower', *honestiores* and *humiliores*, which increasingly found expression, as demonstrated by Garnsey (1970) and Millar (1984), in their treatment by the law,[37] most freedmen ended up among the *humiliores*. However, while freedmen are on the whole likely to have had less *gratia* than their patrons, it cannot be taken for granted that this was universally so, particularly if the patron was also a freedman. Use of the terms 'patrons' and 'freedmen' should not mislead us into thinking that we are speaking of two distinct social categories; they overlapped to a very great extent.

Fabre (1981: 219 ff.) goes further than Duff, and, ignoring the parallel restraints on emancipated children, interprets these restrictions as a privilege for the patron, marking the inferiority of the freedman, or as a duty imposed upon the freedman. For example, in the praetor's edict persons *infames* as the result of a criminal conviction were banned from bringing prosecutions on behalf of other people – with certain exceptions (*D.* 3.1.1.11). The list of excepted persons, on whose behalf such people might sue, includes parents, patrons, patron's children, one's own children, brothers, sisters, wives, in-laws, step-parents and step-children, and so on. Fabre is representing as a duty imposed specifically upon freedmen what is in fact the recognition of a general obligation of *pietas* upon children, parents, siblings, marriage partners and their kin, and freedmen.

The word *obsequium* itself is non-technical, but its appearance also in the first section of *Digest* 38.2 has led a number of modern scholars to presume the existence in the Republic of a virtually unlimited, legally enforceable *right* of the patron to impose duties and services of various sorts on his freedman, as he did during his slavery. This has coloured their interpretation of the edict of the praetor Rutilius, already mentioned. Sometimes, *obsequium* and the even less technical *officium* ('being obliging') are identified, and the latter also represented as something legally enforceable.[38]

EXPLOITATION AND PROTECTION: THE EDICT OF RUTILIUS

The cardinal text is *Digest* 38.2.1, from Book 42 of Ulpian's work on the praetorian edict:

> (pr.) This edict was issued by the praetor for the sake of regulating the respect which freedmen ought to have towards their patrons. For, as Servius writes, previously they were

in the habit of making very serious demands on their freedmen, that is, as repayment for the huge benefit conferred on
the freedmen when they are taken out of slavery into Roman
citizenship.

(1) And indeed the praetor Rutilius first proclaimed that
he would grant the patron no more than an action for
services and for partnership, that is, if a pledge had been
made that, if the freedman did not render him due obedience,
the patron would be admitted into partnership (sc. in the
freedman's property).

(2) Later praetors promised possession of a fixed part of
the estate; for evidently the idea of partnership had led to
rendering the same share, so that [the freedman] rendered
after his death what he had been in the habit of giving while
alive.[39]

Rutilius was praetor about 118 BC (Broughton 1951: 527), and
this text is our only evidence for his momentous edict. Paragraph
(2) concerns our second stage in the development of the patron's
inheritance rights (Gaius 3.40–1), which occurred before 74 BC.[40]
It has been suggested that this was a reaction to the concessions
Rutilius had made to freedmen. The intent of his edict does seem
to have been to make life easier for freedmen. This is how Ulpian
(D. 38.1.2) understood it:

The praetor proposed this edict to restrain the persecution
that was imposed for the sake of freedom; for he observed
that this matter, i.e. the rendering of services imposed as a
condition of liberty, had grown beyond bounds, so that
freed persons were being oppressed and burdened.

Rutilius made it clear that certain demands on freedmen were
not legally enforceable, by specifying the nature of the only ones
which he would be prepared to enforce. In doing so, however,
far from making concessions, he could be regarded as having given
patrons the means to put the squeeze on freedmen, by binding
them contractually to services, operae, with no specified limit, and
partnership, societas. Subsequently, these had to be eliminated
(societas) or restricted (operae).

All that we know about Rutilius' edict is in the Digest passage
quoted above. Unfortunately, its import is not immediately clear.
It has been interpreted in various ways, as evidence for what the

situation regarding freedmen's legal obligations and patron's rights was before the edict. For example, it has been used to put a precise legal significance on Cicero's passing remark in a letter to his brother (*ad Q. fr.* 1.1.13): 'Our ancestors gave orders to their freedmen, more or less like slaves.' So, for instance, we find the notion put forward that earlier patrons had a completely unlimited right to exact obedience (*obsequium*), which Rutilius cut down to specified *operae*; in effect, Rutilius is being credited with inventing the *operae* system. This, for which there is no justification in the sources, is the view of Fabre (1981 317 ff.), rightly dismissed by Waldstein (1986: 125).

The trouble is with the word *obsequium*. For Cosentini (1948), whose view was that the application of the term to the obligations of freedmen was post-classical, the passages in which it occurs were late interpolations. However, whether we suppose that the relevant section of paragraph (1), 'that is ... [property]' (*videlicet ... patronus*),· is to be attributed to Ulpian, or, less probably, is to be regarded as reproducing the original wording of the edict, it is plain that it is intended merely for the sake of example, as an instance of what could be covered in *societatis actiones*, and only a vague and undefined sense can be given to *obsequium*. If any such agreement was ever made, by which a freedman bound himself to give partnership in his property if he defaulted on his obligation, the *obsequium* likewise would have had to be given some specified content, which would vary from one agreement to another.[41]

We cannot use this clause as evidence for a pre-existing generalised and unlimited, but legally enforceable, obligation of something that might be called *obsequium* to a patron – still less one that actually had been in the past regularly enforced by recourse to law, without there having been a previous agreement, *pactum*. If either had been the case, Rutilius' action would have been revolutionary indeed, and the complete absence from the sources of any further evidence on the matter all the more remarkable.

But the last section of (1), from *videlicet*, is suspicious. It looks like an attempt by compilators to explain references to *societas* in earlier texts. Other evidence indicates that patrons had been making *societas* (i.e. partnership in all future acquisitions) a condition of freedom, as a contractual obligation, like that of rendering *operae*. Such partnership agreements were later made unactionable under the praetor's edict, when a ban was introduced

27

on impositions that put a burden on the freedman (*onerandae libertatis causa*). This had occurred by the time of Labeo, i.e. by the end of the Republic.[42]

We might get further by asking what events gave rise to Rutilius' edict. The original motive force must have come from approaches made to the praetor requesting grants of actions, and the tone of the edict suggests that these approaches are likely to have come from patrons. By the end of the second century BC, not only were freedmen numerous, but the characteristics of many freedmen were significantly different from those of the early Republic. Duff (1958: 37), echoed by Kirschenbaum (1987: 133–4), points out how natural it was in the early Republic for the unskilled freedman of Italian origin, with no particular experience other than agricultural and domestic, to remain in a kind of dependent symbiosis with his patron, continuing to perform all sorts of services for him as a matter of course.

By the late second century, however, things have changed. There is a lot more wealth about. There are freedmen of foreign origin, with specialised money-making skills, perfectly capable of going out and making a livelihood apart from their masters. Their prosperity may well have stimulated the greed of the patrons. Some patrons (perhaps themselves more likely to be freedmen) have been binding them by contracts. Others have been going on in the traditional way, expecting their freedmen, as of right, to abandon their own concerns whenever and for whatever purpose the patron requires, and possibly also expecting to avail themselves of the fruits of the freedman's labours without payment.[43] The freedmen themselves are more likely to have seen uncontracted-for demands on their time and labour as an imposition, and to have refused. The origin of many slaves in the Greek East meant that they were familiar with manumission contracts.[44]

The possibility just mentioned – freedmen as patrons – is an important factor. By the late second century BC, we must certainly take into account the fact that very many patron–freedman relationships are not between a freeborn *paterfamilias* and his freed slave, but between a patron who himself had been a slave, and the slave whom he in his turn has freed. What all patron–freedman pairs have in common is not that one of the pair was freeborn, the other not, but that one had held the other in his power and had released him. Much importance was attached to the element of *pietas* in the ideal relationship between patron and freedman. This ideal was already less easy to maintain in practice with the development of large establishments, where there was less personal contact between owner and slave. A patron who had himself been a slave, moreover, was perhaps even less likely to view his relationship with his freedmen as quasi-parental, more aware, from the ex-slave's point of view, of the potential for exploitation inherent in the situation, and more likely to be interested in exploiting others as he himself had been exploited. Freedmen, in turn – especially if they were economically worth exploiting – are likely to have been becoming, by the late second century, both more conscious of exploitation and less amenable and deferential.

In other words, whereas patrons had once been able to get away unchallenged with exactions from their freedmen to which they had no legal entitlement, they are now, by the late second century, increasingly meeting with resistance. They are up against the problem of the recalcitrant freedman, and they try to have recourse to law. Rutilius finds it desirable to spell things out. He will give an action only if there has been a contract, that is, for *operae*, or for *societas*.

It is probably in the period after Rutilius that one should put the appearance of a distinction between two types of *operae*: *operae fabriles* and *operae officiales*.[45] *Fabriles*, as a number of texts makes clear, essentially involve the operation of one's trade or craft, and, as Ulpian says, are classed among things *quae quasi in pecuniae praestatione consistunt*; they can have a cash value set on them, and so can be inherited by a patron's children, whereas *officiales* are specific to the person, i.e. the patron, and cannot be inherited. Patrons, denied by Rutilius' edict the possibility of forcing freedmen to render them unlimited *officia* in the way of general dogsbodying, or attendance of the traditional status-boosting type, such as attendance at the morning levée (*salutatio*), escort in public (*comitatus*), and so on, will have begun to contract for them as well; it is likely that the other type, contracts for an agreed number of days' work at a specific trade, had already begun commonly to form part of manumission agreements. Alfenus Varus, suffect consul in 39 BC, was asked to give an opinion on a contract of this sort, for what could be termed *operae officiales*, since the freedmen in question were not being asked to practise their trade – indeed, quite the contrary. The patron had an ulterior mercenary motive.

A freedman doctor, thinking that he would have many more patients if his own freedmen did not practise as doctors, demanded that they should follow him about and not do any work. Was that legal? The answer was yes, so long as the services were not slavish, that is, so long as he allowed them to rest in the middle of the day and to have regard to their health and their *honestas* (decency?).

(*D*. 38.1.26 pr.)

The patron in question was not using his freedmen on their days of service, as he might have done, to treat additional patients for the benefit of his own practice, so how did he benefit? He was preventing his patients, on those days, from experiencing the medical skills and care available from these rival doctors, and so from perhaps deciding to transfer their custom to them at other times.

Rutilius' edict had given patrons the means of making legally enforceable demands, without restraining the amount, and there are signs that the opportunities were enthusiastically taken up. As we saw, it was soon thought desirable to ban agreements for *societas*; subsequent interpretations of the edict detail the protection to be afforded to freedmen against excessive demands for *operae*, such as would interfere with their ability to earn a livelihood.

Sabinus writes that a freedman should supply his own food and clothes while rendering services; but if he cannot feed himself, his patron is to supply food, or the services are to be exacted in such a way that he is allowed time to earn a living, to enable him to feed himself on those days when he is rendering services. . . . Services should be rendered at the place where the patron resides, and naturally the patron is responsible for travel expenses and transport.[46]

Travel might be necessary, since patron and freedman might not be resident even in the same part of the Roman empire. However, the principle that the freedman's livelihood must not be endangered was upheld. In the first century AD, Proculus said (*D*. 38.1.20) that a freedman ought to come from a province to Rome to fulfil *operae*, but that the days spent in travelling were deducted from what was due to the patron. However, the patron ought to behave reasonably ('like a good man and conscientious head of household', *vir bonus et diligens paterfamilias*), and either stay at Rome or go to the province himself; if he chose to go gadding about all over the world, there was no compulsion on the freedman to go chasing after him.

If a freedman learned a skill or trade after manumission he could be required to fulfil his *operae* by practising it, but not if the work subsequently taken up was disreputable or at the risk of life. Immoral or dangerous activities, such as prostitution or arena combat, were not to be required as *operae*; so a fighter in the arena was not liable to do the same work for his patron as when he was a slave, nor was a prostitute, who continued on the game after manumission, even if she was still making a living by selling her body.[47]

Patrons were expected to use their freedmen's services personally, if at all possible, and not to take advantage of *operae* by selling their work to others, though some concession was allowed where the skill was one of which the patron would not normally be able to avail himself sufficiently. Julian (*D.* 38.1.25 and 27) points out the difficulty where a person of modest means (and therefore, he implies, unable to afford to put on many shows) had a freedman who was a mime actor, or a doctor had a freedman who was also a doctor. In those cases, if they hired them out, they should be deemed to be exacting *operae*, not making a profit. They could, however, lend them gratis to friends, so the freedman, by way of *operae*, should be prepared to put on a performance, or give medical treatment to his patron's friends. 'For', says Julian, with what looks like an attempt, rare among legal commentators, at a joke,[48] 'there is no obligation on a patron, in order to make use of the services of his freedman, to be constantly putting on shows or being ill.'

Hopkins (1978: 130) says that 'such legal regulations were of course for the most part unenforceable; but they reflect . . . the sympathetic concern of lawyers.' Their enforceability, one would suppose, would partly depend on the economic strength, and the confidence, of the individual freedman. The concern of lawyers, which we have seen attested at the very end of the Republic, may have been present earlier in the first century BC, and motivated by more than sympathy for the hard-pressed freedman. The problem of debt was more or less endemic in the first century BC, and it need not be assumed, as is often done, that it was mainly a rural problem. Brunt (1988: 493) points out that the main beneficiaries of Julius Caesar's remission of rents were likely to

include shopkeepers and craftsmen.[49] The civil wars would be a
bad time for them, as would the troubles of the eighties. Too
heavy a burden of demands by patrons could make all the difference between making a go of a business and going under. Excessive
exploitation would be counter-productive, both for patrons themselves and ultimately for society, and needed to be discouraged.
Garnsey (1981: 364) doubts whether the exaction of heavy
obligations from freedmen was at all common; we lack suitable
evidence one way or the other.

PERSONAL RELATIONS BETWEEN PATRONS AND FREEDMEN

Patrons not infrequently showed their appreciation (whether genu-
ine or conventionally expected) of their freedmen both during
their lifetime, with material help, or by leaving them bequests.
These usually took the form of annuities or pensions; many funerary inscriptions describe the monument as built for the deceased,
his family, and his freedmen and freedwomen and their posterity.[50]
The younger Pliny has seen to it that his own generosity in
providing and seeing to the proper exploitation of a piece of
farmland as a 'pension fund' for his old nurse has not gone
unrecorded (*Ep.* 6.3); we also learn from the surviving portions
of his tombstone (*CIL* V. 5262 = *ILS* 2927) that he left the best
part of two million HS for the maintenance of one hundred
freedmen.

Not all patron–freedman relationships were affectionate. The
fond regard of Cicero and his son for his private secretary Tiro,
who evidently continued to live with and work for the family, is
well documented in the orator's correspondence; so is his dislike
of his wife's freedman Philotimus, who ran Cicero's town-house
and kept his accounts.[51] We have many inscriptions concerning
patrons and freedmen, some of which reveal the existence of bonds
of affection, some the reverse; obviously, there is space to cite
only a few here.

For example, the tomb of Zosimus, the orderly of Marcus
Aurelius Cotta (consul in AD 20) records the generosity of his
patron Cotta, who helped to maintain him and his family and
even gave his daughters dowries. The will of the younger Pliny's
contemporary, the upper-class testator 'Dasumius',[52] dated AD 108,
includes bequests of 1,000 denarii each to a number of freedmen

and freedwomen. His old nurse is apparently left two slave fishermen (her sons?), plus some household items, including tableware (perhaps of silver). Some other freedmen are left legacies of maintenance, and one is expressly excluded: Hymnus, '[who although] I showed you very many [. . . you yourself recall what] treatment I had or was apprehensive of having from you.'

The freedman Decimus Otacilius Felix set up a tomb at Ostia for himself, for three other people with the same *nomen*, probably his freed wife and freed children (born as slaves), and his other freedmen and freedwomen, 'excepting those whom I shall exclude in my will'. (Another woman, Luria Musa, called '*uxor*', may have been his second wife.)[53] We do not know what Otacilius worked at, nor whether any of his freed slaves worked with him, either in performance of *operae* or in partnership. This sort of personal and working relationship between owners and owned does not appear, however, to have been uncommon, and it could continue from one generation to another.

A tantalising group of inscriptions from Rome, from the late Republic and the first century AD, attests more than one generation of a group of freedmen and freedwomen, and their freedmen and freedwomen, of the Veturii, and with them other freed slaves, of the Plutii.[54] It is usually assumed that all were connected with the purple trade, perhaps both before and after manumission. In fact, only the woman in the earliest inscription, Veturia Fedra, freedwoman of D. Veturius D. l. Diogenes, and married to her co-freedman, is actually said to have been in the trade (*purpuraria*); another D. Veturius D. l. (Atticus) in the first century AD has a shop in the Vicus Jugarius, and L. Plutius L. l. Eros (undated), husband of a freedwoman Veturia, is from the Vicus Tuscus.

Patrons and freedmen: the Sulpicii at Puteoli

There is one group of texts from which we might hope to find out more about the ordinary activities of patrons and freedmen working together, or at least in association part of the time. For the last twenty years, our knowledge of the operation of credit in Roman business life, and of the rôles played by freedmen and slaves, has been greatly enhanced by the gradual publication of over one hundred and forty wax tablets, found in a villa at Murecine, a suburb of Pompeii.[55] These are from the records of the Sulpicii, a group of financiers, one of them certainly a freedman, with dealings in Puteoli and Pompeii, and many other individuals besides the Sulpicii themselves figure in the texts. Unfortunately, few of the individuals named on these business documents record either filiation or freedman status; those who do are mostly foreigners or imperial freedmen.[56] However, there is, as we shall see, a possibility that one or more of the Sulpicii was freeborn.

The two Sulpicii whose names occur most frequently are C. Sulpicius Faustus (mentioned in tablets dating between AD 26 and 52) and C. Sulpicius Cinnamus (AD 43 to 55). Cinnamus was the freedman of Faustus, to whom he refers in *TP* 30 (= *AE* 1973.151) and also in an unpublished tablet as his patron (Camodeca 1985–6: 20). The absence of filiation in Faustus' name, as in that of Cinnamus and most of the other persons named in the tablets, may indicate that he too was a freedman. An inscription from Cumae (*Eph. Epigr.* VIII. 451) names a C. Sulpicius Faustus and a C. Sulpicius Onirus as sons of freedmen, but we cannot be certain that these are the same as the persons named in the tablets. The tablets stretch over a period of at least thirty-five years, so more than one generation is involved. From their *praenomina*, Camodeca (1985–6) concludes that the Caii Sulpicii are unlikely to have been freedmen of a *gens* of the municipal oligarchy of Puteoli; he suggests an origin in the *familia* of C. Sulpicius Galba, suffect consul in 5 BC. This does not, he adds, necessarily imply that the senatorial patron was involved in their financial activity.

Faustus might have been diversifying from finance into direct trading; in two texts, *AE* 1978.124 (AD 35) and 1986.168 (AD 26) he is apparently described as *m(erc)ator*; in 1978.124 the same term is applied to Faustus and also to another man. However, Camodeca (1983–4: 17) and Bove (1984a: Appendix 1) read *maior* in the latter text. If this were the correct reading, and Faustus was described in AD 26 as *maior*, 'the elder', this might provide a link between the Faustus of the tablets and the freeborn Faustus (his son?) found in the inscription from Cumae alongside a C. Sulpicius Onirus, a name otherwise attested on the tablets in AD 61 (see below). It raises also the possibility that the 'Faustus' named in the tablets is sometimes the elder, sometimes the younger. It would be tempting, but speculative, to see in Onirus also a son of Faustus the elder.

Unfortunately, this alluring genealogical construct is cast in doubt again by the publication of *TP* 136 = *AE* 1984.219 (Landi 1980: 195) dated 14 July AD 29, in which M. Caecilius Maximus acknowledges a debt to C. Sulpicio Fausto Mercato[ri]. It is not clear whether the last word is an occupational description or part of his name.

As more material from the bay of Naples is published additional obvious, or possible, family relationships may emerge.[57] A C. Sulpicius Onirus is named in several Murecine tablets dated to AD 61.[58] Another C. Sulpicius, with the *cognomen* Eutychus, in *TP* 39 (= *AE* 1973.161, dated 30 October AD 51) is said to have appeared in the forum of Puteoli as *procurator* of Cinnamus, making a declaration concerning a forfeit security, probably made on the occasion of the actual sale of the forfeit goods; in the notice of sale, however (*TP* 19 = *AE* 1973.139), dated 5 October, only Cinnamus is mentioned.

It is clear from the dossier as a whole that businessmen such as the Sulpicii performed a variety of functions in facilitating the transactions of the business community in Puteoli. It is less easy to determine the personal and working relationships between the various Sulpicii. Although the tablets concerning Faustus and his freedman Cinnamus overlap in time (Cinnamus first appears sixteen years or so after the earliest tablet mentioning Faustus), so far, they are mentioned together in only three tablets. In *TP* 30 = *AE* 1973.151, Cinnamus records receipt of payment from a third party towards a debt owed to Faustus; we cannot tell from this alone whether Cinnamus is an independent businessman, commissioned by Faustus for this particular piece of debt-collection, or whether he is working off *operae* agreed with his patron, or, indeed, whether the two are in business together, and still less whether they are actually living in the same house, even though the presence of the business documents in the Murecine villa indicates that it belonged to someone associated with the group.

The other two tablets, however, both dated AD 48, do at least indicate that Faustus and Cinnamus were indeed in business jointly. In *TP* 68 = *AE* 1978.138 Cinnamus acknowledges receipt of a sum of money on his own account *and* that of Faustus (*nomine [p]rop[rio] et C. S[ulpic]i Fausti*). The lengthy text of *TP* 47 = *AE* 1974.277 provides more conclusive evidence of joint operations on a regular basis. A certain C. Julius Prudens is acknowledging his obligation under a *stipulatio* administered by Cinnamus to make repayment of the money given by 'him (i.e. Cinnamus) or Eros or anyone of his staff (*si q[ui]d[am] eius*) or his slave Martial or Caius Sulpicius Faustus or anyone else mandated or instructed by any of them'. These tablets, taken with the finding together in one place of large numbers of tablets concerning the transactions of Faustus and Cinnamus acting separately, create a strong presumption that they were in business jointly.

Onirus and Eutychus appear also to be members of the firm. The former at least may be freeborn and perhaps a member of the family (see above); Eutychus' appearance as *procurator* of Cinnamus in *AE* 1973.161 tells us nothing about his status and relation to other members of the group.

From these tablets, and in particular from the three naming both Cinnamus and Faustus and, in the third, some of Cinnamus' slave staff, we may perhaps gain some idea of the way in which freedman-owned businesses perpetuated themselves, and also of the development of the careers of individuals. The Sulpicii tablets extend over thirty-five years. Whatever the original status of Faustus, Cinnamus had been his slave, presumably employed in the business, as later were Cinnamus' own slaves Eros and Martial, and continuing in it after manumission. Eros and Martial, if manumitted, would probably also continue in the firm, and so on. Precise details of the legal arrangements between the free participants are irrecoverable (of course, any *filiifamilias* would own none of the assets), but some sort of *societas* is probable. At any rate, such a set-up, with ex-slave, ex-slave's ex-slave, and present slave working side by side, cannot have been uncommon in Roman business life; nor, in the long run, would it have been good for business had the patrons been unduly exploitative.

'Buying' freedom

Legal evidence indicates that it was not uncommon for slaves to secure manumission by paying a sum of money to their owners. As mentioned above, the requirement of *operae* and the exaction of money payments as a condition of manumission were, in law, mutually exclusive. Crook (1967: 54) suggested that the patron's right to claim a share against a will was grounded in *peculium*, retained by the slave on manumission. He drew attention to the praetorian rule (*D.* 38.2.3.4) that a patron who had accepted money as a condition of manumission (*nummos accepit ut manumitteret*) lost this right. However, although modern studies not uncommonly speak of masters allowing slaves to buy manumission out of their savings, it is important to be clear that payments for manumission were not necessarily made from the *peculium*. Although it was customarily accepted (by how early a date, we do not know) that a slave manumitted in his master's lifetime kept his *peculium*, unless his owner expressly withheld it, a general rule to that effect is not stated until Severus and Caracalla (Buckland 1908: 189). The patron could always keep it if he wished, since it was legally his property. It would be possible for him both to retain the *peculium* and in addition to demand money payment (or *operae*) as the price of freedom.

This in effect (though excluding *operae*) is what happened in the collusive arrangement, mentioned in a number of legal texts, by which a slave was freed upon being 'bought with his own money' (*suis nummis emptus*).[59] These in fact have nothing to do with agreements between the slave and his owner that the latter will free him, and that he will retain only some, or none, of his *peculium*. On the contrary, they refer to a procedure by which an owner sells the slave to a third party, who then, by agreement with the slave, promptly frees him. The whole transaction is one of convenience, and the purchase money is repaid by the freed slave to the purchaser. The latter, and not the former owner, becomes patron, but with only restricted patronal rights.[60]

This may have been a way of inducing a reluctant owner to release a slave. It is true that the various possible sources of money for payment mentioned (*D.* 40.1.4.1) include the *peculium*, with the addition 'belonging to the vendor'. However, since it could be used for this purpose only with the original owner's consent (*CJ* 4.49.7), possibly the lawyers drafting the rescript of the Divine Brothers (Marcus Aurelius and Verus) had in mind a special case, such as the use of such sales as a device to allow owners under the age of 20 to release slaves. The remaining ways mentioned of financing the deal are that money was provided by friends or outsiders, borrowed on security, perhaps even advanced by the buyer, and it seems a fair presumption that resort to purchase was made when a master refused manumission. He kept the *peculium*, and had the slave's price into the bargain.

Another use of the device is suggested by an engaging story in Suetonius (*de gramm.* 13). 'Staberius Eros was bought with his own money from the sale platform (*de catasta*) and manumitted on account of his devotion to literature; amongst others, he taught Brutus and Cassius.' ('Some say', continues Suetonius, 'that he was so honourable that during the Sullan proscriptions he admitted children of the proscribed to his courses free and without any charge.')

Eros, an educated Greek, enterprisingly persuaded a Roman, Staberius, to buy and free him immediately on promise of a reimbursement, doubtless at a substantial profit, from his earnings as a teacher. Suetonius provides no details of Eros' earlier career, or how he came to be a slave. He could, theoretically at least, have done what an unnamed guest at Trimalchio's dinner table (Petron. *Sat.* 57) claimed to have done, that is, deliberately sold himself as a slave in order eventually to become a Roman citizen through manumission. It was a gamble, of course, and for Trimalchio's guest (if he is telling the truth) a rather unsuccessful one – he spent forty years as a slave. No slave could *count* on manumission; that was the safeguard for the Romans against foreigners using the device as a way into Roman citizenship.[61]

Free men sold as slaves could apply to regain their liberty. The law concerned itself with self-sale of free men apparently only where fraud was intended; the perpetrator was punished by being forbidden to reclaim his liberty, and so forced to remain as a slave (unless, that is, his owner chose to manumit him). The details are obscure, and although in Buckland (1908: 427–33) the matter is treated under the heading 'Fraudulent Sale of Freeman', only one type of case is mentioned which is immediately obvious as 'fraud', i.e. where the intention was to share the purchase price.

Another motive was *ad actum gerendum* (*D.* 28.3.6.5), that is to secure the post of *actor*, steward, of a (well-to-do, presumably) owner's household. In a period when free men were not normally considered for such jobs, the only way of getting an audition, so to speak, was to have someone put you on offer as a slave qualified for the job. This could be a good career move for someone of small means, specially because of the chance of ending up as a rich freedman (so Crook 1967: 60); you would then have to wait, however, for the owner to decide to manumit. It was not possible to pick one's own time, and claim freedom. As late as AD 323, Constantine thinks it worth instructing the urban prefect (*C.Th.* 4.6.8) that if someone was knowingly sold when under the age of 14 and later, as it happens, became *actor*, this latter fact was not to be held against him if he wanted to claim his liberty; that he knew of the sale does not count, because he was still a minor.

THE AUGUSTAN REFORMS

Augustus' principate brought far-reaching changes in several aspects of Roman private law, and especially family law. It is a watershed both for the legal determination of relations between patron and freedman and for the status of freedmen in society at large. The most obvious examples of the latter are the bans on marriages between senators and freedwomen and between convicted adulteresses and freeborn Romans.[62] These implicitly attach higher status to free birth, but the grounds for the bans are not necessarily either racial (a motive suggested by Suetonius, *Aug.* 40) or philosophical, such as a belief in a 'slave mentality', *servile ingenium*. The marriage restrictions are more plausibly to be seen as connected with the degree to which the individual is integrated into society via the networks of familial connections. A freed person is connected only to one *familia* (that of his patron) and that not directly by blood, while a freeborn person normally is directly connected to two, through parents. Marrying a freed person would be a handicap for the personal advancement of a senator, as well as weakening the social cohesiveness of the senatorial class as a whole. For adulteresses, at least those of any social standing, part of the punishment consisted in losing the possibility of forming networks of connections in freeborn society through marriage.

However, some of the provisions of the laws on manumission and those of the marriage legislation relating to freedmen have nothing to do with distinctions based on *ingenuitas*. Some are concerned with the quality of the entrants to citizenship, others with the right the ex-owner held over the formerly owned, and both kinds seem aimed ultimately at the restoration and preservation of social stability.

The measure which seems most obviously to have been intended as a means of introducing some kind of quality control on entrance to Roman citizenship through manumission was the *lex Aelia Sentia* of AD 4.[63] Minimum age limits were laid down for both owners (20 years) and slaves (30). If either condition was not fulfilled, demonstration must be made to an official tribunal that there was 'good cause', consisting essentially in close personal service, such as that of a nurse or *paedagogus*, to the owner, or an actual blood relationship, or an intention on the part of a *dominus* to marry his freedwoman; otherwise the slave received freedom but not citizenship. This requirement also effectively ruled out testamentary manumission by owners under the age of 20. Slaves who had been chained, branded, imprisoned, found guilty, after interrogation under torture, of crime, or used as gladiators or beast-fighters, were assigned the status of *dediticii* ('surrendered foreigners'), permanently excluded from Roman citizenship or even Latin status, and barred from approaching within one hundred miles of Rome. In short, owners could as individuals create new citizens only if they themselves had reached an age of reasonable judgment, and their slaves had earned manumission by long service and had clean records; exceptions were made only by a panel of citizens judging the application on its merits. The aim was to exclude the undeserving or undesirable from achieving citizen status.

Some provisions of the legislation of this and the ensuing period were concerned not so much, or not. only, with control at the point of entry to free society, but with the successful integration of the ex-slave into the community.

Non-criminal slaves who had qualified only for informal manumission were encouraged to conform to Roman *mores*, and contribute to the stability of society, by the *lex Junia*,[64] which granted citizenship to those who entered a matrimonial relationship and had a child that reached the age of one year. The provision on inheritance of the *lex Papia Poppaea* which was described above can be regarded as having a similar aim, in that freedmen, especially the more prosperous, were encouraged to settle down and have several children, the better to secure the estate for their offspring and exclude the patron's claim. This provision, however, was nicely double-edged. Either the patron's interests were satisfied by getting a slice of the freedman's estate, or one more ex-slave had settled down into matrimony and family life, and produced several freeborn Romans (the effects on the children's chances of social mobility were probably of secondary concern).

I would go further; as I have argued more fully elsewhere (Gardner 1991), the most satisfactory explanation of the first of the Augustan laws on manumission, the *lex Fufia Caninia* of 2 BC (Gaius 1.42–6), is that it also was concerned with the application of social controls to Roman freedmen. It dealt only with testamentary manumission, to which it set numerical limits, on a sliding scale depending on size of household, up to a maximum of 100 manumissions. Suggested explanations of the law as sumptuary, or as intended to impose some selectivity in manumitting are not very convincing – and the effectiveness of the latter is belied, in the case of some owners at least, by Gaius' evidence for a variety of more or less ingenious attempts to evade the numerical restrictions. These owners did not *want* to be selective.

The law was aimed primarily, I believe, at controlling the numbers of slaves manumitted by childless testators.[65] Childless testators meant unattached freedmen, since there were no *liberi patroni*, patron's children, to inherit the patronal rights. Such freedmen had no bond of loyalty and *pietas* to any members of any existing *familiae*, and were unaffected by the social and legal distinctions between freed slave and patron/patron's child, since there was no one who bore that relationship to them.

The law would serve to control their numbers. It would also have the important, though, I think, secondary effect – more important where testators had family to succeed them – of placing some element of restraint on the depletion of large estates by numerous manumissions. It was intended to preserve and encourage certain influences towards integration and hierarchy, so important for the order and stability that Augustus was trying to establish, or re-establish, in Roman society. This view of the purpose of the *lex Fufia Caninia* has not, so far as I know, previously been put forward, but it seems to me, while fitting in with the social and moral purposes evident in other legislation of the Augustan period, to provide, by considering the actual legal effects in regard to patron–freedman relations and the operation of the law of inheritance, a more coherent and satisfactory explanation of what the law was intended to achieve.

INSTITUTIONALISING RESPECT: THE *ACCUSATIO LIBERI INGRATI*

The *lex Fufia Caninia* and the *lex Aelia Sentia* introduced controls on the creation of new citizens by manumission. A notable provision of the *lex Aelia Sentia*, relatively little commented upon in modern discussion, is that the patrons were for the first time given the possibility of taking legal action to control the behaviour of their freedmen towards them. The kind of behaviour presented in the relevant legal texts as forming the subject-matter, actual or envisaged, of complaints, appears to open a rare window on actual social behaviour. It has little to do with the kinds of obligations and behaviour discussed above under the general term *obsequium*; and it seems to involve not just neglect of symbolic acts of respect or minor serviceableness (*officium*),[66] but rather active disrespect, even, on occasion, violence.

As we saw above, the necessity for Rutilius' edict seems to have arisen because of an increasing recalcitrance on the part of freedmen in face of the demands made on them by their patrons. Since then, Roman society had been through a century of upheaval. Duff (1958: 37) plausibly enough associates the perceived need for such a measure as the introduction of the *actio ingrati*, not merely with the rise of a new type of freedman – the 'ambitious parvenu' – but also with the presumed frequency of cases of disloyalty during the revolutionary times Rome had been through.

The effect on upper-class Roman perceptions by the time of Tiberius may perhaps be seen in Valerius Maximus, who devotes a whole chapter (6.8) to instances of 'unexpected' loyalty of slaves towards their masters during the proscriptions. His final example is Antius Restio, proscribed by the triumvirs (a story told also more briefly, and with different detail, in Dio 47.10). The effect is heightened by making the instrument of Restio's salvation a slave, whom he had punished with fetters and branding. The rest of the household, in contrast to this one (a detail doubtless added for rhetorical effect but not implausible), had taken advantage of the situation to resort to looting. The ingenious device by which the slave saved him was to catch and murder a needy old man and burn him on a pyre. When the soldiers came up, the slave pointed to the pyre and said that his master 'had atoned to him for his cruelty, and was now being burned', implying that he had himself murdered him and was burning the corpse. The soldiers believed him, says Valerius, because what he said had verisimilitude; that is, because that is how they expected a slave to feel towards his owner.

We may also believe, with Duff, that acts of overt disloyalty by freedmen as well as slaves had been not uncommon during the troubles. One famous victim was Cicero, who, according to Plutarch (*Cic.* 48) was betrayed by his brother's freedman, whom he had had educated; Quintus himself had already been betrayed by his slaves. For the traumatic effects on the mentality of owners, we may compare what Eugene Genovese (1976: 97 ff.) calls the 'Moment of Truth' experienced by Southern slave-owners during and after the American Civil War, when their belief in the devotion and loyalty of their slaves was abruptly shattered:

> The experience proved all the more bitter since that organic relationship of master and slave which the slaveholders always celebrated had so clearly rebounded against them; any change in their perception of the slaves intrinsically meant a change in their perception of themselves.

A word reiterated in the owners' correspondence is 'ingratitude'. The *lex Aelia Sentia* in AD 4 allowed a patron to make a formal accusation against a freedman on the grounds of 'ingratitude'. Our legal texts date from considerably later in the empire, and there was development by repeated imperial regulation, so that it is unclear what the original terms were; what offences, if any, were specified, or what penalties prescribed, even what procedure was followed.[67] In the legal texts, the competent magistrates are the *praefectus urbi* at Rome and the *praesides* in the provinces. Initially perhaps the praetor exercised his powers of police jurisdiction, before the development of the *cognitio* system.[68] The variety of grounds of accusation (some accepted, some not) and recommendations on punishment which are mentioned suggest that the law did not specify particular behaviour, and that punishment was left to the magistrate's discretion.

The few relevant literary texts from the first century AD shed little light on the early period of application of the law. By the time of Justinian, the penalty for conviction was re-enslavement (*Inst.* 1.16.1), but although Claudius[69] is credited by Suetonius with having imposed that penalty on (a) certain freedman/men, it did not become a general punishment until the reign of Constantine.

Despite his use of plurals, Suetonius here appears to be generalising from one incident, reported in *D.* 37.14.5 pr.: Claudius ordered to be slave of his patron a freedman, who was proved to have suborned informers to bring a suit against his patron, impugning his status. Just possibly the patron, after his own acquittal, had charged his freedman with ingratitude, using the *actio*; but alternatively the freedman's activities may have become public at the patron's trial and evoked a direct reaction from Claudius. The circumstances, in any case, were exceptional, in view of the possible consequences for the *caput*, the legal status, of the patron, and there is a parallel in Nerva's punishing with death freedmen who had under Domitian informed against their patrons (Dio 68.13). These imperial interventions do not provide evidence for the general implementation of the law in response to complaints from patrons. A generation earlier than Claudius' reign, Valerius Maximus (2.6.6–7) numbers the re-enslavement of ungrateful freedmen among the *prisca instituta*, the ancient practices, of the Greeks, not the Romans.

After Claudius, the next reference to this provision of the *lex Aelia Sentia* is in Tacitus' account (*Annales* 13.26–7) of an appeal to Nero in AD 56 to rule on a proposal widely supported in the senate, that patrons be empowered to re-enslave undeserving ex-slaves. Nero's advisers being divided, he refused to institute this as a general penalty, instructing the senate to consider each case on its merits.

Those advisers who opposed the senate's proposal pointed to the ubiquity of freedmen in Roman society, specially among public servants, and to the freedman ancestry of many knights and senators, and hinted that slave-owners might use informal manumission for preference, rather than granting what was irrevocable (i.e. formal manumission with citizenship). Those favouring the senate's proposal argued that it was necessary as a deterrent, to frighten freedmen into respectful behaviour. The complaints Tacitus mentions are that patrons could assert their rights only by going to law with their freedmen, or using force. Their freedmen even dared to lift their hands against them, and what recourse had an injured patron? All he was allowed was to relegate his freedman a hundred miles from Rome, to the seashore of Campania.

This residence restriction is precisely that mentioned in Gaius 1.27 as imposed by the *lex Aelia Sentia* on all already criminous slaves, who on manumission were classed as *dediticii* and denied access to citizenship. What sort of behaviour by ordinary citizen freedmen could have incurred such a penalty? In the context of Tacitus' account, physical assault is perhaps implied. However, the penalty should perhaps be ascribed to Tacitus' rhetoric, rather than taken to be a quotation from the law. We have no more evidence than this for implementation of the *actio* during the first and most of the second century AD. By the late second century, the penalties magistrates are advised to impose can be rather stiffer, and include corporal punishment. That is not necessarily a reflection of hardening attitudes to freedmen generally, rather of the general trend in punishments.

According to Modestinus (*D.* 37.14.7.1) there had been several imperial instructions that provincial governors also (sc. as well as Rome's magistrates) were to award penalties according to the nature of the offence; as examples of penalties customarily imposed he mentions flogging, and confiscation of part of the freedman's property and giving it to the patron.

Ulpian goes into more detail. When a patron complains to the urban prefect (*D.* 1.12.1.10) that a freedman is disrespectful, and subjects himself, his children or his wife to verbal abuse and insult of more or less seriousness (*contumelia, convicium*) or something of the sort, then it is customary for the prefect to issue a warning (*comminari*) or inflict a flogging, or proceed further, 'for it is often necessary to proceed also to penal measures against freedmen'. If the patron demonstrates that the freedman has informed against him or conspired with his enemies against him, then he ought to be sentenced even to the mines. Similar guidelines are given to proconsuls (*D.* 37.14.1.1, Ulpian), with the addition that they ought to enquire individually into each case. If the freedman is disobliging (*inofficiosus*) he should merely be given a talking to, and warned that he will not get off so lightly next time; this remark perhaps affords a glimpse of the tip of an iceberg of minor complaints. That the law did not specify exactly what constituted an offence for which redress could be sought using this *actio* is suggested by one or two texts which seem to derive from actual enquiries made to magistrates. 'A freedman is ungrateful who does not render *obsequium* to his patron or refuses to administer his property or be tutor to his sons.' 'A freedwoman is not ungrateful because she practises her trade against the wishes of her patron.'[70]

For *convicium* or *contumelia*, Ulpian continues, the freedman ought even to be sent into temporary exile (this is reminiscent of Tacitus' *relegatio*); for physical assault, Ulpian recommends the same penalty as for delation or conspiracy – send him to the mines. Behaviour such as *convicium, contumelia* and assault, on the part of someone not one's own freedman, would allow the aggrieved party to sue on a charge of *iniuria*, 'outrage' (*D.* 47.10).[71] Freedmen could also be sued by their patrons on this charge, and in their case it was regarded as aggravated (*D.* 47.10.7.7–8, Ulpian):

Our emperor has said in a rescript that it is possible today to bring a civil action for *iniuria* even in atrocious cases. 'Atrocious' we understand as meaning an *iniuria* that is greater and more insulting (*contumeliosiorem*) than usual. Labeo says that an outrage becomes atrocious because of the person involved, or the time, or the circumstances (*persona, tempore, re*). An outrage becomes more atrocious in respect of the person when it is inflicted, for instance, upon a magistrate or a parent or patron.

The last sentence appears to be part of the citation of Labeo; Ulpian continues with examples in the categories *tempore* and *re*, repeating 'Labeo says' of the third. Apparently, then, from AD 4 patrons had the choice of either of two actions for use against their freedmen. Since the kinds of behaviour mentioned in the *Digest* title as constituting *iniuria* closely resemble those mentioned as giving rise to an action against a freedman for ingratitude, one wonders why it was thought necessary to create the latter. It may have been done in hope of its deterrent value, or it may have been thought necessary because of pressure of business arising from such complaints. We have no evidence either way.[72] By the early third century AD at least, the urban prefect had some special jurisdiction to deal with verbal or physical abuse of parents by emancipated children (*D.* 37.15.1.2: see Chapter 3 below, page 67), but whether this also had a special *actio* is not known; there is very little evidence on the matter. Since the offence of *iniuria* was aggravated if done by a freedman or emancipated child, presumably the penalty was more severe also; both had acted in violation of *pietas*.

Actions for *iniuria* by a freedman against a patron were possible but not encouraged; this was a defaming action, and freed slaves, like emancipated children, were not allowed to bring such actions (*D.* 37.15.2); this too was a matter of *pietas*. Freedwomen, though, or their husbands, found a loophole.

'We are considered', says Gaius (3.221),

> to suffer injury not only through ourselves, but through the children whom we have in our *potestas*, and likewise through our wives.[73] Therefore if you perform an outrage against my daughter, married to Titius, not only can there be an action against you in her name, but in mine too, and in that of Titius . . .

– or, indeed, of Titius' father too, if he was in power; as Ulpian, in the *persona* of the *pater*, remarks (*D.* 47.10.1.3), he has an action for outrage upon 'my children, my slaves, my wife or my daughter-in-law; for an outrage reflects upon us when it is done to those who are in our power or embraced in our affection (*affectus*).'

So, a freedwoman's husband could apparently sue her patron, who was not *his* patron; Marcellus, a jurist of the generation before Ulpian, had conceded this point (*D.* 47.10.11.7). Ulpian had marked his own copy of Marcellus with a note objecting that this should not apply in all cases; *levis enim coercitio etiam in nuptam vel convici non impudici dictio cur patrono denegetur?* ('Why should a patron be denied the use of moderate correction or strong language, short of the obscene, against a freedwoman who is married?')

Ulpian goes on to say that in his view, with which many agree, if her husband happens to be her fellow freedman, he ought not by any means to be allowed an action.[74] 'From which it appears that our freedmen not only cannot sue us in respect of outrages upon themselves, but also cannot do so on behalf of those (*eas*) in whom they have an interest that they should not be treated in this way.'

At the beginning of the last sentence Ulpian in fact restates the general rule, that freedmen were not granted actions for *iniuria* against their patrons (so they could not sue on behalf of others either). The previous sentence is an example of that rule, where the freedman is the husband of the injured freedwoman who has the same patron.

Ulpian is not at his clearest here; as will be observed also in Chapter 4 below, this tends to happen when he is trying to rationalise conventional reactions to women at law. In objecting to Marcellus' view, he reacts by taking the extreme case, of only very slightly injurious behaviour by the patron. Extreme cases, however, make bad law. Ulpian himself knew perfectly well that established practice was not to refuse freedmen *all* actions against their patrons (*D.* 47.10.7.2), but trivial complaints were rejected. Some protection was given to the freedman against more severe abuse by a patron, as it was also (*D.* 47.10.7.3) to emancipated children.

'It ought to be borne in mind', says Ulpian,

that permission to sue a patron for *iniuria* is granted to a freedman – not indeed always, but from time to time, if the outrage he has suffered is gross, for example, if he has been treated like a slave. But we will allow a patron to exercise a moderate amount of discipline upon a freedman, and the praetor will not put up with a freedman's complaint of an outrage that he has allegedly suffered, unless the severity of it moves him. For the praetor ought not to tolerate someone, who was a slave yesterday and a freedman today, complaining because his master has spoken rudely to him or given him a light slap or corrected him. But if he whipped him or flogged him or wounded him significantly, then it would be most fair that the praetor should come to his aid.

The ultimate sanction: back into slavery

For physical assault upon a patron, Ulpian proposed the severest penalty, condemnation to the mines, which, as remarked by Millar (1984: 138), was tantamount to slavery, and was the penalty for all really serious crime by that time. On actual re-enslavement, imperial policy seems to have fluctuated between the second and fourth centuries.[75] A constitution of Commodus (*D.* 25.3.6.1, Modestinus) prescribed forced service to the freedman's patron and, for persistent offenders, sale and re-enslavement (though to a different owner), not only for *contumelia* and violence but also for failure to provide support to a patron suffering poverty or illness. They were first to be 'restored to the power of patrons and obliged to render service to masters' (*eos in potestate patronorum redigi et ministerium dominis praestare*); if they did not take warning even from this, then the magistrate was to sell them off to a buyer and give the patron the purchase price. In other words, for a first offence, they were to be obliged to render *operae* to their patrons; the penalty for repeated offenders was loss of liberty and sale to someone other than the patron.[76]

Diocletian's references to re-enslavement may be thought ambiguous. In one response (*CJ* 6.3.12), he says that freedmen cannot be obliged to serve (the verb used is *servire*) the children of their patrons 'unless they are proved ungrateful'. However, actual enslavement does not seem to be meant; the passage as a whole denies the right of the children and *a fortiori* of patrons to oblige freedmen to reside with them. Three times he reassures anxious enquirers, probably themselves ex-slaves.

One man is worried about the lack of documentary proof of his manumission (*CJ* 7.16.26): 'Just as a patron cannot take away the liberty given to the manumitted, so he is compelled to provide a document (*instrumentum*) of manumission.'

One woman, Melitiana, is told (*CJ* 7.16.33): 'Even though your master manumitted you in return for money, nevertheless the liberty given you cannot be rescinded', and another, Eutychia (*CJ* 7.16.30): 'Liberty granted cannot be rescinded on the sole pretext of failure to provide *obsequium*.'

Diocletian says clearly, then, that freedom once granted cannot be rescinded by a patron, though the last example seems to imply that in certain circumstances a patron might do so. Constantine, on the other hand, insists on re-enslavement for the *ingratus*, even if the offence is slight (*levis*). However, the rhetorical language in which the rescript, like so many emanating from his office, is cast leaves obscure the nature of the offences meant.[77]

One would really like to know, also, what sort of behaviour Ulpian regarded as relatively innocuous and called *inofficiosum*, and also which of these offences were originally contemplated by the drafters of the *lex Aelia Sentia*. A general remedy in law, for *iniuria*, was already available under the Republic, and may sometimes have been used; there was also a remedy under a law of Sulla, *lex Cornelia de iniuriis*, for offences such as actual physical assault.[78] What is significant is that by AD 4 general standards of behaviour of freedmen towards patrons were perceived as having degenerated to the point where special legal remedy was needed. This was a matter of public concern. One might apply a phrase used by Ulpian (*D.* 37.15.1) with reference to the punishment by the urban praetor of sons for verbal abuse or physical assault against parents: it is a *delictum ad publicam pietatem pertinens*, an offence that affects the proper relationships of respect that ought to exist in society.

Senators are the people making vocal complaint in AD 56, and they were probably also the prime movers in AD 4, but one need not suppose that the phenomenon was confined to their freedmen. I have already remarked on a factor which must have had the effect of eroding the ideal of the quasi-paternal 'family' relationship between patrons and freedmen. More often than not, by the end of the Republic, the patron will himself have been someone who had previously been a slave. Likely effects on the relationship are, on one side, more crude exploitation and, on the other, less deference. These effects, particularly the latter, will have spread, as such changes in social *mores* tend to do.

CONCLUSION

It would be wrong, therefore, to interpret all the legal regulation of freedmen simply as expressive of the attitudes of a superior class towards a lower, as is done, for example, by MacMullen (1974: 104): 'The master class first defined and then punished freedmen. They defined them by law, making of them a separate group that owed reverence, duties and payments to the men they had once served.' The 'master', in one sense, class (i.e. the senatorial élite) formulated the laws, but they did not constitute by themselves the class of 'masters', *domini*. Nor were freedmen a 'separate group' from the masters; for when a *dominus* is also a *libertus*, which group is he in?

It is undeniable that, even where wealth was equal, the prestige ranking and degree of social acceptance of the freedman was lower than that of the freeborn. Social prejudice, particularly in the upper stratum of Roman society (i.e. the one that made the rules) undoubtedly played a part in motivating the imposition and retention of some of the restrictions and disadvantages under civil law which the freedman had to accept in the course of ordinary life. It would be mistaken, however, to assume that such prejudice is either a necessary or a sufficient explanation for the special features of the legal situation of freedmen, many of which seem, so far as our evidence goes, to have existed from the earliest stages of Roman society, while in several respects the freed slave's condition parallels that of certain freeborn citizens, such as emancipated children or women. The legal restraints upon him may have contributed towards lowering the social estimation of the freedman, without necessarily being in themselves an expression of lower esteem.

Although some of the operation of the law was intended to ensure that former owners would not be too much the losers by their generosity in releasing their former property, fairness of treatment for the ex-slave was also a concern. The relationship between freedman and patron was in part reciprocal, the patron having obligations of 'respect' towards the freedman which mirror those of the latter towards him.[79] The most important of these obligations of the patron consisted in duty to respect the freedman's non-servile status (this included allowing him – or her – independence to gain a livelihood) and, in case of need, to provide maintenance, and a ban on testifying against him in criminal cases. The central aim of the regulations concerning relations between patrons and freedmen, and also, as I have argued above, of the important legislation of the Augustan period, appear to have been to maintain stability and harmony in Roman society. In most aspects of civil life, patrons and freedmen, and freedmen and other fellow Romans, were, as citizens, equal before the law.

3

DEPENDENCE: THE ADULT CHILD

A distinctively Roman institution was *patria potestas*. A male head of household, as well as possessing sole ownership rights over the property of the *familia*, had in addition power over the persons not only of his slaves (as also did women owners) but of his children and his sons' children. Gaius (*Inst.* 1.55) observes carefully, perhaps with a slight tinge of regret, that this *potestas* over children was not *quite* unique:

> Also in our power are our children whom we have begotten in lawful marriage (*iustis nuptiis*). This right is peculiar to Roman citizens; for there are virtually no other men who have such power over their sons as we have. And this was stated by the deified Hadrian in the edict he issued regarding those who petitioned him for Roman citizenship for themselves and for their children. (It has not escaped me that the Galatians believe children to be in the power of their parents.)

Surprisingly, he does not mention the existence of *potestas* in provincial communities with Latin rights.[1]

'Over our sons' says Gaius, but daughters were of course also subject to *potestas*; like grammarians, Roman lawyers allowed male to embrace female (*D.* 50.16.1). When the head of household, *paterfamilias* – who was also literally their *pater*, father – died, children of both sexes (*filiifamilias*, *filiaefamilias*) were freed from his *potestas* over their persons and, once they were of age, gained legal capacity as well. Sons, but not daughters, then acquired *potestas* over their children in turn.

The effect of *patria potestas* upon the workings of Roman society can be studied in a number of ways. Particular attention

52

has been paid to it recently in the context of the structure and character of the Roman family. Demographic studies, thought to indicate a generally high age, in the late twenties, for marriage for men (though a decade or so less for women), have suggested the conclusion that only a minority of men were still subject to *potestas* past their mid-twenties. The elderly Roman patriarch is found to be atypical, and the result is to minimise the effects of *patria potestas*.

Although the statistical estimate may, I believe, be somewhat exaggerated,[2] it is more important to observe that to say that this minimised the effects of *potestas* does not necessarily mean that these effects were minimal either for the individual or for society as a whole; especially when one remembers that a Roman woman was legally adult at 12 years old, a man at about 14,[3] and that the average life expectancy may have been as low as 25 (Frier 1982; 1983). For most Romans in *potestas*, the practical importance of this status will in some respects have manifested itself only rarely, on those occasions, relatively infrequent in the course of life (such as marrying and divorcing), when the power of the *pater* over their persons came into play. However, they will more often have had to cope with the effects of the other aspect of a father's power, that over the property of the household, for from that stemmed many of the legal disabilities affecting the dealings of the individual man (or woman) in society at large, that is, the legal capacity of the individual.

One important question, raised by others in the past, that will have to be considered is why *potestas* lasted as long as it did. There appears to be a puzzle there, whether we believe that it was a serious inconvenience for the day-to-day dealings of Romans with each other – in which case it might seem perversity to hang on to it – or whether we choose to stress the various shifts, devices and modifications that were introduced to mitigate it – in which case its eventual retention, becoming apparently ever more pointless, might be ascribed to sheer inertia.[4] Why did the Romans possess and think worth retaining a system which imposed drastic distinctions between the legal capacities of individual Roman citizens, based neither on age, sex nor free birth?

POWER OVER THE PERSON

Stated baldly, and at their theoretical maximum, the effects of *patria potestas* on *filiifamilias* seem rather alarming.[5] However, as Eyben (1991) and Saller (1991) have recently reminded us, a distinction must be made between the formal severity of these powers and their more humane implementation in practice; Saller emphasises in particular the difference between the way in which fathers behaved towards their freeborn children and towards their slaves, despite the similarity of the legal authority they exercised over both.

Moreover, these powers were to some extent modified in the course of Roman history. In the sphere of family law, children could not marry or divorce without the consent of the *pater*, though whether *patres* in general were given to insisting upon their rights in these matters, with complete disregard for their children's opinions on choice of partner, is perhaps doubtful.[6] Eventually Augustus intervened to empower magistrates to override a father's opposition, if it was judged unreasonable, and Marcus Aurelius to prevent disruption of happy marriages by insisting on divorce. These interventions restricted, but by no means abolished, the father's authority,[7] and in themselves they do not represent any very marked inroads upon *patria potestas*. Considerations of property (i.e. the bride's dowry) or personal character were perhaps the most likely motives for parental opposition, and the imperial intention was not to prevent fathers from protecting their children's interests. Formally, the fact that marriage had certain juridical consequences meant that the consent of the holder of *potestas* was necessary, since the parties had no legal capacity to act alone. The consent of the *pater* was also needed because the children of his son's marriage would be additional members of his *familia*, under his *potestas*; as for daughters, in early Rome a daughter had customarily, though not necessarily, passed at marriage out of the *familia* of her birth into the *familia* and *potestas* of her husband or his *paterfamilias*, but this was already very rare by Augustus' time (Gardner 1986: 12–13).

More dramatically, the *pater* had originally had, or so Romans believed, the power of life and death over children, and the power of sale. The power of sale into slavery, or even civil bondage, mentioned in the previous chapter, survived in classical law only as the model for the procedure for emancipation or adoption. By the classical period, the former, the so-called *ius vitae et necis*, survives in full (until AD 374) only as the right of the *pater* to decide not to acknowledge and rear a newly-born child; the punishment of older children must be subject to the judgment of an advisory council of family and friends, or referred to a court of law.[8] Only a handful of instances are attested of fathers inflicting death or banishment on adult children. These are not to be taken as presenting the typical pattern of paternal behaviour. Some of these instances involve public offences, sometimes actually referred by the state to the family for punishment, others (e.g. those in Valerius Maximus 5.8) are cited as examples of exceptional severity. An ambiguous and fragmentary reference to a fifth-century AD commentary on Gaius (*Autun Frag.* 85–6) appears to indicate that even as early as the Twelve Tables some qualification was introduced to the father's power of life and death.[9] The overall impression is that, by the later Republic at least, the exercise of such power was felt to require some strong justification.

PROPERTY POWER

Ownership rights over all the property of the *familia* were vested in the *pater*. Though children (and slaves) could engage in transactions on his behalf, anything they acquired belonged to him alone. The same applied to gifts and bequests. In theory, this could be a source of considerable inconvenience for an adult son or daughter, living perhaps in a separate establishment, even married and a parent and, in the case of some sons, with a public career. In a well-known *reductio ad absurdum*, Daube (1969: 75–6), with a fine disregard for statistical probabilities, envisages a family of five[10] surviving generations, ranging in age from the twenties to 90. 'If the seventy-five-year-old senator or the forty-year-old General or the twenty-year-old student wanted to buy a bar of chocolate, he had to ask the *senex* for the money.' In practice, as he points out, at the lower levels of society, where people had little or no accumulated means, questions of ownership were unlikely to arise. Among the well-to-do, the common solution was to put some means at the disposal of the adult child.

This could be done by making a regular allowance for spending, or by the grant of a *peculium*. Cicero's son received an allowance. The 19-year-old Marcus, about to travel abroad, told his father plainly that he expected it to be a handsome one;[11] his father's reply (reported in *ad Att.* 12.7.1) indicates that upper-class parents were, not surprisingly, guided in these matters by observing the practice of their peers: 'I said I would give him as much as Publius Lentulus or the *flamen* Lentulus gave to their sons.' Generosity was stimulated by concern for public image (*ad Att.* 14.16.4): 'It's not only my duty to see that Cicero wants for nothing, but it affects my reputation as well.'

His friend Atticus handled arrangements for payment of the allowance, which in the summer of 44 BC, if not before, became annual (though Atticus prudently arranged for it to be doled out in instalments). It was funded partly by the rents of some flats owned by Cicero in Rome and partly, no doubt with Terentia's consent, from the rents of some property forming part of her dowry.[12] However, Cicero anticipates reducing (if not actually terminating) the allowance once Marcus will be back in Rome and equipped with a suitably affluent wife.[13] Presumably his intention was to earmark the wife's dowry (which, in the eyes of the law, would while the marriage lasted be the property of Marcus' father) as a source of funds for Marcus.

The *peculium* as a personal fund

An alternative method to making an allowance was to assign a *peculium* – that is, to put at the son's or daughter's disposal a sum of money, or some property which could be used by the latter to generate an income. Cicero perhaps intended to use the anticipated dowry for a *peculium*, rather than an allowance. The former arrangement would give Marcus, the married man, greater practical independence, befitting his mature situation. Roscius of Ameria, for example, at the age of forty was living in the countryside and looking after some farms belonging to his father, which may have constituted his *peculium*; Cicero says he had the usufruct of them (Cic. *pro Rosc. Am.* 39, 42).

Roscius in effect was managing the farms. This would surely have necessitated his keeping some sort of accounts (as we know slaves with a *peculium* did), which is what one would expect. Cicero provides some evidence of the keeping of accounts by *filii*. In the *Verrines* (2.1.60–1), in discrediting Verres' claim that the numerous statues and pictures in his possession were items he had bought, Cicero says, 'I have all his accounts and his father's. I have read and absorbed them most thoroughly, the father's to the end of his life, yours (*turning to Verres*) for the time up to which you say you have kept them.'

It is not unheard of, Cicero admits, for a man to keep no accounts, but quite deplorable, *minime probandum*. (Naturally, he takes a different line speaking for the defence in *pro Caelio* 17, when the prosecutor claims that Cicero's client is in debt and extravagant, and calls for his account books. 'Someone in his father's power keeps no accounts.') It also happens, he says, that men start to keep accounts, not having done so previously, but Verres' claim is something novel: that he kept them for a time, until 73 BC (that is, conveniently, until he started his term of office in Sicily), and then stopped. We do not know when Verres' father died, but it does not matter, for Cicero is talking about Verres' earlier art-collecting activities while legate and proquaestor in Cilicia (80–79 BC), and, as he says, he has the accounts of both father and son for that period. Both are needed, since what the son bought belonged legally to the father.

The use of sons in business life

Provision for living expenses need not, however, be the sole purpose for constituting such a fund. The *peculium* receives a good deal of attention in legal texts, in which the holders of *peculium*, who may be either *filiifamilias* or slaves, are for the most part acting, in effect, as managers (*institores*) of some part of the business interests of the *paterfamilias*.[14] Thomas (1982) has observed that although the lawyers do not distinguish in principle between sons and slaves acting as agents for the *pater*, the overwhelming majority of the cases referred to concern slaves, and some at least of those involving sons concern transactions within the family, such as provision of dowries for sisters. He suggests, therefore, that the *peculium* of *filii* was intended only to provide for living expenses, and not to carry on business activities. He rests his argument chiefly upon the *senatusconsultum Macedonianum*.[15] This Vespasianic enactment directed magistrates to refuse an action, even after the death of the *pater*, to creditors who had lent money to a *filiusfamilias*. Since, it seems at first sight, the effect would be to make it virtually impossible for sons to borrow money, their usefulness as business managers would, Thomas observes, be drastically impaired. One might add that running their domestic affairs would also be more difficult.

However, the law was not quite so much an ass as all that. Somehow, sons in power had to be enabled to carry on with their lives in reasonable independence. Already before the end of the Republic, a number of praetorian actions were available which, according to circumstances, made the *pater* either partially or totally liable for contracts by sons, so that creditors had some guarantee. It should be noticed, also, that the use of slaves as business agents had a similar drawback to that involved in using *filii*. Slaves could not themselves personally be sued on obligations they had contracted, not even after they had been manumitted (*CJ* 4.14.2) – the equivalent, for them, of a son's being emancipated in the lifetime of his *pater* or becoming *sui iuris* at his death. However, we know, from numerous references in legal texts, and now also from the clear evidence of the Murecine tablets, that it was common practice to make use of slaves in this way for the conduct of business. The legal difficulty was equally easily surmounted, whether sons or slaves were used.

A number of praetorian actions were introduced, possibly in the first century BC, which were applicable both to sons and to slaves. The extent of the liability of the *pater* (and so the creditor's chances of recovery) depended on whether his son or slave had acted with or without his knowledge and, in the former case, with or without his express instruction. If the *pater* had given his authority, then he was liable to the full extent of the obligation (*D.* 15.4: *actio quod iussu*). If he did not have knowledge of the transactions entered into by his son or slave, he was liable up to the extent of the *peculium* and also to the extent that his estate had profited (*D.* 15.3: *actio de peculio et in rem verso*). If the *pater* merely knew that his son or slave was trading with all or part of the *peculium*, but had not explicitly authorised a transaction, a creditor could demand distribution of the *peculium* among the creditors, and bring an action against him (*D.* 14.4: *actio tributoria*) if he did not comply. All these actions were equally available whether the transactions were carried out by sons or slaves. In addition, the *actio institoria*, and its more specialised relative the *actio exercitoria* (concerning agents appointed to run a ship), applied whether the agent, or manager (most examples concern businesses), was the principal's own slave or son, or an external person, slave or free.[16] Whether in practice the other party to a transaction regularly ascertained in advance that the slave or *filius* (if indeed it was known that he was a *filius* – concealment was not unknown: *D.* 15.5.6) had paternal consent is unlikely. It would be rather impractical and cumbersome, and in most ordinary instances the principal would be sufficiently well known at least by repute for the creditworthiness of the holder of the *peculium* to be assessed. A remark by the jurist Paul, in his sixth book on the edict, indicates that it was common practice for a *pater* to give a general blanket authorisation of administration, to cover all necessary operations with the *peculium*. What formal procedure, if any, was followed, or what provision was made for verification, we do not know.[17]

It was in fact less convenient to have anyone other than a son or slave as *institor*. Not only did this not automatically, as it would in modern law, create liabilities of the principal to a third party, but it did not give him, for his part, the rights that he had if the agent were his own son or slave (*D.* 14.3.1); a notorious lacuna in Roman law is the lack of development of the concept of agency. In practice, this awkwardness also was overcome by the development of appropriate legal fictions and praetorian procedures, but these were relatively indirect and cumbersome.[18]

The preference for having a son or slave as *institor* is nicely illustrated by a commemorative inscription from Macedonia (*ILS* 7479):

> *Vitalis C. Lavi Fausti ser., idem f., verna domo natus, hic situs est, vixit annos xvi, institor tabernas Aprianas, a populo acceptus, idem ab diis ereptus. Rogo vos, viatores, si quid minus dedi mesura ut patri meo adicere, ignoscatis.*

> Here lies Vitalis, who lived 16 years, Gaius Lavius Faustus' homeborn slave and also his son, manager of the Apriana tavern, popular with the public, carried off by the gods. I ask you, wayfarers, if ever I gave short measure to profit my father, forgive.

The inscription was probably set up by the father, who indulges in a pleasantry in the last line, obviously confident in the trust and goodwill of the neighbours. If his son had given short measure, he, the father, would have been the one responsible for making matters good. But, in view of his evident affection for and confidence in his son, why had he not manumitted him? His age would have been no bar to becoming a citizen, since he was Lavius' son; 'good cause' could have been shown under the terms of the *lex*

59

Aelia Sentia (Gaius 1.19). Certainly, his age might have made him less satisfactory as a business manager. People dealing with a 'minor' (i.e. someone *sui iuris* but under the age of 25) were in general well advised to be cautious and take advantage of the *lex Plaetoria*,[19] by insisting that he use a *curator* for legal transactions; to have to involve someone else (probably Lavius himself) would be bothersome. Part of the reason may have been that once Vitalis was manumitted, Lavius lost any power of direct action to enforce his deals if things went wrong (if, for instance, the wine suppliers defaulted on their deliveries, or the wine was 'off'). That difficulty could have been got round by adopting him (Gardner 1989). Most likely, however, nothing was done simply because of the practical difficulties involved in getting access to the appropriate magistrate and tribunal to secure formal manumission (Weaver 1990).

There was no real hindrance, then, to the use of sons as agents, and we need not follow Thomas (1982) in supposing that the *peculium* of a son was never more than a source of funds for personal expenses. Indeed, the two functions were often likely to overlap, as, for instance, when a son either personally or through his own slave agents (*servi peculiares*), carried on the enterprise which was the source of his income.

In practice, though, we may doubt whether much use is likely to have been made of sons as business managers in the upper classes of Roman society; use would be made of slaves, freedmen and external employees. Lower down the social scale, however, we might well expect to find a son of the house looking after part of the family's income-earning activities. Here again, the Murecine tablets amply illustrate the use of such agents or representatives. These are mostly slaves, possibly reflecting the extent to which the commercial activity of Puteoli was carried on by freedmen businessmen, among whom adult freeborn sons are likely to have been relatively scarcer than among the freeborn population (Treggiari 1969: 212–13). The way in which slaves function in these transactions, however, corresponds to the way in which sons would perform. In the tablets we may note as freeborn Onirus and possibly a Faustus among the Sulpicii (see Chapter 2 above), though whether these are still *filiifamilias* is not indicated.

Slaves appear in the tablets more often acting for creditors than for debtors,[20] and consequently there would appear to be less need for assurance of the authorisation of the *dominus* for the transaction. Particularly interesting, however, is *TP 7*[21] recording a transaction dated 2 July AD 37.

> *Diognetus C. Novi Cypaeri ser(vus) scripsi iussu Cypaeri domini mei coram ipso me locasse Hesycho Ti. Iulii Augusti (liberti) Eueni ser(vo) horreum duodecimum in horreis Bassianis publicis Puteolanorum medi(i)s in quo repositum est triticum Alexandrinum quod pignori accepit hac die a C. Novio Euno, item in iisdem horreis horreis imis inter columnia ubi repositos habet saccos leguminum ducentos quos pignori accepit ab eodem Euno, ex Kal(endis) Iulis in menses singulos sestertiis singulis num(mis). Act(um) Put(eolis).*

I, Diognetus, slave of Gaius Novius Cypaerus, have written on the order of my master that in his presence I have leased to Hesychus, the slave of Tiberius Julius Evenus, freedman of Augustus, the twelfth warehouse in the central Bassian warehouses, community property of the people of Puteoli, in which is stored wheat which he has received as a pledge today from Gaius Novius Eunus, likewise in the same warehouses, on the bottom floor (?), a space between the columns where he has stored 200 sacks of legumes which he has received from the same Eunus as a pledge, from the Kalends of July for one sesterce a month. Done at Puteoli.

This tablet is one of a group of five relating to borrowings by Eunus.[22] On 28 June[23] he borrowed 10,000 sesterces from Evenus, in the latter's absence, through Hesychus, giving various stocks of grain and pulses, stored in this warehouse, as security. On the same date as *TP 7*, he borrows a further 3,000[24] from Hesychus on the same security. Hesychus (on behalf of Evenus) now takes over the rental agreement for the storage of the pledged goods. This is equivalent to the creditor's actually physically taking possession of the goods; they cannot now be removed without his consent, and he is now the leasing tenant.

It is not thought necessary for Evenus to be present (and indeed his obligations to the landlord are of the slightest, since the rent is set at a merely nominal figure). Diognetus' master, however, is specifically stated to be present, although the necessity for his presence is not immediately obvious since the leasing contract is being made by Diognetus, which is something that a slave (or a *filius*) was legally quite capable of doing in the master's absence.

The reason may be, as Serrao (1984) suggests, that in view of the importance of the client and the value of the goods stored, it was thought necessary (or may even have been requested) to receive a specific assurance of the master's authorisation. This would guarantee his liability in full, and not merely to the extent of any *peculium* Diognetus may have had, for the value of the goods stored.[25]

What is true in this text of a slave acting on behalf of his owner could equally well, in fact, apply to a son acting on behalf of his *pater*. We may therefore take the evidence of the Murecine tablets as showing us the way in which, in practice, sons working in the family business carried on from day to day in Roman towns.

They also enable us to see how *filiifamilias* were able, for the most part, to carry on in daily life without much practical inconvenience, though some inconveniences there were. In particular, they could not, with a few exceptions, litigate independently, nor make provision by will for their children nor alienate property (though – what must have been a great convenience – they could buy, even by mancipation, as indeed could slaves, since the title in whatever was acquired belonged to the *pater*: Gaius 2.87).

Special concessions – the *peculium castrense*

Augustus (partly perhaps as a recruiting incentive) removed from serving soldiers still *in potestate* some of the inconveniences to which their absence on service made them more liable than others, by giving a special status to any property which came into their hands, whether directly from the *pater* or in other ways. This was known as the *peculium castrense*, and the soldier (or, after Hadrian, ex-soldier also) had the right not only to dispose of it by will but also to alienate it in his lifetime, and even to bring lawsuits, independently of his *pater*, in its defence. It reverted to his *pater* if he died intestate; if, however, he outlived his *pater*, the property remained his, instead of being absorbed into the paternal estate.

These were marginal concessions, applying only to a small proportion of Roman citizens, and extended (as *peculium quasi castrense*) by Constantine to the inner circle of Palatine staff, and under later emperors to a wider range of public salaried officials and to churchmen.[26] Most citizens were unaffected; for them there was over the centuries even less alteration – and that only at a very late date – to the principle of paternal property-power.

One change of general application was made by Constantine, who, as we shall see below, provided that bequests from a mother should not be absorbed into the paternal estate but must eventually be passed on intact to the child, and it was not until Justinian that this was extended to acquisitions from other sources. Again, however, this is merely a marginal change, as far as the experience of the child in power is concerned; control of this maternal property, as of all the rest of the property of the *familia*, remained with the *pater* during his lifetime.

RELEASE FROM *POTESTAS:* STRIKE THE FATHER DEAD?

There were two ways out of *potestas* into legal independence. One, in the lifetime of the *pater*, was by emancipation. The other was at his death. It has been seriously suggested by more than one scholar[27] that, because of the system that gave the *pater* sole property rights, hostility to fathers, and indeed parricide, were common in ancient Rome. The most extreme statements are perhaps those of Veyne (1978; 1987). Describing the adult male's situation as 'psychologically . . . intolerable', he says (1987: 29–30), 'In these circumstances, the obsession with parricide – a relatively common crime – is not surprising. The reasons for committing such a horrible act are quite comprehensible and require no Freudian feats of explanation.'

According to Veyne (1978), Roman sons who had not been orphaned by the age of 20 resented the half (or so) who had. Parent–child relations were, he says, normally cold and lacking in affection. He ascribes to 'absence of parental instinct' the testamentary practices of the Romans. Certainly, bequests to outsiders, and even their nomination as heirs, are not uncommon. However, one should now read Champlin (1991), whose finding, after a study of more than 1,000 wholly or partly surviving Roman wills, is that in fact children, and sons in particular, were normally preferred by testators to all other heirs. Roman law also worked to protect the inheritance rights of children. Various laws passed in the Republic (*Cincia, Falcidia, Voconia, Furia*), though primarily aimed at minimising fragmentation of estates, irrespective of the identity of the heirs, would obviously tend to benefit *filii*, and

the latter's interests were specifically provided for by the praetorian procedure of *querela inofficiosi testamenti*, 'complaint of
unduteous will'. Children who thought themselves unfairly treated
could challenge the will, and if the petition was accepted, their
share was increased to at least the minimum required by the
Falcidian law, in spite of the will, on the legal fiction that
the testator must have been insane, *color insaniae* (*D.* 5.2.2).

As evidence in support of his belief that parricide was common,
Veyne cites Velleius Paterculus (2.77.2). Concerning the proscriptions of the second triumvirate, Velleius says:

> The point must be noted, however, that towards the pro-
> scribed, the loyalty of wives was greatest, that of freedmen
> moderate, of slaves not negligible, of sons non-existent – so
> difficult is it for men to bear any delay in achieving their
> hopes, however conceived.

The rhetorical intent of the passage is clear. In describing the
horrors and violations of the natural and normal order inflicted
by the proscriptions and the civil wars generally, Roman poets,
historians and moralists commonly exploit for their rhetorical
value allegations of such behaviour – regarded as 'unnatural' – as
that characterised by Velleius. They also, of course, like to offer
instances of the opposite, of self-sacrifice and outstanding *pietas*
in the most adverse circumstances. Individual examples both of
domestic loyalty and of its opposite may be found in the literary
sources for the triumviral proscriptions. Since the triumvirs confiscated the property of the proscribed, hope of accelerating their
inheritance can hardly have been a special motive for sons to
betray their fathers. Much of the 'unnatural' behaviour described
in our sources is not attributed to sons and daughters, but to
other relatives.[28] Moreover, analysis of the events described in
political terms, an aspect neglected by our moralising sources,
reveals in fact a high degree of family solidarity during the troubles
(Hinard 1990). In any case, the period in question can scarcely
be taken to be representative of filial behaviour in normal times.

Among the lawyers, Daube (1969: 88–90) also subscribes, on no
very convincing evidence, to the view that parricide was common,
although in practice he concentrates on the rather special case of
filii ruinously in debt.

Cicero, defending on a charge of parricide a *filius* (aged 40 and
apparently living quietly in the countryside on the proceeds of

farms assigned as *peculium* to him by his father) mentions only in order to reject it a suggestion hypothetically supposed to come from the opposition, that debts engendered by riotous living drove him to it (*pro Rosc. Amer.* 39); the inference, according to Daube, is that these 'ranked as standard motives for parricide in the trials'. What trials? For the period between 200 and 80 BC Mommsen (*Strafr.* 614 n. 1, 644 n. 1) found only five possible instances, not all of which, however, concerned the killing of fathers – and one of which (Val. Max. 6.1.5) actually involved the exercise of paternal authority to put sons to death (see Cloud 1971: 38–47). Daube also mentions a moralising anecdote in Seneca *de Clementia* 1.15 about a plotting son and a forgiving father, but strangely omits the collection in Val. Max. 5.9 of four magnanimous fathers (one of them anonymous) whose sons were suspected of parricidal intent.

Actual parricides, however, are not easy to find in the sources. In the Principate, two passages in Suetonius may relate to actual events. Augustus (Suet. *div. Aug.* 33) was lenient to one man who was 'clearly guilty' according to Suetonius; he was also an assessor on the occasion reported by Seneca *de Clem.* 1.15 (above). Only in *Claudius* 34 does Suetonius use a plural: 'He used to exact interrogation under torture, and the punishment of parricides, immediately and in his presence.'[29] Details are suspiciously lacking. Seneca (*de Clem.* 1.23) alleges that Claudius 'sewed up more men in the sack' (i.e. punished more parricides) within five years than during all previous time; however, as he continues by rhetorically developing a paradox, that the institution of the punishment was what *encouraged* children to the deed, too much reliance cannot be placed on this statement. This is scarcely enough to justify Daube in saying, 'There were enough cases of the crime for a ruler to develop his own style of dealing with it'.

Daube also accepts the tradition that the *senatusconsultum Macedonianum*, mentioned above, was named after a son who murdered his father; though the wording of the *sctum*, as given in *D.* 14.6.1 pr., suggests rather that Macedo was a usurer.

> Whereas in addition to the other causes of crime which nature supplied to Macedo, he also added debt and often supplied means of wrongdoing to evil dispositions, in that he lent money to debtors who were, to say no more, unreliable: it was decided that no action or claim is to be granted

to anyone who has lent money to a *filiusfamilias*, even after the death of the parent in whose power he was, so that pernicious moneylenders may know that no debt of a son in power can be made good by waiting for the father's death.[30]

Daube outlines a melodramatic scenario, a 'Rake's Progress', of *filii* borrowing to finance extravagant lifestyles, then caught in a descending spiral of embezzlement, blackmail by unscrupulous lenders, and ultimately parricide; scarcely the picture that emerges from the cases sedately discussed in *Digest* 14.6, *de senatusconsulto* Macedoniano, and *Codex Justinianus* 4.28. Ulpian (*D.* 14.6.1.3) envisages the possibility of borrowings by *filii* who are senior magistrates, even consuls, and by holders of *peculium castrense* (to whom the *senatusconsultum Macedonianum* does not apply). In any case, the *senatusconsultum*, as we have already seen, was not held to apply to borrowings authorised by a *pater*.

It cannot simply be assumed, on the basis of such evidence, that the parricidal spendthrift is typical of the average Roman *filius*, nor even that among *filii* there was widespread resentment of their status. As we saw above, in the case of Cicero and his son Marcus, public opinion, and the *mores* of one's social peers, were powerful influences both upon the expectations of sons and upon their treatment by their fathers.

EMANCIPATION AND ITS EFFECTS

Departure from *potestas* during a father's lifetime was effected by emancipation (Gaius 1.132 describes the procedure, more elaborate than for the manumission of a slave).[31] In addition, if the child was under age (*impubes*), the manumitting parent became *tutor*, with administrative responsibility over the child's property. The main advantage for the adult child was the achievement of legal independence and the ability to acquire and dispose of property. The main disadvantages were the loss, for the sons, of prospective *potestas* over their children already born (who remained in the *potestas* of the manumitting *pater*) and, for both sons and daughters, of automatic right to part of the family inheritance.

The latter disadvantage, at least, had effectively disappeared by the end of the Republic. Praetorian rules of succession allowed emancipated children to claim a share in an estate against, or in default of, a will; provided, that is, that they added to the total estate any property they had themselves acquired in the meantime (*collatio bonorum*).[32]

The emancipated son or daughter and the parent had certain duties and obligations to each other closely resembling, as we saw in Chapter 2, those between freed slave and patron. The father retained certain rights, even against a will, over any estate left by an emancipated child who predeceased him (*D*. 37.12, *passim*), though these rights were less extensive than those of a patron against a freedman. The emancipated child's brothers and sisters had no claim against his estate (unlike the children of a patron). If he could show intent to defraud, a patron had available the Fabian action, where his freedman had left a will, or the Calvisian, if he was intestate, to make claims against the estate; a manumitting parent could not bring such claims, 'for it is unfair', said Gaius, 'that freeborn men should not be free to alienate what is their own' (*D*. 37.12.2). Fathers were not, however, compelled to honour testamentary requests (*fideicommissa*) and they could, if they wished, claim part of the estate against any instituted heirs, or even all of it against undesirable heirs such as prostitutes (Paconius, cited by Paul, *D*. 37.12.3). Whether such a claim would be upheld where the instituted heirs were also the children of an emancipated son is not stated, but seems unlikely. (See Chapter 2 above, p. 23 and n. 34.)

As we saw in the last chapter, emancipated children, like freedmen, were expected to show *obsequium*, as *pietas* required, to their manumitters (*D*. 37.15), though fathers could not impose conditions, such as *operae*, for emancipation. It is unclear what recourse, if any, parents had in classical law against ungrateful or disrespectful children, such as patrons had had, since AD 4, against freedmen, and there is very little evidence for the later empire. By the early third century, at any rate, they had some recourse. According to Ulpian, the prefect of Rome administered punishment appropriate to the degree of the offence if a son verbally abused or physically assaulted his father or mother, whom he ought to venerate. This Ulpian describes (*D*. 37.15.1.2) as a *delictum ad publicum pietatem pertinens*, an offence affecting the proper relations of respect that should exist in society. He adds that a son who *maleficos appellaverat*, which in context should mean not just had 'called criminal' but 'brought criminal charges against', the parents who he says reared him, is to be judged

unworthy of military service. Much later, in AD 367, a rescript in
the names of Valentinian, Valens and Gratian says that the laws
have willed that children who have insulted or inflicted some
atrocious injury upon their parents are to have their emancipation
cancelled and lose the freedom which they have not deserved (*CJ*
8.49). Since Constantine, ungrateful freedmen had been liable to
re-enslavement, even for slight offences (*CJ* 6.7.2).

Motives for emancipation

How common emancipation was, and the relative frequency of
different reasons for emancipation, are matters on which there can
be no certainty. Clearly, emancipation could serve a number of
purposes.[33] Lacey (1986: 134–5) attaches importance to the fact
that it enabled the emancipated son to 'exercise the *ius commercii*
fully', without adducing any reasons why this should be desired,
other than that the situation of a son in power was 'awkward'.
The limited extent of its inconvenience has already been indicated,
and as we shall see below, evidence for actual emancipations does
not support the idea that consciousness of such awkwardness was
a prime motive. Lacey elaborates:

> It seems to me that the development of the will was to allow
> the *paterfamilias* to emancipate a son so that the son could
> enjoy the *ius commercii* in his father's lifetime without losing
> his succession rights to *paterfamilias* when he became *sui
> iuris*, rather than that the will was developed in order to
> enable the *paterfamilias* to disinherit, wholly or partially,
> one or more of his children.

Neither seems particularly likely to me; just as probable, if not
more so, is that wills developed in order to enable either a childless
pater to benefit someone other than the agnates (e.g. his widow),
if he chose, at his death, or (a related case) one whose only
children were daughters married with *manus* to leave his estate
either to them or to his grandchildren in another *familia*. These
explanations account better than Lacey's for the ancient procedures, in particular for the *testamentum in procinctu*, the will
made on the eve of battle.

Emancipation could be used, for example, to allow the making
of a will (e.g. by a parent), something not possible for anyone
(except, after Augustus, soldiers) subject to *potestas*; or to enable

a child personally to receive a legacy or inheritance. Individual instances of these can be found in the sources; especially frequent is emancipation as a condition of an inheritance, the condition often apparently being motivated by the testator's personal hostility to or mistrust of the child's father.[34] After the *senatusconsultum Orphitianum* (AD 178) made children the heirs on intestacy of their mothers, such a condition became less effective as a means of keeping property bequeathed to them by mothers out of the hands of their fathers.[35] However, it was not until AD 315 that emancipation became unnecessary in order to ensure that what a mother left would (at least ultimately) benefit her child. Constantine provided (*CJ* 6.60.1 = *C.Th.* 8.18.1) that bequests from a mother should form part of the property of the *pater* during his lifetime, but his rights were limited to enjoyment (i.e. he could not sell or otherwise dispose of it), and the property must in due course pass to the children. Although Humbert (1972: 398) calls this 'a revolutionary reform, opening a breach in the authoritarian edifice of the Roman family', on the grounds that it breaks an essential prerogative of the *patria potestas*, he has to acknowledge that, in comparison with a testamentary condition of emancipation, it took less from the *pater*, since it not only left him in enjoyment of the maternal property during his lifetime, but recognised his ownership (*dominium*). In principle, this does not seem to curtail his rights much more than the long-standing rules regarding the rights which as a husband he had over his wife's dowry. If a marriage was ended by the husband's death, the wife or her father could reclaim the dowry from the heirs; however, since it was the husband's property, it did not revert to her or her father automatically, but had to be claimed by bringing an action, the *actio rei uxoriae*, against the heirs. So, likewise, the children are, in Humbert's phrase (p. 400), 'only creditors for the value of the maternal property, not its future proprietors'. This still left the father free to make such inroads on the property as he wished during his lifetime. It was not until nearly twenty years later that this power was curtailed, and then at first only with reference to fathers who remarried (*C.Th.* 8.18.3: AD 334); they were to be deprived of their usufructuary right to the property. They were to regard themselves as merely its guardians (*tutelae vice*) until the children seemed of fit age (*probata aetate esse videantur*). The significance of this last clause is illuminated by a suggestion by Arjava,[36] that after his remarriage the maternal property (*bona materna*) was treated as a kind of *peculium quasi castrense* for the children of the previous marriage – that is, so long as the father did not emancipate them. If he did, I presume he would then be expected to release the maternal property to them in its entirety.

In AD 315, matters had not advanced so far. Just a month or two later than the ruling of July 315 (*C.Th.* 8.18.1), in response to an enquiry from the deputy prefect of Italy (*C.Th.* 8.18.2), Constantine had elaborated further. Fathers were to have possession of the maternal property, but without the power to alienate, 'so that, if the coming of age of their children invites fathers to emancipate them, and they wish to see their children as *patresfamilias*' (apparently sons only are thought of here), then they may assign these children one-third of their maternal property (calculated by independent assessors), though this is done merely as a favour, *muneris causa*, and the father remains owner, while the children are to accept dutifully whatever their father chooses to give them.[37] In itself, emancipation will not have been of financial benefit to the child, and the emperor's provision is perhaps as much in recognition of the situation of need in which some independent children might find themselves, as actuated by respect for testators' wishes or blood relationships. Imperial rescripts from the reign of Marcus Aurelius onwards attest legal recognition of the right of children in power to be maintained by their parents, and vice versa, in case of need, so far as their means allowed; Ulpian's opinion was that the same applied to emancipated children and their parents, and, since this right was based on equity and the affection of blood kin, also to illegitimate children and to mothers.[38] For anything beyond actual maintenance, however, they had no claim upon their father's own property.

For our present discussion, Constantine's response just cited (*C.Th.* 8.18.2) is interesting for its assumption that at least some *patres* preferred to release their children on their attaining adulthood. The motives are not discussed, but we are probably not justified in assuming that their age was the main relevant factor. Here, as in some other examples (*CJ* 3.29.5; 3.29.8.1; 4.19.16), the father's remarriage, actual or anticipated, seems to provide the motive. A *pater* might find it convenient or desirable to keep separate the patrimony of children from an earlier marriage by emancipating them. In these circumstances, it would be natural to make some provision for the children at emancipation.

However, there could be snags later. One father who had, with excessive generosity, exhausted his resources in gifts to his emancipated children sought permission to recover a portion of the gifts he had made them; the danger he apprehended was that one day the children of a subsequent marriage might find themselves left relatively badly off and challenge his will as 'unduteous' (*CJ* 3.29.5). In *CJ* 3.29.8, divorcing parents had come to an agreement, of a not uncommon sort, that what the husband had given to the wife during the marriage was to be hers, and she then with his consent gave it to their emancipated son; another son, apparently not her favourite (his late mother had exhausted her estate in gifts to the emancipated son), is told that what the father had given her counts as part of the father's estate, which meant that he could not benefit from it. The converse could occur. As one or two legal texts indicate (see n. 38), fathers who subsequently fell on hard times and became financially embarrassed might find their emancipated sons less than willing to help, and have to resort to law to make them fulfil their filial duty.

The above concerns possible motives for emancipation on the part of fathers. However, an equally important question (whatever one's view of the ideas about parricide discussed above) is how much active pressure, or even desire, there was on the part of children *in potestate* themselves to be emancipated. References to *emancipati* are frequent in legal sources, but this is in part a reflection, not of the actual incidence of the emancipation of children, but of the thoroughness of lawyers, when discussing a particular topic, in covering all possible contingencies.

The frequency of emancipation

Alan Watson (1973: 23–6; 1977: 24–5) has suggested that emancipation was, or became, very common in the third century AD, being present or implied, he says, in 14 of the 53 imperial rescripts beteen AD 235 and 284, and in 36 of the 112 from the reign of Diocletian, dealing in any way with parent and child (and possibly present, though not mentioned because irrelevant, in some others). His conclusion is: 'At the very least, one can say that during the third century very many Romans preferred not to live with the much-vaunted *patria potestas*.' Watson's main concern is with the practical effects of the son's lack of independent legal capacity, rather than with his financial dependence. His way of putting it, that very many Romans 'preferred not to live with' *patria potestas*, is in line with the general tenor of his argument, that the institution of *patria potestas*, being fundamentally inconvenient, survived only by inertia, because law was out of step with the needs and actual lifestyle of the Romans themselves. As we have seen, however, many of the practical inconveniences were routinely circumvented, and need not have interfered too much with the lifestyle. We shall consider in a moment some further difficulties which might have arisen.

First, however, Watson's claim itself must be challenged. If one looks more closely at the rescripts he cites, it will be found that they do not all involve actual emancipations. Where there is emancipation, most give no indication of the reasons, and where reasons are given or implied, these usually do not seem particularly relevant to Watson's general thesis.

One type of response is that in which an enquirer is told: 'The answer to your query depends on whether the person in question is *in potestate* or emancipated'.[39] Clearly, these cannot be counted as actual instances of emancipation. Nor can the inconvenience (for a son or daughter) of living with *patria potestas* be claimed as a motive for emancipations made by a *pater* on the insistence of a mother wishing a child to benefit financially (a sizeable group),[40] or as a way of dispersing the family property, for example in order to avoid the father's liability to public duties, *civilia munera*,[41] or, as mentioned above, in anticipation of remarriage.

In short, where we have any evidence at all of the reasons for emancipation, they seem usually to have to do with property. There is no sign that the awkwardness or inconvenience in ordinary life of the legal disabilities of the *filiusfamilias* was a widespread or common motive for emancipation.

LEGAL DISABILITIES OF THE *FILIUSFAMILIAS*

Outside the family, the *pater*, and only the *pater*, had the legal capacity to be a party to transactions with other Roman citizens. In early Rome, offences within the *familia* were for the *pater* to deal with. We have already seen how this was modified, already in the Republic, in the case of the 'right of life and death' (*ius vitae et necis*); serious criminal offences such as parricide, incest and adultery – all matters which can be regarded as involving not only the family itself, but public order and stability[42] – also in due course came under the jurisdiction of the state.

In civil law matters, however, the *familia* was the basic legal unit, and all valid legal relations with other *familiae* were mediated through its head. It would be an exaggeration, but not a great one, to say that he was the only member of the *familia* whose existence was legally recognised. Like the slave, in any transactions with others which created rights for the *pater*, the child in power was legally transparent, acting on behalf of the *pater*. All rights in relation to other citizens vested in the *pater*. Only he could own property; only he, therefore, could alienate or acquire property. Only he could sue on the results of these transactions. The position regarding his liabilities is a little more complicated.

Any offence or damage to his children or his slaves, or to property which might be currently in their hands, was committed upon the *pater* himself; similarly, he was personally liable for any offence or damage done outside the *familia* by son or slave.

Normal daily life was full of transactions which gave rise to legal contractual relationships. As we have seen, praetorian law developed a number of procedures which enabled third parties to obtain against a *pater* legal enforcement of contracts made either by sons or by slaves. This was necessary because of the particular feature of Roman law, that rights and liabilities came into existence only between the two parties directly involved in making a contract. Slaves were legally non-persons, but it was accepted that while their contracts could give a master rights of action, they did not impose obligations on him. Hence the development of the various praetorian actions already discussed. Sons, on the other hand, could themselves incur obligations in making contracts, but could not be sued upon them while they were still in power. (Daughters could not incur such obligations; see the excursus at the end of this chapter.)

Sons, like most people, would tend to be more concerned about securing performance of the obligations undertaken by others towards them, and this – for example, when a *filiusfamilias* had to chase up unsatisfactory tradesmen – is where the inconveniences of his position might have been expected to make themselves felt. Much of the time it might be possible for matters to be privately settled, but if it was necessary to resort to litigation, he was in theory dependent on his *pater* being available and willing to act, since the rights to all acquisitions belonged to the *pater*, not to him.

Coping independently: possibilities of action

In practice, however, for some matters at least, as so often where there was no right in Roman civil law, effective remedies were provided by praetorian jurisdiction. Ulpian (*D.* 44.7.13) remarks that 'even *filiifamilias* may exercise *actiones in factum*'. An *actio in factum* was one in which a plaintiff's claim was not formulated in terms of a legal right; instead, the facts were alleged, and the *iudex* was instructed to give judgment according as he found these facts proved or not. The *actio in factum* was not a device invented solely to help *filiifamilias*; rather, it was part of the enormous armoury of devices by which praetorian jurisdiction, in Papinian's famous definition (*D.* 1.1.7), was used to 'assist or to supplement or correct the civil law, for the public utility'.

Elsewhere (*D.* 44.7.9) Paul gives a list of praetorian actions which he says are available to a son, in his own name: *iniuriae*, *quod vi aut clam, depositum* and (according to Julian) *commodatum*. Ulpian (*D.* 2.4.12) adds that, in the absence of a *pater*, a patron's son can also be granted a penal action for 50 *aurei*[43] against a freedman who is suing him.

This last, taking thought for the *pietas* which a freedman is expected to show both towards his patron and his patron's children, is obviously an action thought of as affecting the person rather than property, as is the action for *iniuria*. The rationale of the others is less obvious. Buckland (1966: 102) suggests 'convenience', which is quite plausible, since the three types of suit listed were likely to be routine and frequent, at most levels of society.

Depositum, in legal terms, was one of several types of contract (there were four, none of them in themselves very important) created *re*,[44] that is, by actual delivery, physical handing over, of an object. *Depositum* was when something was handed over for safe-keeping (not lent for use). Although socially important, and quite likely to give rise to litigation if you trusted the wrong people, it was not legally very important, since it did not transfer ownership or possession, and no payment was involved. The same was true of *commodatum*, loan (free of charge) for use. Borrowing a spade from a neighbour created *commodatum*.

Quod vi aut clam was a form of possessory interdict[45] which someone could use to prevent others from interfering with his possession of property, and to recover possession from any dispossessor. Only two facts had to be proved: that his occupancy was possession in law; and that he had not gained possession *vi aut clam*, by force or by stealth. *Ownership* did not have to be proved; that would come into play only if either party contested the judgment, and wanted to claim actual title to the property. Even if one of the parties to the dispute was a *filiusfamilias*, there was no need to involve the *pater* at the stage concerning *possessio*, but only if it came to a question of ownership. The convenience for someone like Roscius of Ameria, farming land owned by his father, is obvious.

So, for some at least of the minor ordinary business of life, the child in power was able to look after his person, and his means of livelihood, without having to depend upon his *pater* to act for him. These exceptions, though (apart perhaps from *iniuria*, a term covering harm both to person and to reputation), are relatively trivial; anything more serious, and especially anything involving money or ownership, might require the *pater* to take action. Not merely that, but, given the nature of Roman legal procedure, the actual personal participation of the *pater* was necessary and, often, his willingness or ability to travel to Rome or to the local seat of government to engage in litigation.

This was obviously an inconvenient situation; however, it was *not* an inconvenience which arose solely from the effects of *patria potestas*. Difficulties must often have arisen for the Romans in securing the attendance of other parties to lawsuits and of witnesses; hence the regularity of the practice of setting bail for appearance, attested both in many of the Murecine tablets and in the dossier from Herculaneum of 'the woman calling herself Petronia Justa'.[46] Even manumitting a slave (or, for a Junian Latin, as Weaver (1990) points out, securing full citizenship by 'iteration' after informal manumission or by *anniculi probatio*), or claiming an inheritance, similarly involved securing the attendance and participation of a number of other persons. These were inconveniences which the Romans were apparently content to live with.

Even where money was involved, however, this would not necessarily mean involving the *pater*. Here again the Murecine tablets are instructive. When goods were sold, or money advanced, or any other transaction for which payment was due, it was usual to create a contract for payment by making a *stipulatio*.⁴⁷ A son or a slave could make a *stipulatio* for payment to be made to them by another person. Neither, however, could proceed to law for recovery of the debt. This was not a problem. As the Murecine tablets demonstrate, it was common to engage the activities of professionals like the financial firm of the Sulpicii to pursue the fulfilment of contracts on behalf of the principals. All that was necessary was to secure a *stipulatio* from the debtor that he would pay either to the creditor or to Sulpicius.

This is exactly what happens, in the end, in the case of the credit which, as we saw above, had been extended to Eunus, apparently a grain-dealer, by the slave Hesychus acting on behalf of his owner, the imperial freedman Evenus. Eunus had borrowed 10,000 sesterces, and a few days later a further 3,000. Fifteen months after the original loans, we find that Eunus still has an outstanding debt of something over one thousand, which he is being pressed to pay. By this time, however, Evenus is apparently dead. The debt, and the slave Hesychus, have been taken over by no less a person than the emperor Gaius. Obviously, the emperor is not going to go to law in person to pursue such a petty sum, but Hesychus the slave cannot sue. What was done is revealed in *TP* 18:⁴⁸

I, C. Novius Eunus, have written that I owe Hesychus, slave of C. Caesar Augustus Germanicus, (formerly) of Evenus, an outstanding 1,250 HS net, which I received as a loan from him; which sum I have promised on oath that I will repay either to Hesychus himself or to C. Sulpicius Faustus before 1 November next . . . and that if I do not pay on that day, not only am I liable on grounds of perjury but as penalty I will also be obliged to pay 20 HS per day.

The text records that a fresh *stipulatio* was taken, by which Eunus contracted to pay either Hesychus or Sulpicius, so enabling Sulpicius to take legal action if Eunus defaulted. There will also have been a *stipulatio* in which Sulpicius contracted to pay over to Hesychus any sums he succeeded in recovering from Eunus.

Similarly, one or other of the Sulpicii is often employed, as *coactor*, to handle the sale of goods seized from defaulting debtors. He organises the sale, and handles all the financial and judicial matters. He makes a *stipulatio* with the seller to pay him the proceeds of the sale, less his fee; he also acts as creditor for the buyer, again with a *stipulatio*.[49]

What was useful, as well as socially desirable, for an independent principal was equally useful – as well as necessary – for a slave or a Roman in power. People like the Sulpicii filled a need, but a need that existed, not because of *patria potestas*, but because of the desire of many Romans, particularly the better-off, to distance themselves from the petty details of financial and commercial business. Sons in power obviously benefited from the facility of being able to handle most of their financial business without having to involve father.

Nevertheless, father controlled the family purse-strings, and for the senatorial classes at least Daube (1969: 84 ff.) regards the consequences, in the late Republic, as momentous (it would be less easy to apply his argument to the political conditions of the Principate). Large sums of money were needed to fund the progress through the magistracies that constituted a political career, and father, in Daube's scenario, is the sole source of funds. (Verres, whose activities we glanced at earlier, is assumed to be untypically unscrupulous.) 'It is difficult to conceive of a more powerful brake on any deviation from traditional family politics, or, indeed, on any tendency to detract in a thoroughgoing way from the old-established scope of *patria potestas*.'

'Traditional family politics' is, as Roman historians are now well aware, an elusive (even, perhaps, illusory) creature to try and track down in what evidence we have for the day-to-day politics of the Republic. More importantly, it is simply not true that the only financial resource of a *filius* in politics was his father or, failing that, extortionate moneylenders. Lending money, at very easy or even non-existent rates of interest, and without pressure for repayment, was in itself, for the lenders, part of the process of building up political and social influence and standing, and there was no shortage of persons to whom the *filius* could turn.[50]

Watson (1977: 27–8), in what is intended as a counter to Daube, says that if the *filius* was short of money, this should not simply be blamed on *patria potestas*. 'In any family which derives its income from property, children remain economically dependent so long as their father is alive, unless they acquire a trade.' This takes too narrow a view of 'property'; the model envisaged by Watson seems essentially to be that of the child's income consisting entirely in a fixed allowance, doled out by a landowning father, and spent as received. He compares ancient Rome with Anthony Trollope's England, as a society 'where gentlemen from well-to-do families do not usually earn their living by trade, commerce or industry'. It is now generally recognised, however, that upper-class Romans might derive at least some of their income from a variety of economic enterprises,[51] and, as we have seen, there is no reason why sons[52] could not also turn their allowances to economic profit, and indeed, for much of the time and in ordinary circumstances, manage their domestic affairs and live off their income in much the same way as other Roman citizens who were not *in potestate*. The main difference, at least for the upper classes, was that the sons constituted an extra, middle layer between the *pater* and his *institor* or agent. Lower down the social scale, the son *was* in effect the agent, and it would usually be in the interests of the *pater* to consent to further his enterprises.

PATRIA POTESTAS AND CITIZENSHIP

It is time to return to the question raised at the beginning: why the Romans maintained in existence a system which imposed such great differences between the legal capacity of individual Roman citizens. To formulate the question with reference to the supposed convenience or inconvenience occasioned in practice by the existence of *patria potestas*, and then to blame the Romans, as Watson (1977) does, for supposed inertia and inadequate use of legislation for radical law reform, is, I think, a mistaken approach. Most of the supposed inconveniences were already, in the Republic, routinely overcome by applying praetorian rules. This was in any case the Roman way, to rely on the magistracy to make an existing system work in practice, rather than to have unnecessarily frequent recourse to legislation (one might call it 'remedial legislation') to obviate difficulties and anomalies as they came to notice. The latter method is not in itself (*pace* Watson) intrinsically more responsive to the actual current needs and desires of society. The development of magisterial law under the Republic and Principate, and the emergence of the emperor (through decree, edict or, especially, rescript) and the pronouncements of imperially authorised jurists as in effect new sources of law in the empire, are the consequence of day-to-day response to actual conditions in society.[53] However numerous the detailed modifications, the fundamental principle of any institution felt to be important would be retained as a safeguard.[54] In the case of *patria potestas*, the institution survived very largely intact.

The *filiusfamilias* in civil law was – to repeat a phrase already used – 'legally transparent'. That is, he had relatively little in the way of acknowledged rights, or existence, apart from his *pater*. Public law, however, was a different matter, especially, but not only, in regard to political life. In a revealing phrase, the second-century AD jurist Pomponius remarks (*D.* 1.6.9.1): 'In public matters, the son in power is regarded as equivalent to a *paterfamilias*, for example so that he may hold office, or be assigned as *tutor*.'[55] What may be covered by *publicae causae*, other than the examples given, is further elucidated by Hermogenianus' long list (*D.* 50.4.1), and the even longer list given by Arcadius Charisius[56] (*D.* 50.4.18) of the public duties, *munera*, that might be required of local councillors by the time of Diocletian. These are divided into two categories, the patrimonial and the personal (Arcadius adds a third, 'mixed' category, since some civic duties might involve elements of both). The former consisted essentially of expenditure from one's personal property. A *pater* was responsible for his son's fulfilment of patrimonial *munera*, unless he expressly objected to his son's appointment; this was an acceptable defence for him, but did not remove the son's liability (presumably to the extent of the *peculium* at least, and, if he became *sui iuris*, for the full amount). Personal *munera*, on the other hand, required some personal physical or, especially, mental effort and imposed an administrative responsibility.[57] To be a *tutor* or *curator* also fell under 'public' responsibilities no doubt because it could be assigned by a magistrate, and because it involved intervention in the affairs of another *familia*.[58]

The conflict of authorities

The most important *publica causa* which a *filiusfamilias* might be called upon to undertake was the holding of office. This could potentially involve a clash between the paternal authority over a son in power, and the authority of the state's officer over an individual citizen, his father. The piquant conflict is one which naturally appealed to Roman moralists; analysis of the stories, however, reveals that the piquancy derives, not from the conflict of authorities, but from the strains placed on the affective relation presumed to exist between parent and child, that is, on *pietas*. Valerius Maximus, in his collection of *Memorable Deeds and Sayings* dedicated to the emperor Tiberius, presents several anecdotes.

In 5.4.5 he relates that C. Flaminius as tribune of the plebs (232 BC) tried to push through a law for the distribution of the *ager Gallicus*, land south of Ariminum confiscated from the Senones, maintaining his attempt despite bitter senatorial opposition and even the threat of armed force. At the very moment when he put the proposal to the vote of the people, his father laid his hand upon him (*manum iniecit*; as it were, 'arrested' him), and he promptly desisted and left the rostrum. The assemblage thus deserted, says Valerius, made not the least murmur of reproach (he omits to mention that the bill was in fact carried: Polybius 2.21). This story resembles that of Coriolanus' yielding to his mother (told at 5.4.1; cf. Livy 2.40). Coriolanus, of course, was moved by *pietas* towards his mother – a mother had no *potestas* – and both stories are in fact grouped under the general heading '*Pietas* towards Parents'. Though *patria potestas* is not directly mentioned, Valerius using instead at the start the phrase *auctoritas* (strictly, 'unofficial influence') *patria*, he comes closer at the end, describing Flaminius as *privato fractus imperio*, 'yielding to a private authority'. The son's authority in the state yields – exceptionally – to the father's private authority over him within the *familia*. Valerius obviously regards the father's action as being more closely in accord with the true interest of the *res publica*, implicitly acknowledging its technical illegality (an idea exploited by Cicero).[59]

The first of Valerius' examples of 'Parents' Love and Indulgence towards their Children' is (5.7.1) Fabius Rullianus, five times consul, who in 295 BC, at an age when he was more fit for resting in bed than campaigning, accompanied his son to war as his *legatus*, and was content to follow on horseback in his triumph – and was the main centre of atraction. What makes this an appropriate item under this heading is the contrast, this time implicit, between the deference due to an officer of the state and that due by a son to the personal authority of his father. In this case, of course, there is no real conflict, and the situation need never have arisen; the behaviour of the *pater* arises from affection, and is meant to enhance his son's achievement in the eyes of others.

An example of paternal severity, on the other hand, is Cassius, father of Spurius Cassius (5.8.2), who summoned a council of friends and relatives *after* his son's demagogic tribunate (486 BC) had come to an end, condemned him of aspiring to royalty, had him beaten to death with rods, and dedicated his *peculium* to Ceres. (In 6.3.1, Valerius tells the story differently. This time, Cassius was condemned and punished by the Senate and people of Rome, who also destroyed his house; this is one of a group of examples of severity exercised by the state.) Again, as in the story of C. Flaminius, the father is represented as acting in the public interest, against a son's misuse of public authority.[60]

The story of Titus Manlius Torquatus (5.8.3) is similar. When his son – who was no longer in his power, having been adopted by D. Junius Silanus – was accused by the Macedonians after his praetorship there (141 BC), Torquatus obtained the senate's consent to delay judgment until he himself had conducted an enquiry. This he did, found him guilty of extortion from the provincials and announced, 'I judge him unworthy of the Republic and of my house, and bid him depart from my sight', a judgment which so shattered Silanus that he hanged himself the next night.

Only in the first of these anecdotes are we offered a situation in which a father intervenes to impede the action of a son actually in office. However, the son, as tribune (a rather suspect and demagogic office anyway), was, it is made clear, misusing his authority. This story does not, any more than the others, challenge the acknowledged truth that the state's authority was legally superior to that of the individual.[61] This is *not* the same as to say, as one recent writer[62] misleadingly puts it, that 'a father's authority did not legally extend over a son in office'. In all aspects of life in which he was behaving as a private individual, a *filiusfamilias* who happened to be a magistrate was still, like Verres, in his father's *potestas*, and lacked independent legal capacity. As a magistrate, on the other hand, he could in various ways exercise his public authority over others, whether or not they were *patres*, and even over his own father.

Sons, *patresfamilias* and the franchise

This brings us back to what was described above as Pomponius' revealing choice of words (*D.* 1.6.9.1): 'In public matters, the son in power is regarded as equivalent to a *paterfamilias*.' The Romans

knew perfectly well that a magistrate with a living father was not really a *paterfamilias*. This resort to a legal fiction to justify his exercise of authority seems to reveal an underlying, probably ancient, concept of citizenship in which the citizens, in the fullest sense of the word, were those who alone were entitled to transact independently and on a basis of equality in matters both public and private with other citizens – in other words, the *patres*, heads of household.

The idea that in early Rome only these had the franchise is not a new one, and has been put forward by numerous scholars. It would not be surprising if the military necessities of the developing state and the demands made on individuals, including those in power, resulted in the admission of sons to the voting body. Our literary sources assume the existence of popular assemblies from the earliest days of regnal Rome, but without committing themselves to any specific account of their composition. They also preserve[63] a tradition of a linked military and political reorganisation of the people by king Servius on the basis of gradations of wealth, a forerunner of the centuriate system of historical times. How historical the 'Servian' reorganisation, or even king Servius himself, was, I do not wish to speculate. What is evident, however, is that at some early point in Rome's history, franchise was linked with military service, and obviously *filiifamilias*, as well as *patres*, fought under arms.

They therefore acquired public capacity – i.e. the vote – but without private. That remained the prerogative of the *pater*.

Daughters, who had no part in military service of the state, were not included. However, women *sui iuris* had not the franchise either, since they were not heads of household in the fullest sense, having no *potestas* over children, and over property a *potestas* that was limited by restraints, originally far-reaching, over their ability of control and disposal (details in Gardner 1986: 14–22). They were 'heads of household' only in a very limited sense. Restraints on women's legal capacity will be discussed in the next chapter.

CONCLUSION

The *potestas* of a *paterfamilias*, as we saw, extended both over property and over persons. Blood relationship was neither a sufficient nor a necessary condition to identify these persons, whose relationship to the father was a legal one and required his personal decision; they comprised acknowledged children born of a legal marriage, adopted children, and wives formally taken into *manus*. They, in turn, had primary right of hereditary succession to the property. Economically, as well as socially, the *familia* was structurally basic to the community, and the composition of the *familia* was determined by its head. How he chose to do it was also up to him. Serial marriage for the production of heirs was one method, the effects of which on the composition of upper-class households in the late Republic have been studied by Bradley (1991); another was adoption, though the stress laid on it by Garnsey and Saller (1987: 144) as a deliberate preference, involving rejection of the alternative of children, and as an index of individualism, should perhaps be reviewed in the light of recent work on the family and of Champlin (1991) on wills.

The extreme rigour of the system of *patria potestas* relaxes, but only to a limited extent, with the development of society. The law intervenes from time to time over such matters as succession to property[64] or the exercise of the harsher extremes of power over the person. These changes reflect changes in Roman society and Roman attitudes, but in themselves barely affect the legal nature of *patria potestas*. Socially, the *familia* was, as already said, a force for coherence and stability. It was a focus of loyalties for both present and past members, and also a means of exercising control over them at need; over the former directly, through *potestas*; over the latter less directly, but through the socially and, increasingly, legally recognised obligations of *pietas*. This was an important factor in a society where law enforcement was left mainly to the initiative of the individual, and there was relatively little even in the way of police provision.[65] The low level of public interference with the internal self-government of the *familia* should also be linked with its economic autonomy. This is in contrast to a modern industrial society, such as Britain, in which a high level of state involvement in family finances, both as debtor and creditor (making payments in kind, public services, and cash, e.g. income supplements, and exacting claims of taxation), is accompanied by extensive and detailed legal regulation of behaviour within the family. The system of *patria potestas* fulfilled many of the functions now assumed by the state and its agencies.[66]

EXCURSUS: CONTRACTS MADE BY DAUGHTERS IN POWER

Oddly, though sons in power could incur obligations to others, daughters in power, *filiaefamilias*, like slaves, according to Gaius (3.104), could not incur obligations in this way. This is strange, since several texts appear to accept the possibility of their having a *peculium* (*D.* 15.1.1.2–3, 27 pr.; 23.3.24), and so engaging in contractual undertakings. With or without a *peculium*, and whether married or not, women could scarcely provide even for their ordinary needs without some commercial transactions which involved contractual obligations of some sort. While the woman remained in power, the other party to the contract would have available the praetorian actions described in the text above, but would be unable to pursue the matter further if it was still outstanding when the woman became *sui iuris*.

The reason for the differentiation between sons and daughters is not immediately obvious. Girard (1911: 467 n. 4) links it plausibly with the incapacity of women *sui iuris* to bind themselves contractually without tutorial authority. Certainly, at the time when their *tutela* was still a powerful restraint, it would have been paradoxical if women in power had greater capacity. Although *tutela* of women lost much of its force to compel, it did not entirely disappear until Theodosius and Honorius in AD 410 made a blanket grant of the *ius liberorum*, which exempted from *tutela*, to all women in the Empire (*CJ* 8.58(59).1). Additionally, in early Rome and for much of the Republic, women were commonly married with *manus*; that is, they passed from the power of their fathers into that of their husbands (who certainly could not be held liable for obligations contracted while a woman was under another's power), or even, if unmarried at their fathers' death, became briefly *sui iuris* and then passed into power again; remarriage of widows was also regular. In these circumstances, it would not be surprising if some women were prevented from incurring obligations which it might never be possible to pursue against them personally.

4

GENDER: THE
INDEPENDENT WOMAN

'In many articles of our law', said the jurist Papinian at the
beginning of the third century AD, 'the condition of females is
worse than that of males' (D. 1.5.9). In some points, indeed, it
was better; for example, although in Roman law, as in other legal
systems, ignorance of the law was not an acceptable excuse, in a
few instances exceptions were made for certain categories of
people, and these included women.[1] The legal situation of Roman
women has been studied in some detail elsewhere (Gardner 1986);
attention will now be turned to a topic only briefly considered in
the earlier study, that is, the legal *capacity* of women. There were
certain areas in which the capacity of Roman women to engage
in legal transactions was restricted in comparison with other citizens, or non-existent, and the reason for this differentiation (for
obvious reasons, I prefer to avoid the loaded term 'discrimination')
needs to be examined.

It will be as well to start by summarising briefly what these
restrictions and exclusions amounted to; the reasons for them will
be considered later. One group may be described as 'political'.
Roman women had a disability common to women in most
societies and at most periods, indeed in some societies until well
into the twentieth century, that is, the lack of the franchise.
Women had no part in the *comitia*, the voting assemblies of the
Roman people, which were active until the end of the Republic
(though not much longer). Consequently, they had no part in
those public activities which formed part of the *political* aspect of
being a citizen. They could not take part in the popular legislative
or electoral procedures which still existed under the Republic and
they could not elect, or be, magistrates; moreover, they could not
serve on criminal court juries.[2] As citizens, women themselves

85

could be tried by such courts. They could bring prosecutions in them, but this right was limited to those cases in which they had a direct personal interest, i.e. for redress for offences against themselves or close relatives.

Criminal justice had a political[3] dimension, and women were excluded from political life. Condemnation in a criminal court, especially if it was for a so-called 'capital' crime, would result in loss or curtailment of the *caput* of a citizen; that is, not necessarily of life, but of legal status. At the very least, there would be some loss of legal capacity, since the condemned person became *infamis*.[4] Significantly, some of the more important disabilities incurred by becoming *infamis* applied to women anyway, simply by virtue of their sex. *Infames* might suffer temporary or permanent exclusion from the right to hold office; women were not allowed to hold office at all. *Infames* might lose the right of good (male) citizens to bring criminal prosecutions where not personally involved (and, if the offence was really severe, even to seek redress for personal injuries); in criminal justice, women were not denied *self*-protection, even at the expense of others, but that was all.

In private law also, women's legal capacity was subject to certain restrictions. In the civil courts, women could bring prosecutions on their own account, but not on behalf of others (again a disability shared with *infames*); under the praetor's edict, some loss of legal capacity was incurred by condemnation in certain civil actions, which rendered the convicted person *infamis*.[5] Women had no *potestas* over other free citizens, so not only had they no legal authority or control over their own children, but they could not adopt children. They were subject to *tutela*, i.e. they had to have the authorisation of a male tutor for certain legal transactions, but they themselves could not be tutors to others. There were also certain restrictions on their capacity to take on financial responsibilities for others; they were not, it seems, allowed to act as bankers, and an enactment of the middle of the first century AD, the *senatusconsultum Velleianum*, limited their capacity to undertake responsibility for the debts of others.[6]

The foregoing, of course, concerns only women who were legally independent (*sui iuris*), i.e. freedwomen or freeborn women whose fathers had already died, or emancipated them. Independent women could own property and dispose of it, they could engage in litigation, and they could marry and divorce at will, none of which was possible for women (or men) *in potestate*. Sons in power could not (with the few exceptions already noted) engage in litigation, nor could they possess and transmit property; on the other hand, they had public capacity. They could vote, hold office, serve on juries and even, as we saw above, be tutors.

GENDER AND PUBLIC CAPACITY

Gender, however, was not the sole determinant of public capacity. Birth, for example, counted; freedmen also were excluded from political life, at least partially. Their effective voting power in the assemblies was for a long time restricted in the Republic, and they could not hold magistracies or state priesthoods, restrictions which may have had something to do with the fact that they were less completely integrated than the freeborn into the network of familial kinship connections. In the religious life of the state, although the performance of certain rituals was reserved to women (and in particular, to the six Vestal Virgins), all the powerful top-level state priesthoods, the pontificate, were held by freeborn men and were, at least notionally, filled by popular election; state religion was part of politics.

Free birth was not necessarily enough; plebeian freeborn men were for a long time denied access to public office, which was confined to members of the exclusive circle of patrician families. As mentioned in the previous chapter, sons in power may originally have lacked any public capacity, gaining it partly in consideration of their military importance but also, it seems likely, because unlike daughters they had the prospect of themselves in due course having *potestas* and heading *familiae* in their own right.

However, free birth, even patrician birth, made no difference at all to the public capacity of Roman women. A woman, whether freeborn, after the death of her father, or freed, had personal capacity, like a man, to own and dispose of property, to engage in legal contracts, to bring prosecutions and so on, but she was not in the full sense a 'head of household'. She controlled a *familia*, in the sense of a property unit, but she did not count as head of, and had no *potestas*, legal control over, a *familia* in the sense of a descent-group.[7] She herself was, as one lawyer put it, 'the source and end of her own *familia*'.[8]

This, it seems, is the basic reason why a woman could not act on a footing of equality with other heads of *familiae* in ways that involved taking responsibility for, or actively intervening (save in

87

defence of her own interests) in, the affairs of other *familiae*. This would exclude public activity such as passing legislation, exercising magisterial authority or appointing others to do so, or giving judgment.

The Romans themselves in the historical period do not appear to have questioned the reasons for the exclusion of women from these public activities. It was simply taken as given fact. There are a few texts, the earliest no earlier than the late second century AD, in which Roman jurists attempt to assign reasons for the accepted public incapacities of women, but these 'reasons' amount to no more than an assertion of the existing state of affairs.

Thus Paul states (*D*. 5.1.12.2):

> Not everyone is eligible to be appointed to judge lawsuits by those (i.e. praetors or provincial magistrates) who have the authority to appoint judges. Some are barred from being judges by law, some by nature, some by custom (*moribus*). By nature – e.g. the deaf and dumb; also the incurably insane and the under-age, since they lack judgment. By law – someone who has been expelled from the senate. By custom – women and slaves, not because they do not have judgment, but because it is received practice (*receptum est*) that they do not perform civil functions.

Similarly, he says in passing (*D*. 16.1.1), 'By custom (*moribus*) civil duties (*civilia officia*) are taken out of the sphere of women and are for the most part not valid by the operation of law (sc. if done by women).'

Moribus can be translated, as here, 'by custom', or 'by convention', but we should not take this to mean 'merely by convention', i.e. either in the absence of any reason or without any sense of binding obligation. 'Custom', in the mouth of a Roman lawyer, is one of the accepted sources of law (*D*. 1.3.32, 33), and the older an institution is the less likely there is to be any written record of a law setting it up. What Paul is saying is, 'This is the way things are and, as far as we know, always have been'. Ulpian does not refer to *mores*, but in a chapter of the *Digest* whose title, significantly, is 'Concerning various rules of ancient law' he is cited as saying:

> Women are excluded from all civil or public functions and therefore they can neither be judges nor hold magistracies

nor litigate nor intervene on behalf of someone else nor be agents for others. Likewise someone below puberty ought to refrain from all civil functions.[9]

Ulpian's list includes not only public functions, but some private ones as well, from which women were excluded, and these latter will be considered further below. To be a *tutor*, i.e. guardian (which, as we saw above, was also regarded as being in a sense a public function), whether of a child or another woman, would also be ruled out, since it involved intervention in, and, in the case of the *tutela* of minors, responsibility for, the property affairs of another *familia*. Four legal texts concur that exercise of *tutela* is 'men's business'.[10] Eventually individual permission was given to women, on appeal to the emperor, to act as tutors for their own children, but our earliest clear evidence for this (*C.Th.* 3.17.4; AD 390) specifies that this is to be allowed only if no *tutor legitimus* (i.e. no agnate) is available, and only if the woman undertakes not to remarry; if she does remarry, her second husband's property is to be pledged and held as security. There was no abandonment of the general principle that women were excluded from the exercise of *tutela*.[11]

Of women's incapacities in private law, lawyers say (what amounts to the same thing as asserting the status quo) that certain activities are 'men's business', or they reiterate what were by then conventional attitudes – the justification is women's weakness (*infirmitas*), or their 'light-mindedness' (*levitas animi*), roughly 'irresponsibility'.[12]

THE PURPOSE OF GUARDIANSHIP

A particular restraint on the legal capacity of Roman women which has attracted much attention recently among social historians is *tutela*, the requirement to have a guardian to authorise certain legal transactions.[13] As noted by Dixon, 'Legal historians are generally agreed that the origin of *tutela mulierum* (the guardianship of women) is to be explained in terms of the early Roman system of inheritance'.[14] In this early system, as we find it in the Twelve Tables, the first claimants to the estate of a *man* were his *sui heredes*, i.e. those persons in his *potestas* who became legally independent at his death – in effect his children or grandchildren (and his wife, if she was *in manu*). Women, like minors (*impuberes*), did not have *potestas*, so the first claimants to their estates were the people who came second in the order of succession to a man, the nearest agnates. Accordingly, the tutors of women during their lifetimes (and children of either sex during their minority) were originally their nearest (male) agnates, and these were known as *tutores legitimi*. Patrons, similarly, were tutors for their freed slaves (as ex-slaves had no agnates). The purpose of this *tutela legitima* is clearly stated by Ulpian (*D. 26.4.1 pr.*): 'that those with expectation of inheriting should also look after the property *ne dilapidarentur* (lit. "to prevent its being scattered like stones", i.e. frittered away or depleted)'.[15]

Tutela legitima of freeborn women (though not of freedwomen) had disappeared long before Ulpian's time; those women who had tutors for the most part either had persons nominated in the will of their *pater*, or appointed by the praetor. The institution of *tutela* for women had become severely eroded, along with awareness of its *raison d'être*, and although Ulpian is quite clear (see above) about the purpose of *tutela legitima*, he can nevertheless say (Ulp. *Reg.* 11.1), 'Roman women were given guardians because of the weakness of their sex and because of their ignorance of legal matters.' Gaius assigns a similar reason: 'The early jurists thought that women, even if they had reached majority, ought to be in *tutela* because of their lack of serious judgment (*propter animi levitatem*)'; though he admits elsewhere that this estimation of women does not correspond either with their actual performance or with the attitudes of tutors and of magistrates towards them in his own day: 'In certain instances, the guardian gives his authorisation as a matter of form, and often he is actually obliged by the praetor to give authorisation, even against his will' (Gaius 1.144, 190). Gaius makes it clear, however (1.192), that *tutores legitimi*, because of their reversionary interest in the intestate estate, could not normally be compelled in this way to give authorisation, unless for very strong reason.

Recently Evans (1991: 21–6) has argued that belief that women were unreliable was in fact the original reason for the creation of the institution of *tutela*. He points out, correctly, that although the charge of 'light-mindedness' against Roman women is first attested in Cicero, it is an *argumentum ex silentio* to assume that that marks its first appearance in Roman thought.[16] However, he adduces no strong evidence for his view that it was generally believed among men in early Rome that women, as a sex, were unstable and irresponsible. First, there is the notorious group of anecdotes about the severity with which the ancients allegedly regarded wine-drinking by women.[17] Second, there is a law of the Twelve Tables, which Cicero tells us (*de leg.* 2.59) forbade women to tear their cheeks or make excessive displays of lamentation.[18] Though Evans regards this as embodying 'an aversion to excessive display of feminine passion', it seems rather to be a piece of sumptuary legislation. It is only one of a number of provisions which Cicero himself says were intended to limit the expense and the lamentation at funerals. Expense is limited by restricting the number of musicians and the quantity of mourning garments; the women, clearly, are to be thought of as hired professional mourners, whose business it was to make an overt display of acted sorrow.

Evans accepts that the provisions of the Twelve Tables regarding *tutela* reflect a determination to safeguard the intestate succession for male kinsmen. This he insists, however, is only a half-truth. As well as women, lunatics and spendthrifts, whose incompetence had been demonstrated, were subject to *tutela*, and since gender was not the determining factor in their case, we should suspect, he believes, that with regard to women as well it was not gender but some persisting disability which rendered them incompetent ever to manage their own affairs. This argument is obviously open to criticism. The end (protection of the property) is admittedly the same. The means employed, however, are not identical. The *curatores* appointed to madmen and prodigals, like tutors of chil-den, had a duty of administration, but tutors of women did not. The range of transactions covered is also much wider for these others than for tutors of women. For example, women, unlike madmen, could litigate in their own persons in matters concerning their property, and it was no part of their tutors' obligations to do it for them. There is no justification for assuming that the reasons for assigning guardians in all these transactions are the same.[19]

Property and marriage in early Rome

Institutions, as Evans rightly observes, do not exist *in vacuo*, and we ought to look at *tutela* in the context not only of the legal situation concerning property ownership and transmission, but also of the social conditions, in regard to property itself and to marriage, in early Rome, even before the Twelve Tables. (Though *tutela*, like many other institutions, is first attested in that code, this does not necessarily mean that it came into existence only then.)

Certain important points must be borne in mind. The making of a will was an exceptional procedure in early Rome; most succession was intestate. Second, marriages were normally accompanied or followed by the passing of the wife into *manus*,[20] and so into the *familia* of her husband and into his *potestas* or that of his *pater*, ranking among his *sui heredes* for intestate succession. Third, the kinds of property which a woman required tutor's authority to dispose of, *res mancipi*, comprised essentially the only kinds of property of any value that there were in primitive Rome – land in Italy with the buildings on it, working animals, and slaves – and these were the bases of production in a peasant economy. In this situation, the long-term economic interests of any *familia* demanded some control on the way its female members disposed of their property once they became legally independent. In primitive Rome, this would have left women with very little freedom in disposing of their property (e.g. by sale, pledge, dowry or bequest, all actions requiring tutorial authorisation). Nevertheless, unlike minors, they had autonomy as far as its internal organisation and management were concerned, since their tutors' authority did not extend to administration. This does not suggest that they were regarded as incompetent.

A question of loyalties

Both the original wish to have some control over women's disposal of property, and subsequent developments during the Republic, were occasioned, I believe, by concern arising from the inevitable conflict of loyalties to which women were exposed, i.e. between loyalty to their natal families and to those into which they were married.

Before the development of will-making, a daughter still unmarried at the death of her *pater* automatically shared the inheritance equally with her brothers, and was so provided for. At her marriage (and marriage was universal, at an early age, and an accepted social necessity) she would normally, in early Rome, enter into *manus*. All her property then went with her into another *familia*, that of her husband, and ceased to be hers, since she was now in power again. A daughter already married at her father's death would be in power in another *familia*, and ineligible to inherit from him, though some portion of his property would already have gone with her as dowry, and been absorbed in the property of her new *familia*. As a widow, she inherited equally with her sons and daughters from her husband. At her death, her intestate heirs would be her children, or other members of her marital *familia*.

Even before the development of 'free' marriage, i.e. marriage without entry into *manus*, and of testamentary procedures available to women,[21] the ownership of property by legally independent women (mainly, in the nature of things, widows) was a potential threat to the economic stability of a family group. Part of the property of the *familia*, on which it depended for very survival, was now in the hands of the widow (as one of those who inherited a share automatically), and she had divided personal loyalties – both to members of her marital *familia*, especially her children, and to her own blood kindred in her family of origin. The situation was even more dangerous if she was childless. It was in the interest of her marital *familia* that there be some control on her disposal of this property during her lifetime; that was the rôle of the agnate tutor. Once it became possible to leave property by will, this also had to be controlled in the interest of the *familia* to which her intestate heirs belonged.

Avoidance of automatic entry into *manus* was already a possibility by the time of the Twelve Tables, and this was obviously introduced in the interests of women's natal families. The law as we have it in the classical period says merely that the tutor had to authorise the constitution of a dowry (since dowry became the husband's property for the duration of the marriage). It does not say that the tutor had to consent to the marriage – quite rightly, since the woman was now *sui iuris*, legally independent. How early the possibility of withholding entry into *manus* appeared, we do not know. What is clear is that in the early Republic, and for a variously estimated length of time thereafter, it was accepted that marriage would normally be accompanied by the transfer of the wife (and so of all her property) into her husband's *familia*, and the 'dowry' would in practice be the whole of her property. In such a situation, tutors would in effect (though whether it was ever stated in these terms we do not know) have the power to give or to withhold their consent to a particular marriage, not merely to haggle about the amount of the dowry.[22] Women might appear to be effectively denied any power to make their own choice of husbands. On the other hand, daughters still unmarried when their fathers died will have been very young, with little acquaintance with males outside the household, and are unlikely to have been in a position to make any sort of informed choice of husband for themselves.

In 'free' marriage, the property inherited by an unmarried daughter at her father's death would not simply be lost to her family when she married. The problem of divided loyalties was still present, however, since ties would be developed, particularly through children, with her husband's family. Again, the rôle of the agnate tutor (who would belong to her natal family) was vital.

The relaxation of *tutela*

The origin of *tutela*, then, in a basically rural society of discrete property-owning kinship groups, is explicable in the above terms. Its progressive weakening is one aspect of the decline in importance of agnate connections, and the increased emphasis on co-operation as well as, to use the modern term, 'networking' between familial groups, in the political and social conditions of urban imperial Rome.

Champlin (1991) repeatedly draws attention (14, 17, 147) to the honorific aspect of the naming of friends as tutors to one's children. Like leaving them legacies, it conveyed social recognition and thanks; it also had the advantage of avoiding 'the conflict of interests which might beset (sc. as *tutor*) a potential heir on intestacy'. The Hannibalic war and the wars of Rome's expansion may also have encouraged the trend to some extent. When nominating in their wills tutors for their daughters, some fathers who might otherwise have preferred to choose close relatives would be obliged, since the latter had been killed, to go outside the immediate family. Similar considerations, one may speculatively suggest, encouraged the practice of husbands allowing their widows, who had been *in manu*, to choose their own tutors; the extent of risk to the estate was within the testator's control (cf. Gardner 1986: 15), since he could choose how much he wished to leave to her. Champlin (1991: 121–2) observes that, in attested testamentary practice, wives were not normally shown special favour in the matter of inheritance, especially where there were children: 'Wives were fondly remembered and their welfare carefully considered, but they were firmly separated from the bulk of the patrimony.' The effect of war in depriving women of tutors already appointed, and the practical inconveniences this caused, perhaps was what prompted the passing of the *lex Atilia*, providing for the appointment of tutors by magistrates.[23]

The persistence of *tutela* – protecting the property

To explain the persistence of *tutela* (other than *tutela legitima*) it is not necessary to invoke either Roman male chauvinism or conservatism; it was retained, rather, as a safeguard, to be called upon if needed, when a woman's proposed actions seemed likely to endanger her economic situation.

The need would be perceived only in the case where a woman had any property worth protecting. Champlin (1991: 46–9) has calculated that among testators attested, whether in literary, legal or epigraphic sources, where sex is determinable men outnumber women by three or four to one. From this he draws the conclusion that many more women than men must have died intestate, suggesting as the most likely reason for this phenomenon that women owned less property (proportionately) than men.[24] This does not mean that we need assume that women had less interest in the disposal of what they had (Champlin rightly rejects passivity as an explanation). If the relatively small proportion of women testators attested accurately represents reality (and of that we cannot be sure), the explanation may be that many had little or nothing to leave, a situation to which a number of factors could have contributed.

Of course, all women who died *in potestate* (and not necessarily very young, like Cicero's daughter, over thirty at her time of death) were excluded from testating, as were men (except, after Augustus, soldiers) dying as *filiifamilias*. Though we cannot say with any confidence that there was a statistical probability of more women than men predeceasing their fathers, the risks attendant on early marriage and pregnancy might have had this consequence.[25] Outside the ranks of the wealthy, many of those who married in the lifetimes of their fathers but died in those of their husbands may have had little or nothing to leave, since the dowry (still in their husbands' hands) probably represented most, or even all, of their fathers' provision for them, and their opportunities of acquiring more once legally independent were limited. Widows, other than those of independent means, were largely dependent on their late husbands' generosity, but generally were not preferred to the latter's children or blood relatives.[26]

Whether in marriage with *manus* or in free marriage, one way, it would seem, of preventing dispersal of property, via women, beyond the group of those who would inherit by right of legal kinship would be to arrange marriage only within the *gens* (roughly 'clan'), the group next in line of succession to the agnates. Watson (1974) argued for the prevalence of this type of marriage, at least within the wealthier classes. Though this idea has some degree of inherent probability, it rests on little concrete evidence beyond the inclusion, among the rewards granted in 186 BC to a freedwoman who gave information about the Bacchanalia, of *enuptio gentis*, 'marriage outside the *gens*'.[27] From about the same period, there is some evidence of aristocratic endogamy; however, this occurs not only within a given *gens*, but also between *gentes*, drawing upon relationships both in the paternal line and through cognates on the mother's side, and the evidence extends only to a few families.[28] In the later Republic, those few noble families who appear to have confined themselves to intermarriage only with other noble *gentes*, and those, still fewer, who occasionally contracted marriages within their own *gens*, were the exception rather than the rule (Wiseman 1971: 53).

Of course, the Romans need not in the first place have adopted a system of succession which gave women equal rights of intestate succession with men. That they did should perhaps cast further doubt upon the idea that they distrusted female competence. A *tutor*, after all, as already remarked, did not take over the administration of a woman's property. Although, because of the factors mentioned above, the area of a tutor's authority was *de facto* wider in early Rome than later, his was essentially only a watching brief, to intervene if anything a woman proposed to do seemed likely to risk serious depletion of the property, and his responsibility was in large part to her eventual heirs. Men did not have tutors, because men had *potestas*, and therefore perpetuated the *familiae* (in the sense of a descent-line) of which each severally became head; this meant that they had *sui heredes*, immediate heirs upon intestacy (i.e. their children, natural or adopted, and wife *in manu*), and agnates' claim to the inheritance was secondary to these. The agnates' claim was based on blood kinship; but the primary claim was based not on blood but on *potestas* and if blood-heirs were lacking, others could be acquired by adoption (i.e. the taking of an outsider into one's *potestas*).[29]

Women did not have *potestas* over free persons, only over property, and could not perpetuate a *familia*, either by birth or by adoption. It was only by a legal fiction that a woman could be said to be head of a *familia*; her descent-line stopped with her.

MEN'S BUSINESS: GUARANTORS AND SURETIES

In a sense, therefore, it was not possible for women to engage in legal transactions on a basis of equality with men, since what was at stake was not equal. It becomes understandable that the Romans found it acceptable for one *paterfamilias* to act on behalf of another, or to intervene in the affairs of another even when his own interests were not directly involved, but not for a woman to do so.

We have already found jurists talking of 'women's weakness' when discussing guardianship over women, and of 'men's business' when rejecting guardianship by women. 'Men's business' also appears as the primary reason alleged for certain restrictions upon women's capacity in matters of private law. These are of two kinds: taking responsibility for the debts of others, and representing others in litigation.

According to Ulpian, the wording of the *senatusconsultum Velleianum*,[30] a decree of the senate passed about the middle of the first century AD, was as follows (*D.* 16.1.2.1):

> With respect to guarantees and loans by which women intervene on behalf of others, although already the practice of the courts appears to have been to refuse suit against women in such undertaking, since it is not equitable that women should undertake men's duties (*virilibus officiis fungi*) and become bound by obligations of such a kind, the senate's opinion is that those to whom legal application is made in such cases will do well and properly if they see to it that the senate's wish is upheld.[31]

Earlier, he tells us (*D.* 16.1.2 pr.), first Augustus and then Claudius had issued edicts banning women from standing surety for their husbands. He says that by the senate's decree women in general were given judicial assistance (*subventum est*). Later on (*D.*

16.1.2.2), he expresses approval of the farsightedness of the senate in bringing aid to women 'who are exposed and a prey to many cases of this kind because of the weakness of their sex (*propter sexus imbecillitatem*)'. On examination, however, it does not appear that the measure was originally motivated by a belief that women in general were incompetent to handle finance; nor can the alleged reason, that it is not equitable that women should undertake men's work, have formed part of the original wording of the decree.

First, the measure is expressed in a typically Roman way. Women are not henceforth *forbidden* to stand surety for others; they are not banned from engaging in those business and commercial activities in which they have been engaging and in which, in fact, they continue to engage. The magistrates in civil courts are encouraged to use their discretion to refuse to recognise creditors' claims against women guarantors. What this meant in practice was that if a creditor brought a claim against a woman guarantor, the latter could bring a barring counter-claim (*exceptio*), which the praetor might decide to allow. He would not do so if it was plain that the woman understood perfectly well the consequences of her undertaking, but was deliberately attempting to evade, or help others to evade, liability. Indeed, two emperors, Pius and Severus, found it necessary to issue rescripts stating that women attempting fraud were not to be allowed the benefit of the *senatusconsultum*. So Ulpian tells us, with the comment, 'For it was the weakness of women, not their shrewdness, that deserved help' (*infirmitas enim feminarum, non calliditas auxilium demeruit*). Protection, that is, was to be available only where it was necessary. Some women were perfectly capable of understanding and handling such matters; others were understandably at risk through their inexperience. The intention of the *senatusconsultum* resembles that of the Republican *lex (P)laetoria* and subsequent measures,[32] which did not prevent persons of both sexes under the age of 25 from making contracts, but allowed them to protect their youth and inexperience against deceit or exploitation (though not to exploit their protection fraudulently).

Second, who or what is it that is being protected by the *senatusconsultum Velleianum*? The property, according to Paul (*D.* 16.1.1), in whose view the chief consideration motivating the legislators was that standing surety for others actually endangered the family fortune (*res familiaris*, a significant phrase, i.e. the property possessed by the woman in regard to which she had a responsibility to her *familiares*). The decree comes third in a series of enactments which reflect the concomitant decline in the ability or concern of tutors to intervene to protect the property in which a woman's kinfolk had an interest. Augustus had removed *tutela* entirely from women who produced three children (four for freedwomen); Claudius had abolished agnate *tutela*. Tutor's authority would normally have been needed to undertake surety. First Augustus, then Claudius, intervened in the area where requests for such assistance to be given by women were most likely to arise, i.e. between husband and wife. Meanwhile, women had been going on standing surety for others, sometimes with authorisation (now perhaps more readily obtainable) from tutors, others without any longer having to obtain such authorisation; and for some, perhaps, the financial results had been disastrous. Magistrates had presumably been going on in their usual way, handling individual cases at their discretion. It is difficult to know how much or how little to read into the phrase presented by Ulpian as from the *senatusconsultum* itself: 'It appears that heretofore the practice in giving judgment has been not to allow claims or actions against them.' This need not necessarily mean a blanket refusal by praetors to accept such actions by creditors, though the tendency may have developed to play safe by doing so. That the situation was evidently thought to be unsatisfactory, and a policy recommendation sought from the senate, suggests rather a recognition of the necessity and desirability of women continuing to participate financially in business and commercial activities, than the reverse. Confidence in credit needed to be restored.

The ban on women being bankers (*argentarii*) – obviously a blanket ban intended to cover a range of activities under that heading – though first attested under the Severi,[33] may have followed fairly soon after the senate's decree. *Argentarius*, however, is to be understood in the strict sense. There seems to be nothing in law to prevent women, in principle, from engaging, for example, in the kind of transaction documented above for Sulpicius Faustus (*TP* 18 = *AE* 1973.138), acting as go-between in debt-collecting, and giving and taking stipulations for payment,[34] though if they did so professionally the frequency of demands upon the offices of tutors (for those who had them) might be thought burdensome. Andreau (1987: esp. 139 ff.) carefully distinguishes this and similar activities, with corresponding differences in the description of the person involved – *coactor, coactor argentarius* – from those of the banker proper, *argentarius*. The obligations of the former were in general clear-cut and defined by *stipulatio*; they acted as go-betweens and their liability to one party was direct and personal, and offset by a matching *stipulatio* taken from the other party. Bankers, however, offered the service of underwriting clients' debts by formless promises, rendering themselves liable for payment under an *actio recepticia* granted by the praetor, and the obligations thus created were potentially open-ended.[35] Whether the ban reported by Callistratus was the subject of a separate enactment, or, perhaps more probably, the result of interpretation of the *senatusconsultum*, we do not know, but clearly it also is directed at the undertaking of obligations on behalf of others, and the danger to the *res familiaris*.

WOMEN AT LAW

There could be no question of Roman women sitting in judgment upon their fellow citizens. Paul (*D.* 5.1.12.2) lists women among the categories of people ineligible to be selected by praetors to judge civil lawsuits. Ulpian's wider formulation (*D.* 50.17.2), 'Women are excluded from all civil and public offices, and therefore they can neither be judges nor hold magistracies', would presumably cover criminal courts as well as civil, and with even more reason. As mentioned above, condemnation in a criminal court usually meant some degree of impairment of the defendant's legal capacity. Condemnation in certain civil suits also resulted in legal disabilities;[36] in most, the loser's property was affected. Judging, then, was an activity that interfered not only with the legal status of other citizens, but also with the property belonging to other *familiae*, in matters which were no direct personal concern of the judges. To the Roman way of thinking, clearly, only full-blown heads of household (or potential *patresfamiliarum*, since sons were not excluded) ought to exercise such power.

Similarly, the right to bring prosecutions, whether civil or criminal, was restricted for women to those cases in which they had a direct personal interest; nor could they appear on behalf of others.[37] Tutor's consent was required for bringing a lawsuit, presumably because of the possible effects on the *res familiaris* if they lost.

The list of 'civil and public offices' from which women were excluded (Ulpian, *D.* 50.176.2 pr., above) continues: 'nor [can they] intervene on behalf of another nor be procurators.' Women were unable to appear in court on behalf of others either as *cognitor* or *procurator*. Both were representatives of parties to a lawsuit, with the difference that a case brought through a *cognitor* could not be brought again by the principal, whereas a *procurator* had to give security that the principal would ratify the actions taken, since it was possible for the principal to sue afresh. If they were appearing for the defence, again the procurator had to give security. Judgment was normally given to or against them, not the principal.[38]

Women's exclusion from bringing civil suits on behalf of others was specifically mentioned, Ulpian says, in the praetor's edict (*D.* 3.1.1.5).[39] The reasons he gives are (mildly) entertaining, but also oddly inapposite:

> The reason for the ban is so that they shall not, contrary to the modesty befitting their sex, involve themselves in the cases of others, nor, as women, carry out men's work (*virilibus officiis fungantur*). The cause for the ban was a certain Carfania, a woman of the utmost effrontery, whose shameless litigation and pestering of the magistrate gave rise to the edict.[40]

'Carfania', otherwise unknown, may be a garbled reminiscence of the C. Afrania castigated by Valerius Maximus (8.3.2) for her persistence in bringing lawsuits before the praetor, in which she spoke herself; but, as she plainly was litigating on her own behalf, her activity is irrelevant to the ban discussed by Ulpian.

More relevant as a reason is that it was 'men's work', a term whose significance for the Romans is by now evident. The three types of activity just discussed – acting as tutors, taking responsibility for the financial obligations of others, and engaging in litigation on behalf of others – all involve either active intervention in, or taking responsibility for, the affairs of another *familia*.

WOMEN'S WEAKNESS AND WOMEN'S MODESTY

Ulpian begins, however, by citing another reason, which the story of Carfania is presumably meant to substantiate – that involving themselves in the cases of others is 'contrary to the modesty

101

befitting their sex'. Such a social prejudice seems both bathetic and inadequate as the origin of a legal discrimination. Ulpian's phrase might almost be echoing Valerius Maximus' introduction (8.3 pr.) to his group of anecdotes: 'Mention must be made of those women upon whom their natural condition and the modesty (*verecundia*) appropriate to the matron's dress did not prevail to make them keep silence in the forum and law-courts.' This chapter of Valerius is headed 'Women who pleaded causes before magistrates on their own behalf or on that of others', and the last phrase, if this *was* Ulpian's source, may have misled him. Ulpian's reading would have had to be rather careless, however, since Valerius' first two examples, Afrania and Maesia of Sentinum, are explicitly said to have spoken on their own behalf; while the third, that of Hortensia, daughter of the famous late Republican orator, addressing the triumvirs on behalf of the matrons subjected to a wealth tax, has nothing to do with ordinary lawsuits.

What Valerius thinks is improper, even if not illegal, is the appearance of women in public venues. In 8.3 it is their pushiness that he objects to, taking a point of view similar to that attributed by Livy, in his account of the debate on the repeal of the *lex Oppia* (34.1–8), to the elder Cato. Valerius Maximus' own comment on the repeal (9.1.3) ignores the sympathetic (and successful) speech Livy assigns to the tribune L. Valerius, proposer of the repeal, and is modelled on the sentiments in part of the speech Livy gives Cato. In this passage, he concentrates on the theme of extravagance and *luxuria*. The women got their way, he says,

> for the men of that age did not foresee towards what extravagance the headstrong enthusiasm of this unprecedented mass assemblage was tending, nor to what length audacity would go once it had succeeded in defeating the law. . . . But why say more about women, whose weakness of mind (*imbecillitas mentis*) and exclusion from important business impels to devote all their attention to elaborating their *cultus* (self-presentation; i.e. clothes, hairdo and make-up) – when I see that men of reason and excellent character in times past have gone astray into this sort of extravagance that was unknown to the simplicity of old?[41]

Another important theme in the Livy speech, however, the undesirability of women's gadding about in public, surfaces elsewhere in Valerius. In 6.3.10–12 Valerius adds to the story of

Egnatius Mecenius, already cited (n. 17), three examples of husbands who divorced their wives, one because she had gone to the games without his knowledge, one because she had gone about unveiled in public ('You should wish', said her husband, 'to seem beautiful only to my eyes'), one because she had been seen whispering in public to a low-class freedwoman. These divorces may be apocryphal; the stories seem a little too obviously made to point a moral. Though they are presented by Valerius as examples of exceptional severity, he stresses their importance and effectiveness in maintaining women in the obedience, as well as chastity, proper to wives. Cato's speech in Livy (34.2) also links the ideas of obedience and chastity to remaining modestly within the confines of the home:[42]

> As things are, our independence, overpowered in the home by female indiscipline, is now being crushed and trampled upon in the forum . . . I might have said to them: 'What do you mean by rushing out in public in this unprecedented way, blocking the streets and accosting men not your husbands? Could you not have asked these questions at home, of your husbands? Or are you more attractive in public than at home, more appealing to other women's husbands than to your own?'

And if things go on like this, he says, women will seize complete licence, and end up controlling men, and indeed the state: 'What they want is complete liberty, or, to speak the truth, complete licence. . . . Once they begin to be your equals, they will be your masters' – and then public order and the rule of law will be overthrown.

In these passages from two authors of the early Principate, certain stereotypes are exemplified. Women are weak-minded, i.e. they are self-willed and lack control. This is manifested in such traits as being extravagant, self-indulgent, sexually rampant and disobedient. Therefore they present a danger to domestic economy and values – and to public as well, if they become active in that arena.

Dixon (1984: 361) describes Ulpian's strictures on Carfania and the rhetoric Livy gives Cato as 'the remarks of a ruling group defending the bastions of privilege against real or anticipated assault'. She points out, correctly, that 'the idea that modesty in public is proper for women . . . is not linked with female vulnerability or incapacity', adding, however, 'so much as an insistence on excluding from the public sphere women who are only too likely to force their way into it'. The two cannot really be linked in this way.[43] The excited rhetoric of Livy's Cato does indeed include the idea that women, as a group, have ambitions to do something which they are not legally entitled to, i.e. to participate actively in political decision-making. Ulpian, on the other hand, is not so much 'defending a bastion of privilege' as trying to suggest an explanation – that it is not becoming to feminine modesty – for a rule (in this case, the ban on bringing suit on behalf of another person),[44] the original purpose of which has long been lost sight of and which was not, so far as we know, the object of any overt protest by women of Ulpian's own time (so perhaps unlikely to be felt in need of defence). The women criticised by Valerius Maximus (in a passage, 8.3.2, which, as we saw above, may have been the garbled source of Ulpian's account) for speaking in public were *not* trying to force their way in where they had no right to be. Hortensia's action, which most nearly approaches that of the women in Livy's account of the *lex Oppia* protests and was undertaken, as Valerius points out, because no man was bold enough to support the women against the triumvirs, is recounted with no word of blame, merely of regret that there were no *male* descendants of Hortensius willing to take up the inheritance of eloquence. This was a one-off, as was the action of the defendant (not litigant) Maesia,[45] Valerius' reaction to which recalls that of Dr Johnson to women preaching: 'Because, under her female appearance, she bore the mind of a man, they nicknamed her Androgyne (Man-woman).' His fire is reserved for Afrania, who was doing only what women were, and continued to be, perfectly entitled to do. What Valerius objects to is that she did it so *often*, which he takes as a mark of effrontery (*impudentia*).

The idea of modesty introduced by Ulpian, as by Valerius, carries the implication (underscored by Valerius' use of *impudentia* of Afrania) that there is some moral impropriety in women's presenting themselves in public when they need not do so. Appearing in a public court, even in one's own behalf, was not an absolute necessity for most people; they had the choice of appointing a representative. The women who appeared personally in court because they had no choice but to do so were those who for one reason or another belonged among the disgraced (*infames*) listed in the praetor's edict (see next chapter).

As observed above, the notion of chastity is linked with staying at home, away, that is, from the eye of men other than husbands. Women who *voluntarily* offer themselves to public view raise doubts, it is suggested, about their morals. That this social taboo derived not solely from masculine prejudice but had some foundation also in social conditions, in particular female vulnerability amid what was regarded as perfectly normal, if not entirely acceptable, male behaviour, is suggested by the praetorian edict on sexual harassment (*de adtemptata pudicitia*).[46] It was thought necessary to introduce some deterrent to men who pestered women in public, though plenty of loopholes were provided for evading retribution. Mere jest, or intended helpfulness, were acceptable excuses, and it was made clear that approaching women who – at least in appearance – were slaves or prostitutes was unlikely to get a man into trouble.

The corollary to this is the idea that women were particularly vulnerable to abuse and should not be *obliged* to appear in public. The law of the Twelve Tables (I.2) allowed a plaintiff to use force to compel a reluctant defendant to appear in court, but Valerius Maximus claims:

> In order that the decency of married women might be made more secure by the protection of being afforded proper respect, they [the early Romans] did not allow anyone summoning a married woman to law to touch her person, so that the matron's gown might be left unviolated by the contact of another's hand.[47]

Both strands of thought are combined in another passage. 'What', he begins (3.8.6), 'have women to do with public meetings?' This is by way of introduction to the story of how Sempronia, sister of the Gracchi, refused in 102 BC to support the fraudulent claim of the tribune Equitius to be the son of Tiberius Gracchus, against his rejection by the censor. Valerius intends to praise Sempronia for her steadfastness, and the way she lived up to the greatness of her family, but he does so in a singularly indirect way:

> What have women to do with public meetings? Nothing, if traditional custom were preserved – but when domestic peace is tossed in the waves of sedition, and the authority of

ancient custom is ripped to shreds, the compulsion of violence prevails over the persuasive precepts of *verecundia*. So,
far be it from me, Sempronia, to give a hostile account of
you, as absurdly pushing yourself into the most serious
business of men. Rather, I record you with honour. You
were forced to appear before the people by a tribune, in a
place where the chief men of the state were wont to feel
nervous.

He piles on details to emphasise the frightening aspects of such a
situation: confusion, official intimidation and the clamour of the
mob. Here the assumed emotional, as well as physical fragility of
women is emphasised. The rough and tumble of the forum is no
place for the delicate sex; but at the same time their toughness in
pushing themselves in there is equally deplored. Too much logic
should not be looked for in moralists.

Feminine fragility becomes something of a stock 'reason' in
legal texts of the third century AD and later, even in contexts to
which it is not especially appropriate.[48] Particularly piquant is the
imperial instruction issued in AD 397 to the praetorian prefect
Eutychianus:

> The sons of those found guilty under the Julian treason law
> are to be allowed to live (though they ought to die like their
> fathers, as there is apprehension of their displaying inherited
> criminal behaviour), but they are barred from inheriting from
> their mothers, grandmothers or other relatives or receiving
> bequests from non-relatives; they are also perpetually barred
> from public office and sacraments, so that they may be
> forever indigent and find death a solace and life a torture.
> Daughters, however, irrespective of their number, are to be
> allowed only the Falcidian share (i.e. one-quarter) of their
> mother's estate, whether there is a will or not, so that they
> may have a modest subsistence, rather than have intact the
> benefit and name of heir. For the sentence ought to be
> milder in respect of those who, in view of the weakness of
> their sex (*infirmitate sexus*), we are confident are less likely
> to attempt anything.
>
> (*CJ* 9.8.5.3).

It is unclear whether the emperors supposed women to be temperamentally too timid to attempt rebellion, or simply presumed their lack of opportunity.

CONCLUSION

As readers will have observed, the argument in the above chapter is that the common element to all the restrictions upon the legal capacity of Roman women, and their *raison d'être*, is women's lack of *potestas*. This conclusion, though, tempts one to push the question back a stage. Why did men have *potestas*, and not women?

According to Maine, the reason for agnation being determined only through the male line was to avoid a conflict of domestic authorities, i.e. between the *potestas* of the husband and that of the wife's father (not between the wife and her husband).[49] He does not in the context explicitly entertain the idea of women having *potestas*; indeed, it is not clear what he thought would happen, in a system in which agnation passed through both lines of descent, when a woman's *pater* died. Since his model of ancient society is patriarchal, he probably assumed that *potestas* over her children would pass to their maternal uncles – though obviously the conflict of authorities would have recurred, and even more forcibly, if the woman herself inherited *potestas*.

However, we have no reason to suppose that the Romans ever consciously put the question to themselves in terms of alternatives, and took a decision to transmit *potestas* through males only. The primitive (though we cannot say for certain how primitive) institution of *manus*,[50] which transferred not only authority over, but responsibility for, women on marriage to the *familiae* of their husbands, suggests the contrary; i.e. that it was simply taken for granted in early Rome that society consisted of discrete patriarchal groups headed by males, never females. The reason was probably pragmatic. Before the development of community justice, authority would naturally tend to belong to those capable of physically protecting the members of their group, a task for which women were obviously less suited.

An economic explanation of the origin of differentiation in public and social status between men and women in certain societies (though not specifically with regard to ancient Rome) was put forward by Sacks (1974), based on the evolutionary theory of Engels (1891). Briefly, Engels posited an initial state of society of communal groups (of hunter-gatherers) producing only for subsistence, and without the concepts of private property or the family. Private property (land and animals) and the family were the result of the development of agriculture. Women's work, which he took for granted was domestic, was of less significance to the productive unit than the agricultural work (which now produced a surplus for exchange) of men, and the latter alone owned property. Out of private property and production for exchange developed class society.

Sacks identifies a flaw in Engels' evolutionary theory, namely the observable fact that exclusive male ownership of private property and the subordinate status of women do not universally coexist in all societies (as we saw was the case among the Romans, who from the earliest time of which we have information practised divergent devolution of property in intestate succession, but excluded women entirely from political participation). Nevertheless she still retains to some extent a belief 'that women in general stand in more equal relationship to men in nonclass societies than in class societies.' She herself puts forward a theory of female subordination in *class* societies, but in terms of labour rather than property. Men's labour is valued by rulers, who exploit their surplus production; women's labour is domestic and non-productive, save for subsistence, so they are not socially valued. It is not my business here to criticise in detail this view, which, while apparently dating the inception of female subordination at a considerably later stage in societal development than Engels', equally assumes an early stage of complete societal equality; it is also implicitly framed in terms of the nuclear family (see especially Sacks's p. 221), not of the patriarchally dependent kinship group which is the basis of the Roman system. However, Sacks is aware that there is still a question to be answered: why were men, rather than women, the external workers par excellence?[51] Men, it turns out (p. 220), were more mobile and capable of being more intensively exploited, not having to rear and nurse children. In other words the answer is, yet again, the physical difference between the sexes.

As I briefly suggested above, the most likely reason why, as far back as we can trace, *potestas* among the Romans was reserved for males was that their greater physical robustness and freedom from the demands of gestation and child nurture made them more capable of protecting the interests of the descent-group against outsiders. That it was confined to the *pater*, i.e. to the earliest living male ancestor of the group, avoided conflict of authority within the group itself.

This explanation in terms of women's weakness differs from that of the jurists. They name women's weakness, which they evidently think of as mental as much as, or even more than, physical, as an explanation for what, I have argued above, were various *consequences* of women's not having *potestas*. I offer their physical weakness as an explanation for the lack of *potestas* itself.

5

BEHAVIOUR: DISGRACE
AND DISREPUTE

We have seen that the legal capacity of ex-slaves, sons (and daughters) in power, and women was limited simply in virtue of their condition. The reason for these limitations, it is suggested, is that the freeborn *pater* was the standard, by reference to which certain legal powers were considered inappropriate for and withheld from persons in those categories. These limitations were inherent in the person's condition; there were certain other legal disabilities, however, which could be incurred as the result of a person's own behaviour. Conviction in some civil and all criminal trials resulted in the loss of certain private rights, and especially in the curtailment, to greater or less extent, of the power of action through the courts of law; some of these also caused exclusion from public office or service. The same was true of the pursuit of some trades or occupations; even one's way of life could affect one's legal capacity.

The activities mentioned are numerous, though not all are liable (or at least, are specified in our sources as liable) to incur all of the same penalties.[1] There is a certain amount of overlapping between texts, and the tendency in modern studies has been to discuss all of these under the heading *infamia*,[2] and to assume that all are grounded in society's general moral disapprobation. This approach is encouraged, and indeed almost enforced, by the pervasiveness of non-technical, non-legal use of terms such as *infamia*, *ignominia* and their corresponding adjectives.[3] There is little or no attempt at closer enquiry into the reasons for the application of the penalty in specific instances.[4] For some allegedly, and for most fairly self-evidently, the grounds are moral (though it should not simply be assumed that a given restriction is necessarily intended to be penal for all to whom it applies),[5] but the nature of the moral objections needs some investigation. In addition, since the strongly derogatory tone of *infamia*, *infamis* and cognate words in their non-technical usage can be misleading as an index to the severity of the legal penalties involved, and so to the degree of seriousness with which such activities were regarded, we must enquire into the practical effects of *infamia*. How disabling was it for the conduct of ordinary life? In order to approach these questions, it will be as well to start with some account of the restrictions that might be placed on the individual's rights in civil law, and with the types of behaviour which incurred them.

THE RESTRICTIONS

The restrictions themselves are mentioned in legal sources, some-times with a very brief comment on the supposed reason for them. However, we are not told their actual effects on the lives of those to whom they are applied, and this is something which ought to be considered, in order to try to evaluate their significance.

They mainly concern private rights, although, as already mentioned, there also could be exclusion from certain public functions such as central or local office-holding, military service, or acting as a *iudex*.[6] The power of the individual to participate in legal proceedings could be limited in several ways. No persons were denied the right to obtain legal redress in civil law for themselves[7] or to defend themselves in court; those considered unable to do so at all on grounds of physical handicap, such as deafness, or legal immaturity, were required to use the aid of an *advocatus*, provided if necessary by the praetor. The edict went on to specify two further broad categories: those who were not allowed to represent *any* other persons in court, and those who were allowed to represent only certain others.

Legal representation

Both personal misfortune (*casus*), further described in terms of physical handicap, and, as we saw above (Chapter 4), gender, were specified as grounds for excluding some people from going to law on behalf of others. However, the praetor's edict also placed restrictions on certain persons on the grounds of their own past or continuing behaviour. Their right to appear in court on behalf of other people might be removed or limited. Those merely limited could appear only for (i) close relatives and/or (ex-) members of the same *familia* (i.e. parents, children, brothers and sisters, patrons and their parents and children), (ii) relatives by marriage (in-laws, step-parents and stepchildren), (iii) wards or persons under their care (such as the insane); those totally excluded from acting for others were nevertheless allowed to represent this third group, if they already were exercising the functions of *tutor* or *curator*. Moreover, some were denied the right to be represented themselves by others appointed for the purpose (*cognitores, procuratores*; see below). These rules applied to both plaintiffs and defendants.[8]

Anyone shown to have acted in contravention of the ban would be refused permission to proceed, and in addition consigned to a judge who would assess an appropriate financial penalty. As the wording of this provision indicates, the praetor (or, later, the appropriate magistrate to whom the would-be litigant applied) did not necessarily take the initiative in implementing the ban. This could hardly have been expected, given the lack of provision for any sort of record-keeping for many of the categories affected, and the variety of sources from which disqualification might arise. If the magistrate himself knew that an individual was disqualified, he would no doubt refuse to accept him as a contestant in an action; otherwise it was apparently up to the adversary (if he knew of the disqualification) to challenge by an objection, *exceptio*, which must be examined before the case could proceed.[9] No doubt it was possible for some people who were technically disqualified nevertheless to slip through the net.

This is only one of several considerations that should make us doubt the appropriateness of the reasons alleged by Ulpian for the inclusion in the praetor's edict of restrictions on the right of certain categories of people to 'postulate' (i.e. to appear and plead in court):

> *hunc titulum praetor proposuit habendae rationis causa suae-que dignitatis tuendae et decoris sui causa, ne sine delectu passim apud se postuletur.*
>
> (*D*. 3.1.1 pr.).

The praetor issued this title for the sake of taking into account and protecting his position and for the sake of his own dignity, to prevent applications being made before him indiscriminately by all and sundry.[10]

In fact, it appears that his 'dignity' could sometimes be violated without anyone being aware of the fact. Though this was less likely when the penalty arose from something such as a judicial conviction or practice of a particular profession, the spread of Roman citizens and citizenship even through Italy, and even more so the Mediterranean world, meant that the disqualification might not always be known of locally in the community where the lawsuit occurred. Most cases, however, will have occurred between members of the same local community.

Ulpian goes on to mention, supposedly to illustrate the ban on representing others on account of one's sex or personal misfortune (*casus*), two examples of undignified situations which allegedly occurred in the past. One is the rather suspect 'Carfania' story, discussed above. The other – apparently intended to illustrate Ulpian's purported explanation, that the praetor rejects a blind man as advocate because he is unable to see and show respect to the magisterial insignia – is an anecdote of ambiguous significance ascribed to Labeo, about a blind man on whom the presiding magistrate turned his back (or who had his back to the magistrate, who therefore abandoned him; either translation is possible). The latter version fits the 'dignity of the court' idea better, the former merely exemplifies the praetorian practice of rejecting blind men as advocates. We are not told the reason for the magistrate's behaviour, and the whole story is very strange. However, both stories have to do with situations which could equally well have occurred when women and blind people were appearing on their own behalf. This was something which both were and continued to be entitled to do; so it cannot be the case that the mere presence of women and the blind was held to be inimical to the dignity of the court.[11] Nor, it may be observed, would the edict as a whole prevent the appearance in court, on their own account, of *any* of the categories mentioned (other than the deaf and the under-age); indeed, it positively required the personal appearance of those who were banned from using others to represent them. The motive for these prohibitions does not seem, then, to be the protection of the dignity of either the praetor or the court.

Excluding those with a physical handicap, such as blindness, from being representatives protects the interests of those in need of adequate representation; the exclusion of women, as we have seen, has to do with the autonomy of the *familia*. In the remaining instances the ban on representing others seems intended to be penal. Of the total ban, Ulpian says that in the edict the praetor specified sex and *casus*. 'He also stigmatised (the word used is *notavit*, suggesting the censor's mark of disapproval) those *notabiles* ('notorious'? or 'deserving to be stigmatised'?) for their moral baseness (*turpitudine*).' The remaining category suffered only a partial ban, 'as though (*quasi*) they were less delinquent than those stigmatised in the previous clauses'.

These moral grounds appear as part of Ulpian's editorial comment, not as part of the wording of the edict. However, his interpretation, at least to the extent that some sort of disapproval is indicated (so implying that the restriction is intended to be penal), appears to be supported by what he goes on to cite as an actual quotation from the edict (*D*. 3.1.1. 8); the third category, those partially excluded, includes all those declared *infames*, 'infamous', in the praetor's edict.

The use of representatives in litigation was common. Before the supersession of the *legis actio* by the more convenient and flexible formulary system, a process probably made general, if not initiated, by the *lex Aebutia* in the latter half of the second century BC,[12] participants to lawsuits had to press their claims in person. However, the development of *formulae* (standard forms of words in which the praetor defined for the judges the matter at issue and gave directions on the proper way in which judgments in either direction should be expressed) made representation not only possible but easy, since the praetor could secure implementation of the judgment by inserting the name of the representative, whether for prosecution or defence, at the appropriate place in the *formula*. There were two types of representative, the *cognitor* and the *procurator*, the former always appointed to deal with a specific case, the latter in Cicero's time looking after the principal's interests in a general way, which might or might not involve going to law.[13] The appointment of a *cognitor* formed part of the litigation procedure, and was done by application to the praetor in the presence of the other party to the case, before the drafting of the *formula*. Since, according to Gaius's description of the procedure (4.83), the representative, though not necessarily present, was named, there was opportunity for objecting at this stage, with procurators only later. Cognitors and procurators appeared *instead* of the litigant; it is possible that the edict's ban on postulating for others also excluded appearing and pleading alongside a litigant as a *patronus* (distinguished in the Republic from the *advocatus*).

No text, however, mentions a ban on using someone as *patronus* in one's own case, presumably since the litigant still had to appear and bring the case in person.[14]

The bans both on being and on having a legal representative were meant to be in some way penal. What were the disadvantages incurred?

The practical inconvenience of not having representation is obvious, in so far as it might involve having to devote time and effort to arrange to be at the praetor's court, possibly from a long way away, and also to attend the trial in person. There could be some actual material loss, more especially for those obliged to interrupt the exercise of business on which they depended for a livelihood. For persons of high status, there could be significant social consequences, such as a certain loss of face, especially if it were suspected or known (something the opposition would doubtless try to ensure) why the litigant was acting in person, and that it was not from choice. There could be difficulty as well in securing the co-operation of skilful advocates to increase chances of winning. Their use was not, it seems, excluded, as they were technically merely assisting the principal, but they might prefer not to be associated with someone of already doubtful reputation (which their refusal might in turn lower still further). As a penalty, the inability to appoint legal representatives would bite only intermittently, when and if occasions should arise when litigation was necessary.

However, it is interesting to note that it did not affect both sexes to the same extent. The appearance of men in court, whether on their own behalf or that of someone else, was normal and unremarkable; but Roman social *mores* and the attitude to appearances by women in public places, discussed in the previous chapter, meant that for those women who were obliged to litigate personally, because they did not have the option of being represented, an appearance in court made their disgrace conspicuous. Whether the possibility of being suspected of being *infamis* discouraged the untainted from appearing is probable, if not provable; and so the social expectations were strengthened by being constantly fulfilled.

For men, on the other hand, not being allowed either to be a representative (that is, to 'postulate' on behalf of others, whether as a pleader in support of a litigant or appearing in his stead as an appointed representative) or to have a representative (that is, to appoint someone else to appear in one's place) had potentially far-reaching social effects, although, for most of the individuals banned, there are unlikely to have been serious effects on their financial and property interests. However, representatives had obvious practical and commercial use, for others as well as the blameworthy, and there were many in business life, such as the Sulpicii, who spent much of their time professionally engaged in carrying out transactions on behalf of other people, which could include having to litigate. At first sight, it might seem that, if any of them incurred a ban on acting as a representative in court, this could seriously interfere with his means of earning a livelihood.

However, the effects of this restriction were easily avoided, at least as far as contractual dealings were concerned; indeed, Justinian eventually abolished the procedure for objecting to procurators (the term had by then absorbed 'cognitors'), as being little used (*Inst.* 4.13.11). A practice commonplace in business life was the use of *stipulatio*, one form of which, *adstipulatio*, we have seen in use in connection with the transactions of Hesychus and Sulpicius in Chapter 3. Gaius describes it (3.110–11):

> When we stipulate we may bring in another person to stipulate for the same thing; this person we commonly call an *adstipulator*. An action can be brought by him and payment can lawfully be made to him exactly as to ourselves; but by the action of mandate he will be obliged to pay over to us whatever he obtains.

If it proved necessary to sue the debtor C. Novius Eunus, Sulpicius could do so in his own name, not as a representative; indeed, his whole business career as a middleman is made possible by the giving and taking of the *stipulatio*, which enables him to sue and be sued directly, in his own name.

Likewise, a client under a ban could still use the services of a representative in this way. Being banned under the praetor's edict from being or appointing a representative in court, therefore, did not interfere with the pursuit of any litigation arising out of contractual dealings (though if the ban arose from discreditable behaviour, and was known of, it could impair one's business credit).

Not all litigation, however, was contractual, and there also are other possible effects to be considered. *Postulatio* in general is one of those friendly services important for Roman men in building

116

and maintaining status and cementing alliances in public life (not only in politics, but in the broad sense of 'public', i.e. extra-familial). Exclusion from this form of 'networking' was a handicap, and one whose effect would be greatest among the élite, especially, though not solely, those whose forensic activities, though ostensibly gratis and done out of friendship, in fact were a source of some material as well as social gain. Even these, however, were not dependent on this activity for a living. As a social handicap, it may be compared with that imposed by the Augustan adultery law on adultresses, who were forbidden marriage with the freeborn; the same emperor, it will be remembered, prevented senators from inflicting handicaps upon themselves by imprudent marriages to the socially limited, i.e. freed slaves, and the disreputable or judicially disgraced.[15] We shall return to marriage restrictions later.

The worst cases, those allegedly of outstanding moral baseness (*in turpitudine notabiles*, to use Ulpian's phrase), were not permitted to represent even those persons whom the third edictal group could represent. It is important, however, to remember that although these excepted persons on whose behalf the third group could appear (that is, various relatives by birth or marriage or patrons and their children) were closely connected to the penalised person, and some of them at least had once been in the same *familia*, all were now heads of other *familiae* and so *extranei*, outsiders. Those less penalised were, in effect, allowed still to render the service to the people outside their own immediate *familia* with whom they had some bond of *pietas*.

Even that was not allowed to the worst cases; they were allowed to act only in matters affecting themselves and those in their power (who were, in the eyes of the law, part of themselves). There was one small exception. If a man was already tutor of a minor, or guardian of someone mentally ill, he was allowed, apparently by later interpretation of the edict,[16] to represent them. It is probable, however, though not expressly stated in the legal sources, that the magistrate would refuse to appoint such a person as *tutor* or *curator*, though the testamentary appointment by a *pater* would be respected, and *legitima tutela* (i.e. by an agnate or patron) would stand.[17] In the former case, the *pater* had himself given the direction for the administration of the *familia* which he was bequeathing; in the latter, the *tutor legitimus* was assigned to look after the property which would automatically come to him at the death of the owner, becoming part of his own *familia*.

It seems, therefore, that being banned from having or providing legal representation would not have serious effects on a person's economic situation, and that that was not intended. Rather, it amounted to a degree of social ostracism, cutting off the banned person from some of the interaction between peers (i.e. heads of *familiae*) in Roman society. The effect would be felt mainly by members of the élite, and no doubt that was the intention. For those among the élite who were interested in pursuing a public career, exclusion from office-holding would be a serious penalty. Whether, as is sometimes assumed, becoming *infamis* under the terms of the praetor's edict carried with it more than these inconvenient restrictions on legal capacity, but meant also, for those of equestrian and senatorial rank, loss of that status, is a question to be further considered below.

Witnessing

Another restriction, whose scope is not entirely clear, was to be declared *intestabilis*. The penalty, again social rather than directly material, was to be excluded from being a witness (*testis*). Some were not allowed to give evidence in criminal cases.[18] It could also apply to being a witness in certain important formal acts of private law, such as the conveying of property (*mancipatio*) and the making of wills; the latter is mentioned by Pliny (*Ep.* 1.9), along with supporting someone in court, as a typical time-wasting social duty.[19]

What is much more doubtful, however, is whether, as is asserted by later jurists, *intestabilis* was originally also taken to mean 'incapable of *having* witnesses'. The first evidence for this is Gaius, who says (*D.* 28.1.26), 'This means that his testimony is not to be accepted, and further, as some think, that witness is not to be given for him.' 'As some think' indicates that there was no positive rule on the matter, and that opinion among jurists was divided. Ulpian drew the specific inference that this meant that the *intestabilis* could not make a will – presumably since a will, to be valid, required the attendance of seven witnesses (see references in n. 19) – and this became the accepted legal view (*Inst.* 2.10.6).[20]

This means that, from the late second century at any rate, being under this particular legal disability caused rather more inconvenience than before. Just how serious was this inconvenience, and whom did it affect?

Inability to make a will would matter only if there were no pre-existing will, or if someone particularly wished to change an existing will. In the former case, the rules of intestacy would presumably come into play. One effect on the thwarted testator during his lifetime would perhaps be the frustration, for us incalculable, of anticipating the potential damage to his posthumous reputation of being unable to use his will in socially commended ways. Of more practical importance, perhaps, for some would be the loss of the security for proper care and concern from others in old age that the ability to make, or indeed to change, a will could bring. This is a factor stressed by Champlin (1991: 22–3), though as present wealth could, one supposes, to some extent compensate by purchasing care, the effects might be greater on those of relatively modest means.

However, that is not necessarily to say that the jurists' main intention was to cause the penalised persons either physical hardship in actuality, or mental distress in the apprehension of being deprived of the self-interested care of potential beneficiaries. Such a consideration would be alien to Roman ideals of *pietas* and *magnanimitas*. It would be tantamount to tacitly approving the moral crime of *captatio*, inheritance-hunting. As Champlin (1991) has demonstrated,[21] this practice, the rendering of services by 'extraneous parasites' in the hope of receiving testamentary benefits, although little attested in reality, was held in abhorrence by the Romans, to the extent of becoming a common literary motif. It is these would-be beneficiaries, as Champlin remarks (p. 92), who receive the execration of writers, rather than the testator who is prepared in their favour to ignore the claims of duty or *pietas*.

The effects of being *intestabilis* were briefly considered by Westrup (1939: vol. 3, p. 171). He, however, assumed (*a*) that it was accepted as early as the Twelve Tables that the person declared *intestabilis* could not summon witnesses and (*b*) that this meant that he could not summon witnesses *at all*. He draws a lurid picture of the presumed consequences:

> He was excluded from any judicial act in which the co-operation of witnesses was necessary; that is to say, he was really excluded from all legal protection in civil economic intercourse, not only in the archaic legal system with the

regulated 'self-help' in which witnesses in the primitive sense, aggressive as well as defensive witnesses (retribution, blood-revenge), were the indispensable 'assistance' in the maintenance of Law, but also in early historical Roman law when all the most important judicial acts carried out *per aes et libram*, mancipation, *nexum* etc. required the co-operation of witnesses.

The consequences of inability to call witnesses, in early Roman society, would indeed have been extremely serious; but the penalty seems quite out of proportion to the offence for which, according to Aulus Gellius (see n. 18), the Twelve Tables imposed it – that of being a defaulting witness to a mancipation or mancipatory will – and there is no evidence to support Westrup's belief that it was imposed at so early a period. Under the established legal practice of classical Rome, the effects would have been somewhat less devastating. The latter part of Westrup's description (concerning 'important judicial acts') is relevant but far from complete. Such a restriction as inability to have witnesses, if applied generally and not only to the making of wills, would have made some property transfers more difficult. Mancipation was used for conveying property to a new owner with full legal ownership, and required the presence of six citizen witnesses (Gaius 1.119). It was required, however, only for certain types of property (land and buildings in Italy, slaves, horses, oxen, mules and asses). Even these could be conveyed by the procedure known as *in iure cessio* (Gaius 2.24), though both the person obliged to use this and the other party to the transaction would be put to some inconvenience, since it was necessary to come into the presence of a magistrate in order to carry it out. Emancipation of his children, however, would no longer be possible, nor adoption, nor could he manumit slaves, either in his lifetime or by will; though these are inconveniences whose effects, one would think, fell more directly upon the children or slaves than on the person supposedly penalised.

Again, although witnesses were not necessary for contracts to be legally valid, we know from documents such as *Tab. Herc.* 15, recording a *stipulatio* setting bail for appearance in the case of the woman calling herself Petronia Justa,[22] and from Murecine tablet *TP 7 = AE.*1973.43, recording the leasing of a warehouse, that written records of transactions were sometimes sealed by witnesses. How common the practice was, however, and to what range of transactions it was applied, is not entirely certain, given the state of the evidence. Although the surviving portions of most of the Murecine tablets published do not contain lists of witnesses, they occur frequently, on the other hand, in the tablets relating to the business dealings of another Pompeian inhabitant, L. Caecilius Jucundus (Andreau 1974) and also in the Transylvanian tablets (page 229, n. 2 below) and one has the impression that the use of witnesses was a customary precaution in daily business life. In the event of the transaction later being disputed, inability to call witnesses could constitute a disadvantage.

A general ban on having witnesses, then, could potentially have introduced to the conduct of one's family and financial affairs a range of difficulties, though these were not necessarily serious in their effects, As far as our evidence goes, however, the ban on having witnesses (which, in any case, arose from legal interpretation) was late in origin, and confined to the making of wills.

Nevertheless, there is something startling in this juristic interpretation, which in effect denies the penalised person not only, as before, the right to interfere in various ways with the affairs of someone else, but the right to dispose of his own *familia*. It should perhaps be seen as one aspect of the increasing hardening under the empire of the attitude of the state towards offenders, which included both 'criminalisation' and punishment by the state of many offences which had previously been pursued privately under civil law, and harshening of penalties (accompanied by differential treatment according to status).[23] There is also what may perhaps be regarded as a partial precedent for this interference by the state with the liberty of the individual to dispose of his own property. According to Gaius (*D.* 28.1.8.1), those condemned to the two severer categories of exile, deportation to an island and 'banning from fire and water' (*si cui aqua et igni interdictum sit*), not only have their property confiscated, but neither any subsequently made will nor any previously existing one is valid (those merely 'relegated' to an island, on the other hand, or exiled from Italy or their home province, retain the right to make a will).

How and when the view first came to be taken by some that a ban on having witnesses, at least for the making of wills, should be included in the consequences of being *intestabilis* is not known. It may go back, at least as a juristic opinion, to the early Principate, which is the period at which we find the application of the ban on *being* a witness extended as a penalty to apply in some new situations (e.g. condemnation for adultery). However, Gaius' insistence (above) on the distinction between those deported, who could not make wills, and those merely *relegati*, who could, indicates that the opinion had not yet hardened into law by his time (*relegatio* was a penalty under the *lex Julia* on adultery). In the third century, Paul (*Sent.* 2.26.13 = *Coll.* 5.2.2) says that a man who voluntarily submitted to a homosexual act (*stuprum flagitiumque impurum*) lost half his property and was not allowed to make a will.

The ban on being a witness is mentioned in the *Digest* as a penalty for serious crimes (see further below).[24] This appears at the end of the Republic and beginning of the Principate as a penalty imposed in connection with three crimes – *repetundae*, adultery and assault – the first a public crime, the second and third offences against the individual and his *familia*. In the first case, the penalty fits the crime; those perverting the course of justice by selling their testimony are no longer to be allowed to give it in court.[25] Adultery first became a crime under Augustus. Ulpian says (*D.* 28.1.20.6) that a *woman* condemned for adultery is not to be allowed to be a witness; however, this is mentioned in the context as an exception to prove the rule that women were normally allowed to give evidence in court, so although the penalties for adultery were in general lighter for men than women, this does not necessarily mean that men did not also come under the same ban.

There were apparently two Julian laws on *vis*, violence, public and private (*D.* 48.6 and 7 respectively), of which the first is perhaps to be attributed to Julius Caesar, the second to Augustus.[26] The former was concerned mainly with armed sedition and riot, and the destruction of property in the course of such events (though the offences of rape of either sex and abduction of females were included); the latter with attacks on private persons or property. Later they are sometimes referred to under a combined title, *lex Julia de vi publica et privata*, or simply *lex Julia de vi* as in *D.* 22.5.3.5 (Callistratus). It is not clear to which law Callistratus refers (possibly to both) when he tells us that under the *lex Julia de vi* certain people are not allowed to give evidence for the prosecution. It is likely, however, that this explicit restriction (on giving evidence for the prosecution only, not as defence witness) applies only to the first group of people he mentions, freedmen and emancipated children. These are not allowed to give evidence against those from whom they have liberated themselves, or against their children, *propter reverentiam personarum*, ('because of the reverence due to persons') – i.e. it is a matter of *pietas* not to harm them; but support of *pietas* would surely equally require that they be allowed to give evidence in their favour. Minors are excluded from being prosecution witnesses, he says, 'because of the instability of their judgment', *propter lubricum consilii*; but minors, it seems, were not allowed to be witnesses at all.[27] The third group, the one which interests us and overlaps to a considerable extent with those banned under the praetor's edict from litigating on behalf of others, consists of people who *propter notam et infamiam vitae suae admittendi non sunt ad testimonii fidem* ('on account of the stigma and disgrace of their lives are not to be admitted to the giving of evidence to be taken on trust'). It is obvious that such people should not be allowed to have the chance of harming others by their testimony; but it is no more obvious that they are to be trusted as witnesses on their behalf – and they are, by and large, the same people as we know from other sources are not allowed to present a case on behalf of the accused. The likelihood is that they were not allowed to appear at all.

The ban on being a witness, then, is specifically introduced as a penalty under two laws on serious crimes (one of which creates a new public crime out of what had previously not constituted even a civil offence) of the late Republic or very early empire, and is extended by a third to persons already subjected to other penal restrictions of their legal capacity, simply in virtue of their pre-existing status.

Marriage

Finally, to conclude this section, one may mention a further restriction. As mentioned above, the Augustan law banned women (though not, apparently, men) convicted of adultery from marriage with freeborn persons; certain others either were under the original law, or later became, liable to the same penalty (Ulpian, *Reg.* 13.2). Presumably, under later interpretations of the law, the same applied to women convicted of *lenocinium* (pandering) for abetting adultery, since the same penalties were imposed as for adultery.[28]

Clearly, the effect of this penalty would vary according to the status of the woman. For a freedwoman and a freeborn woman of low status, this limited the possibility of extending her connections among families in freeborn society, and could impose a check on her upward social mobility. A freeborn woman belonging to the élite was in effect rendered *déclassée*.

Ulpian (*D*. 23.2.43, on the *lex Julia et Papia*) casually supplies the information (§ 10) that a senatorial decree (of unspecified date) stated that it was not 'fitting', *conveniens*, for a senator to marry or to remain married to, a woman who had been condemned in a *iudicium publicum* (excluding the two legal-procedural offences of *calumnia* and *praevaricatio*; respectively, vexatious and collusive prosecution). He is mainly concerned to make a point about adulterous women; the marriage ban, he insists, applies not only to the woman actually condemned for adultery, but also to one actually caught in the act (*deprehensam*), *quia factum lex, non sententiam notaverit* ('because what the law (i.e. the *lex Julia*) stigmatises is the deed, not the judicial verdict'); that is, such women were *already* banned, even if never brought to trial. What we should very much like to know is the date of the *senatusconsultum*; when it was decided that this particular social handicap should be added to those consequent upon a criminal conviction; and, even more, what provoked its passage.

In a text doubtfully attributed to Ulpian[29] we are apparently told (Ulp. *Reg.* 13.2) that the Augustan legislation itself had already banned marriage between freeborn persons *other* than senators (*ceteri ingenui*) and women condemned in the criminal courts. Nevertheless it would seem very strange indeed if Augustus regarded them as unfit partners for freeborn Romans of lower rank, yet fit to be the wives of senators. However, it has been observed also that in Ulp. *Reg.* 13.2 prostitutes are included in the list of marriage partners banned to senators, and missing from the list of those banned to other freeborn Romans.[30] Mommsen and Huschke both proposed transposing the relevant phrase, and the list of those banned to *ceteri* would then read: prostitutes, bawds and pimps and their freedwomen, women taken in adultery, women condemned in a *iudicium publicum* (or by the senate; see below), and actresses. Clearly, there is still something wrong with this text (and note that actresses appear in both the senatorial list and the 'others' list).

First, the word *ceteri* is misleading, since it could mean, taken literally, that some groups of women are off-limits only to senators, others to 'the others', i.e. to all other freeborn citizens but *not* to senators, so that senators could marry bawds, adulteresses, and so on; clearly an absurd inference, though such a mistake would not be without precedent.[31] Rather, the reverse is to be understood: all the groups listed, under both heads, are excluded from marriage with senators, but *other* freeborn citizens may marry those specifically mentioned only as not available to senators.

Second, the text includes, under the heading of the *lex Julia* on marriage, matter certainly not contained in the law. There is a provision belonging to other legislation (i.e. the *lex Julia* on adultery), and the passage ends with a later juristic interpretation by Mauricianus (adding women condemned by a senatorial court). There is no necessity to assume, then, that the reference to women condemned in a *iudicium publicum* also belongs to the original Julian law. If it did belong to the law, this would not only enormously expand the range of the marriage bans imposed by Augustus, it would also add very greatly to the handicaps imposed on women by becoming *infames*; note, however, that Ulpian himself (*D.* 23.2.43.10, cited above) ascribes it to a *senatusconsultum*, which was not apparently of general application, but related specifically to the marriages of senators, and merely said that such marriages were 'unsuitable'.

There does not seem to be any justification for assuming that, from the time of Augustus, no woman condemned of any criminal offence could marry any freeborn man. Indeed, that Gellius (2.7.20), in a philosophical discussion of the duty of a son, can contemplate the opposite – 'If [your father] orders you *uxorem ducere infamem, propudiosam, criminosam* (to marry a wife who is infamous, shameful or criminal) . . . then of course you should not obey him' – tells against such an assumption. Certainly, if it had been the case that every woman with a freeborn husband found, on her conviction in a *iudicium publicum*, that her marriage was invalidated, the effects on society would have been disruptive.

What the *senatusconsultum* mentioned by Ulpian did, therefore, was to introduce yet another means of discrimination between the senatorial order and the lower ranks of Roman society. How effective it was is another matter. We have very little information about specific individual Roman divorces, let alone their causes;

and whether this was actually the cause of (or even the pretext for) breaking up any marriages is unknown. In the nature of things, evidence linking it with marriages which did not take place, as the cause of their failure, is even less likely to be forthcoming. The *senatusconsultum* may perhaps belong to the reign of Septimius Severus, a period of considerable legal reform; however, Dio's comments on that emperor's attempts to implement the Julian adultery law (77.16) give little cause for confidence that this further attempt to regulate Roman marriages was any more successful.

The texts cited above list various categories of *women* prohibited from marrying freeborn *men*. Except for senators (to whose descendants of both sexes in the male line for three generations the ban applied by the time of Marcus Aurelius at least; Gardner 1986: 33 with references at n. 8), we have no texts to inform us whether there was a corresponding set of prohibitions on marriages with freeborn women. Treggiari (1991: 63) presumes that they were at least forbidden to marry pimps and actors. We may guess, however, that in practice under the empire little concern was taken over the marriages of the lower orders, since neither politically nor privately, for such matters as property rights, was their married status particularly important.

THE SOURCES

The main sources are as follows:

(i) *Digest* 3.1 *de postulando*, especially section 1, from Ulpian's commentary on that part of the praetor's edict specifying which persons were not to have unrestricted right of *postulatio*, pleading in court; parts of the actual edict are quoted, including a cross-reference to the part of the edict discussed in *Digest* 3.2.

(ii) *Digest* 3.2, *de his qui notantur infamia*. Section 1, from a commentary by Julian, quotes the relevant words from the edict, listing those categories of people who are 'noted with infamy'.

(iii) A number of legal texts. Some mention restrictions, specified under particular laws, on being a witness (for which, see above). Some give partial lists of those not allowed to bring accusations, as in *Digest* 48.2 *de accusationibus et inscriptionibus*, Sections 4, from Ulpian's commentary on the adultery law, and 8, from a work of more general application, Macer on *iudicia publica*.

Some concern condemnation for offences mentioned in the praetor's edict. See Macer (from the same work as above) in *D*. 47.2.64(63): *infamia* is incurred as the result of condemnation for theft; in *D*. 47.15.4 for *praevaricatio* (collusive prosecution). In *D*. 47.12.8, according to Macer, *infamia* results from condemnation for violation of a tomb, when regarded as technically falling under the *lex Julia de vi publica*; it also carried *infamia* when prosecuted as an extraordinary delict under the praetor's edict (so Ulpian, *D*. 47.12.1 and 3). So did the extraordinary delict of *stellionatus* (fraudulent pledging of the same security to more than one creditor): *D*. 3.2.13.8 (Ulpian), with Greenidge (1894: 143 n. 3).

It is also worth noting, for its correspondence with part of the praetorian list of *infames*, the list given by Macer (*D*. 48.5.25(24) pr. *lib. primo publicorum*) of those whom, under the Julian adultery law, injured husbands may with impunity kill if they catch them in the act of adultery. Paul (*Sent.* 2.26.4) says generally *infames*, and adds male prostitutes.

(iv) Last but not least, there is a group of partially preserved inscriptions of laws containing regulations on municipal government, of which the so-called *Tabula Heracleensis* (containing the *lex Julia municipalis*,[32] which concerns towns in Italy) has a very extensive list, only partly coextensive with the praetorian lists in *D*. 3.1.1 (the 'postulation edict') and 3.2.1 (the list of *infames*), of those ineligible for membership of local senates. The precise relationship of this to the praetor's edict is uncertain. For a detailed comparison, see Kaser (1956: 241–5). Though there is considerable agreement between them, the extent of the differences leads him to the conclusion that the two were separately constructed, and that therefore it remains doubtful whether and to what extent either can have influenced the other.[33] He refuses to speculate in detail on the reasons for the differences, apart from the inherently very plausible suggestion that these may lie in the different areas of operation of the two and in the differences in the concrete consequences of *infamia*. The inscription is concerned with political qualifications, not with the legal capacity to manage one's private affairs.

The laws in the remaining inscriptions contain regulations for municipal government in towns in Spain and Cisalpine Gaul,[34] of which the relevant parts contain lists of actions which are not to be within the legal jurisdiction of local magistrates. The most extensive list is that in the law from Irni (ch. 84), and it is clear that these actions correspond closely with the so-called *actiones famosae*, i.e. those carrying *infamia* as a result of condemnation. This and the other lists are discussed by d'Ors (1984). For the relative chronology of these and the praetor's edict, with some other texts, see Gonzalez (1986: 228).

THE BEHAVIOUR PENALISED

Who were the people liable to these various bans? Did all apply to all of them? That is, was there a general concept of *infamia*, disgrace, which could be incurred in various ways, but which carried the same range of penalties in all cases? As mentioned above, though the types of behaviour mentioned are numerous, not all are listed in each of our several sources as liable to incur the penalty or exclusion mentioned under that source. Sometimes this is because it is unnecessary. Female prostitutes, for example, are listed among those whom, as mentioned above, Callistratus tells us (*D.* 22.5.3.5) the *lex Julia de vi* bars from appearing as witnesses for the prosecution in cases brought under the law. However, although he apparently groups them among those excluded on the ground of what he called the *nota* and the *infamia* of their way of life, they are not mentioned in Ulpian's account of those barred from 'postulating' (*D.* 3.1.1). The reason is that they are already barred as women, and do not need separate mention. Nor do they appear (though *male* prostitutes do) among those whom the *lex Julia municipalis* says are not to be admitted to membership of local councils, because, as women, they are ineligible for public office anyway. Though they do not appear among the *infames* discussed in *D.* 3.2, the presence of pimps makes it probable that prostitutes also were included in the edict; Julian's quotation may be incomplete. Pimps, however, appear in the lists both of *infames* and of the *lex Julia municipalis*, but surprisingly not in *D.* 22.5.3.5, which suggests that Callistratus here is merely giving examples of those excluded, not attempting to provide an exhaustive list. The activities of gladiators and beast-fighters have a certain kinship, but only the latter occur in the *Digest*. Gladiators occur in the *lex Julia municipalis* (first century

BC) and in a *senatusconsultum* of AD 19 found at Larinum (on which more below), but not in the *Digest*, an omission which Greenidge (1894: 121) explains by their being edited out of juristic texts after the abolition of gladiatorial combats in the Christian empire.[35] Gladiatorial games were abolished by Constantine in AD 325, a ban which was effective only in the Eastern empire; in the West they were abolished in the early fifth century by Honorius. Wild beast shows, however, continued in the West until the time of Anastasius (AD 499), and were still given in the East under Justinian.[36]

However, it would certainly not be safe to assume that all discrepancies between the various lists found in the sources are simply to be attributed to partial citation of a hypothetical common list. Different lists were, as Kaser (1956) observes, created for different purposes, and at different times.[37] Nevertheless, certain groupings are discernible in the various lists; three groups in particular seem always to be regarded as in some way morally reprehensible. Of these, one consists of people condemned of certain offences, the other two (to which we shall turn our attention first) of those practising certain means of earning a living, or engaging in certain behaviour (such as admitting homosexual penetration), that were represented in some contexts as morally disreputable.

The edict on 'postulating' (*D*. 3.1.1, Ulpian) mentions *qui corpore suo muliebria passus est* ('he who has been physically treated like a woman'), and someone who has hired himself as a beast-fighter. The praetor's edict lists among those 'noted' with *infamia* (*D*. 3.2.1, Julian) entertainers, and specifically (?) dramatic actors (those engaged in *ars ludicra* or coming on stage to speak, *pronuntiandi causa*) and pimps. The *lex Julia de vi* (*D*. 22.5.3.5, Callistratus) names beast-fighters again and female prostitutes. Other legal texts (described under 'Sources' (iii) above) give: beast-fighters, actors and pimps (*D*. 48.2.4); *turpis quaestus* – disreputable earnings, unspecified (*D*. 48.2.8). Those whom the law allowed a husband to kill when he took them in adultery (*D*. 48.5.25(24). pr.) were pimps, those in *ars ludicra*, singers and dancers; Paul adds (*Sent*. 2.26.4) male prostitutes and elsewhere (*Coll*. 4.3.2) gladiators and beast-fighters.

Among the lists in laws limiting membership of juries, or of local senates (see 'Sources' (iv) and nn. 35–6 above), most extensive is the list of those excluded from membership of the local senate in the surviving text of the *lex Julia municipalis*: male prostitutes, gladiators, gladiatorial trainers, those in *ars ludicra*, and pimps (lines 122–5). These are preceded by a long list, to be discussed further presently, of those condemned for various offences, to which are added bankrupts and people whose status is variously impaired, mainly as a result of some conviction or judicial decision (lines 110–21).

Preceding all these in the *lex*, and separately mentioned in the previous section (lines 94–7, 104–7) as ineligible, like the under-30s, to hold or to be selected for local office or membership of the local senate, are those engaged in *praeconium*, *dissignatio* and *libitina*, for as long as they do such work. They are quite clearly separated from the condemned criminals and others in the succeeding part of the law; a new section, with a new rubric, starts at line 108. The order of the inscription, as Hinard (1976: 741) observes, resembles that in which Cicero (*Verr.* 2.2.122) lists the criteria given in regulations for selection of a local senate, namely age, *quaestus* (lucrative occupation), *census*[38] (wealth-rating) and 'other matters'. The three occupations follow in the inscription immediately after those persons excluded on grounds of age. There is no obvious reason, therefore, to suppose that their exclusion is based on their being regarded as in some way reprehensible or morally undesirable, like those in the following section. However, since such suggestion is sometimes made, it will be as well to deal with them first, before returning to the 'undesirables'.

Auctioneers, undertakers, ushers and umpires

Three occupations are mentioned, those of *praeco*, *dissignator* and *libitinarius*. Of these, the *praeco* is the one most frequently mentioned in classical literature, and usually in a derogatory manner. For this attitude there are a number of reasons. As auctioneers, they were inevitably associated with the collapse of the fortunes of those whose goods were sold up. Being present at the enforced sale of one's own property is compared by Cicero (*pro Quinctio* 49–50) with witnessing one's own funeral. Auctioneers, like undertakers (*libitinarii*; also in this group), were unpopular because they reminded people of things they would prefer not to think about. Both as auctioneers and in their other main rôle, as heralds and criers, their calling demanded noisy, brash behaviour and, or so common belief went, a constant use of glib misrepresentation.[39] This alone, however, scarcely seems enough to warrant their wholesale exclusion from local élites, particularly as there were among the *praecones* some striking instances of upward social mobility, thanks to their additional public rôle as officials in the service corps (*apparitores*) assisting magistrates (Purcell 1983; Rauh 1989).[40] Although most attested *praecones* are freedmen, the freeborn did not disdain this relatively low-grade post on the magisterial staff, as is apparent from the appearance of freeborn *praecones* in inscriptions,[41] and their mention in the *Tabula Heracleensis*. That, unlike the *ars ludicra*, the profession did not automatically carry a stigma over to the next generation is shown by the adlection of the son of a *praeco* to the town council of Puteoli; his father had been a member of the corps assisting the emperor.[42]

The exclusion of *dissignatores* from office is at first sight no easier to understand. They are mentioned in a variety of contexts, assigning seats at the theatre, marshalling funeral processions, and, apparently, acting as referees at games. The question arose, Ulpian tells us (*D.* 3.2.4.1) whether, in this last capacity, they were to be counted among those *qui artem ludicram exerceant* and therefore classed among the *infames* of the praetor's edict. The Hadrianic jurist Celsus established that they should not, since they did not practice the *ars*, but merely provided a support service – along with musicians, grooms, and some whom we would class as performers, such as chariot-drivers and athletes. These categories were generally exempted by juristic opinion, and 'this appears expedient', said Ulpian, 'because they provide a service at the sacred contests'. (Sabinus and Cassius presented the more high-minded view that athletes were exempt because they were motivated by honour, *virtus*.)

Both *praecones* and *dissignatores* are mentioned as sometimes working with funerals and undertakers, the former in delivering public announcements of funerals,[43] the latter in marshalling the procession; if this common factor for the group is taken as relevant,[44] the exclusion of undertakers still has to be explained. They are the only ones of the three who are directly involved with the handling of dead bodies. We must not, however, jump to the conclusion that, to Roman ideas, this necessarily involved some sort of religious pollution, for them directly and for their working associates indirectly. One of the chief officers of the state religion, the priest of Jupiter, *flamen Dialis*, was indeed under a long list of interdictions which included being forbidden to touch a corpse; but magistrates in general were under no such taboo, and other evidence indicates that, for the rest of the population, the public nuisance and danger to health from corpses was their main concern.

Cicero, discussing the Julian municipal law (*Fam.* 6.18.1) might just possibly be alluding to the funerary rôle of the *praeco*,[45] though if this is indeed the aspect of their work foremost in his mind, he does not seem unduly perturbed by any idea of religious pollution. The point of comparison might rather be supposed to be the more gruesome and physically unpleasant aspects of the religious duties of certain Roman senators: 'It would have been intolerable if those who had (in the past) practised as auctioneers were not allowed to be in local councils, while people exercising the art of *haruspicina* are enrolled into the Roman Senate.'

Haruspicina does literally mean 'divination by inspection of entrails', but the word is so common a technical term that its corporeal associations need not have been uppermost in Cicero's mind. *Haruspices* received some payment for their service. His words would make equally good sense if he were taken to be simply remarking on the incongruity of denying membership of one public body to persons who had in the past performed certain work for it, but were no longer doing so, while allowing others to exercise the two rôles simultaneously.

Amenity, rather than religious dread, appears to be the main concern of a notice put up by a praetor in the early first century BC on each of two stones marking the boundary of a communal dumping-ground for corpses near the Esquiline gate:[46]

L. Sentius son of Gaius, praetor, by decree of the senate, has given order for the fixing of boundaries. For the public good. No burning to be undertaken beyond the markers in the direction of the city. No dumping of refuse or corpses.

To one of the inscriptions was added, in red paint:

Take shit well away, if you do not want trouble.
(*CIL.* VI. 31614, 31615 = *ILS* 8208)

The absence of religious horror is further shown in the fact that in the time of Augustus this burial-ground for the destitute was turned into a public park (Horace *Sat.* 1.8). Witches, Horace makes a statue of Priapus complain, still come there as a traditional collecting-site for suitable ingredients for their spells and potions; otherwise, he has nothing more eerie to object to than thieves and animals, and the unsightliness of the bones that used to litter the place.

An inscription from Puteoli,[47] laying down local regulations for the management and conduct of undertakers' businesses, imposes certain restrictions:

> The workforce is not to live on this side of the tower where the grove of Libitina stands today. They are to take their bath after the first hour of the night. They are to enter the town only for the purpose of collecting or disposing of corpses, and on condition that whenever any of them enters or is in the town, then he is to wear on his head a distinctive (*coloratum*) cap.

Later on, the text appears to specify that if a corpse is to be dragged away with a hook, the workers are to be brightly dressed in red and ring a bell. Bodies not receiving ceremonial funerals are to be removed within a few hours. All these requirements can also be explained as intended to safeguard the population at large from the physical unpleasantness of contact with cadavers. The workers are to be readily identifiable, and (doubtless because their occupation would tend to leave them offensive to the senses of others) they are not to frequent the town at other times, and to bathe only at set times.

The unpleasantness of the tasks carried out by the slave workforce, however, does not seem an adequate reason for excluding the proprietors of the business from membership of the local council, still less for the exclusion of the much more remotely involved criers and marshals, for whom it is not even their principal activity. In the search for a common factor linking the three, the association with the rituals accompanying death appears to be a red herring.

In fact, disposal of the dead is not the sole occupation of the *libitinarii*; like *praecones* and *dissignatores*, they have a number of functions. This is made explicit in the inscription from Puteoli just mentioned. The other main business which such firms contract to perform is the administration of punishment and torture and even the carrying out of executions, and this is done both for private individuals and for officials. The regulations detail the contractors' obligations, both towards anyone who wishes to have a slave punished privately, and towards a magistrate who gives orders for such punishments as he wishes to exact in his public capacity.

This last clause, I suspect, provides the necessary clue to explain both the exclusion from municipal office of the whole group, and their eligibility (unlike pimps, etc.) once they had ceased to practise their respective occupations. All three, for at least part of their time,[48] did paid work for the local authority. This is surely the correct interpretation of *quaestus* in Cic. *Verr.* 2.2.122; not, as Hinard (1976: 741) assumes, that people were excluded from membership of a local senate simply because they 'pratiquaient un métier' (i.e. did *any* sort of work for which they were paid); the purpose of the scrutiny was rather to establish whether the particular line of business of a candidate, like his age and his *census*, made him eligible or ineligible. The reason for the ineligibility of *praecones* was, I suggest, that since they were from time to time engaged in the performance of contracted work for the local council, there was the possibility of a conflict of interest[49] (a difficulty which in modern councils is handled by having the councillor 'declare an interest' when the occasion arises). *Praecones* could be called upon to attend local officials on public occasions, or, in their other main capacity, to conduct auction sales on behalf of the local authority. *Dissignatores*, as we have seen, had a function in the theatre and at the games. *Libitinarii* were hired both to execute publicly imposed punishments and to remove corpses from the streets. Once they had given up their respective occupations, they were free to present themselves for selection to the local council. Their previous callings caused no prejudice against them as persons afterwards, nor, while they were engaged in these occupations, I have argued, was disapproval of how they earned a living the reason for their exclusion. They do not present themselves in any of the contexts in which curtailment of legal capacity, or designation as *infamis*, is in question, except for *dissignatores*, who are the exception proving the rule. They are mentioned in interpretations of the edict *de infamia* only because of their professional connection with the *ars ludicra*, and legal opinion is agreed that the edict should *not* be held to apply to them.

The 'undesirables': shameful professions

The same cannot be said for the other occupations mentioned in the Julian law and in other texts (see above). They and their practitioners clearly attract disapproval. Again, one must enquire into the nature of this disapproval, and in particular whether its nature and cause are the same for each.

An investigation into the possibility of there being a common factor linking three of these – actors, gladiators and prostitutes – has recently been made by Catharine Edwards.[50] Her paper, which lays a good deal of stress on the evocative use of these characters by Roman moralising authors of the early empire to castigate the alleged moral and physical degradation of their contemporary society, performs a valuable function both in demonstrating in detail how these authors use them to create a kind of composite stereotype of depravity (as she remarks, there is a conceptual link between actors, gladiators, prostitutes and their associates), and in identifying some of the elements out of which this picture is composed. These texts reveal how such persons are perceived as threatening to the values of Roman society, and she analyses in some detail the grounds of this perception, without, however, suggesting that this is in itself the *reason* for their being subjected to legal restrictions. It is not part of the intended scope of her paper to attempt to draw firm conclusions as to the specific grounds for categorising each as *infamis*.[51]

Indeed, it is not easy to determine the reasons. Pleasure, as Edwards points out, is routinely contrasted by Roman moralists with duty (especially public duty). All three – actors, prostitutes, gladiators – minister to pleasures, but of different kinds. That provided by the prostitute is, obviously, directly sexual, and all three may be linked as somehow emblematic of corrupt sexuality. The commodity of the prostitute – sex – serves, Edwards suggests, as a metonymy for the sensual pleasure purveyed by all those Romans labelled infamous. Hence the erotic associations of actors and gladiators. Those who sell their bodies for public exhibition in the theatre or arena are assumed to be sexually available.

It is important to distinguish between two different ideas: one, that the public performance itself is in some way erotic (or at any rate provides a 'sensual pleasure'); the other that, off-duty, the performers are (or are thought to be) sexually promiscuous. To take the latter point first, although gladiators and actors are mentioned frequently in literary texts from Cicero onwards as typical objects or instigators of alleged irregular and disreputable sexual indulgence by the Roman élite, we do not know of what proportion of performers this was actually true, nor (more relevantly for the present discussion) do legal texts specify sexual misbehaviour as the ground for the imposition of these performers' legal disabilities. If it were, then it is not easy to see why the occupation of the perpetrator is relevant. We have virtually no evidence for attempts by the state, prior to the Augustan legislation, to regulate by legislation the sexual behaviour of the Romans, other than a single sentence in a legal writer of the late second century AD.[52] Besides, there are other, related types of performer, who also incur legal disabilities, but are not similarly treated in literature – the beast-fighter, for instance (Ville 1981: 335) – or performers in other types of *ars ludicra* than acting and dancing.

In the case of gladiators, moreover, although there are numerous references to the attraction they are said to hold for women, deliberate eroticism is not a characteristic ascribed to their performances (unlike some stage performances). Edwards finds it in the aggressive masculinity of which they were emblematic;[53] she also points out that both gladiators and actors, like prostitutes, put their bodies on display,[54] and contrasts with these the chariot-drivers, who are not among the lists of *infames*, and the backstage trainers and service workers, about whom jurists were doubtful. These characteristics, however, are true only of some arena performers. Juvenal (4.99 ff.) mentions the nudity of an aristocratic *bestiarius*, but twice (2.143 ff.; 8.199–210) draws attention to the effeminacy of a tunic-clad *retiarius*; there seems to be an inverse correlation between the level of masculinity and the amount of bodily covering worn. To the law, however, all are *infames*, and distinctions between them are made, as we shall see, upon other grounds.

There are valuable remarks in Wiedemann (1992)[55] on the psychology of spectators of the shows, especially as revealed in comments in literary sources (and it has to be borne in mind that the authors of these, like the drafters of the laws, are males of the Roman governing classes). What is chiefly dwelt upon is not lustful attraction, but the ambivalent attraction of the physical horror of the arena, the bloodiness and the cruelty. This clearly fascinates even those who profess to abhor it; see, for example, Seneca *de ira* 3.3.3 (and compare 3.3.17–18).

As to their 'off-duty' lives, although Ville (1981: 329–31) cites some Pompeian graffiti celebrating gladiators' supposed success with women, and a handful of anecdotes alleging the fathering of babies by gladiators upon upper-class Roman matrons, he also lists a number of funerary inscriptions mentioning not only wives of gladiators but also their children. The presence of the latter, particularly where they join with their mother in commemorating their dead gladiator father, casts some doubt on his confident assertion that these were not 'des ménages bourgeois', and that the women were for the most part merely 'groupies', *ludiae*, passing from man to man. Though not all of the unions will have been legally recognised marriages (which was not possible where the gladiator was a slave, e.g. *ILS* 5091), this does not prevent them from having been stable and loyal relationships. Some men may have acquired wives and families only after retirement from the arena. This could be the case with the ex-gladiator of the 'Thracian' type, M. Antonius Niger, dying at the age of 38 as a *veteranus* after eighteen appearances, and commemorated by his *coniunx* Flavia (*ILS* 5090); but it is unlikely of Iuvenis, dead at 21 after five fights and only four years in the business (*ILS* 5107).

Some of the families attested belong to men who were in the less glamorous side of the business, working as trainers or possibly umpires.[56] The imperial slave Threption, trainer of 'Thracians', may have had a free 'wife'; he commemorated at Puteoli, as well as several males with single names (possibly fellow slaves in the gladiatorial school), a little boy, L. Tettius Alexander, dead at 5 years 11 days (*ILS* 5091). The imperial freedman Trophimus, a *secunda rudis* (see n. 56) at Rome, had a freeborn wife and set up a memorial to himself, his wife, his freeborn *nutricius* (male child-minder), and his freedman, who had been a homeborn slave (*ILS* 5129). It is perhaps less remarkable to find evidences of domesticity in the lives of men performing the more humdrum tasks of the arena. Very striking, however, is the memorial at Milan to Urbicus, the sword-fighter (*ILS* 5115):

> *Urbico secutori primo palo, nation. Florentin., qui pugnavit*
> *XIII, vixsit ann. XXII, Olympias filia quem reliquit mesi.*
> *V, et Fortunesis filiae, et Lauricia uxsor marito benemerenti,*

cum quo vixsit ann. VII. Te moneo, ut quis quem vic[e]rit occidat. Colant Manes amatores ipsius.

To Urbicus, *secutor* of the first grade,[57] from Florentia by birth, who fought 13 times and lived 22 years. Set up by his daughter Olympias, whom he left at the age of five months, and Fortunesis, belonging to his daughter (i.e. a slave), and Lauricia his wife, to her well-deserving husband, with whom she lived seven years. I advise you, let each man kill the one he conquers. May those who love him reverence his Manes.

Clearly, not all gladiators spent their leisure time servicing high-class Roman ladies.

More direct connection can be perceived between overt sexuality and the stage. Some theatrical entertainments (though not all) appear to have been designedly erotic in nature, such as the dancing girls referred to more than once by Martial, or the (fictional, but perhaps based on reality) balletic performance described by Apuleius (*Metamorphoses* 10.29–34), in which the actress playing Venus was costumed (if that is the appropriate word) in a fashion similar to the Venus later painted by Botticelli.

The association of theatrical entertainments with eroticism and self-indulgence (*luxuria*) on the part of the Roman upper classes, especially in their exotic (sc. Greek, i.e. un-Roman) private amusements, is discussed by Wiseman (1985: ch. 2) in his study of the lifestyle of Clodia Metelli and others of her time and milieu. When the aristocratic employers themselves decided to participate and perform, society reacted with overt disapproval. Cicero represents Catiline's special cronies as effete and degenerate, spending their energies on all-night parties. Eroticism and the arts of the stage are linked.

These pretty young voluptuaries (*pueri lepidi ac delicati*) have not only learned all about making love and having love made to them, and dancing and singing, but they have also learned to wave daggers about and sprinkle poisons.... How will they endure the Apennines and all that frost and snow? Unless perhaps they suppose that they will tolerate wintry conditions more easily because they have got used to dancing naked at parties.

Even to call a respectable Roman a 'dancer' was an insult belonging to the language of street corners and buffoonery (*ex trivio aut ex scurrarum aliquo convicio*), because of its association with lust, wild parties and extravagant spending.[58]

Descriptions of real or alleged private 'theatricals' appear to have formed part of the warfare of character denigration between Octavian and Antony. A party given by Octavian where he and the guests dressed up as the Olympian gods caused, says Suetonius (*div. Aug.* 70), general gossip, especially happening as it did in a time of dearth. It was the subject of anonymous verses, while Antony deliberately in his letters gave the names of all the guests, and added the detail that Octavian had cast himself as Apollo. This is countered by a story told by Velleius Paterculus (2.83). The degradation in which Antony, in his debauched dalliance with Cleopatra, involved his noble Roman associates is illustrated by the shameful behaviour of Lucius Plancus. Once Plancus, along with M. Titius, had abandoned Antony and Cleopatra and thrown in his lot with Octavian (Dio 50.3.2), the latter, says Dio, 'was very glad to receive them and learned from them all about Antony's actions and intentions'. Any discreditable stories they had to tell (doubtless heightened in the telling) would be well received and would form a useful store of counter-propaganda against Antony. Plancus, says Velleius, had himself painted blue and danced the part of the sea-god Glaucus at a banquet, naked except for a fishtail and a garland of reeds. This, however, was not, according to Velleius, what had led to the breach between him and Antony, but rather the latter's discovery of Plancus' unscrupulous venality. Antony's most debauched (*obscenissimae*) doings had Plancus, he says, both as instigator and accomplice.

In these two instances, however, it is not altogether clear that an erotic element is given particular prominence (is blue skin erotic?). Plancus' performance is an offence against the *dignitas* proper to his status. Suetonius seems more concerned with the tactless expense, and this, strikingly, is the element singled out by the writer one may almost call the historian-laureate of the Augustan principate, Livy, at the end of his potted history of the theatre in Italy (7.2.13): *ut appareret quam ab sano initio res in hanc vix opulentis regnis tolerabilem insaniam venerit* ('to show from what sober beginnings things have now come to the present madness, which even wealthy realms could scarcely support').

The sentences immediately preceding this comment are relevant to the present discussion. According to Livy, the Atellane farces had for a long time retained their essentially amateur character, and were not performed by professional actors; and that, he says, is why it is still the custom that actors in Atellane farces are not excluded from tribes (i.e. from the electoral assemblies of the Roman people, soon to become obsolete under the Principate) and from the army.[59] Valerius Maximus (2.4.4) copies Livy's account closely, but the exceptional treatment of the Atellani, according to him, was because that genre of entertainment, coming from the Oscans, was 'tempered with Italic austerity, and therefore carried no stigma' (*Italica severitate temperatum vacuum nota est*). He substitutes the commonplace notion of old-fashioned *gravitas* for Livy's much more interesting statement that what made the difference was whether or not performers were paid. The questionable historicity of their accounts of the past of the Italian stage does not matter here; what is important is what they reveal of the attitudes of the élite in the early Principate. I shall return to the matter of payment later.

There is certainly a conceptual link between sex (other than marital, for procreation), the theatre and the arena as areas of activity not proper to be indulged in by a good citizen, and especially inappropriate to the *dignitas* of the ruling classes. It cannot be accidental that all three figure among the iniquities stereotypically attributed to the 'tyrant' figure, such as the various 'bad' emperors, especially Caligula and Nero, though even Caligula is credited with the expulsion from Rome of certain entertainers specialising in sex acts.[60] The equivocal attitude to Julius Caesar and Augustus in later tradition appears in the sexual appetites that are attributed to them – though to the latter only in his youth and 'from policy' (Suetonius *div. Jul.* 49–52; *div. Aug.* 68–70) – and both are credited with attempting to impose some control upon the conduct of public performances and on appearances by members of the élite, while sometimes countenancing these.[61]

The Larinum decree and official attitudes

Ancient sources enable us to follow in some detail the vacillations of official policy towards public appearances, both on stage and in the arena, by upper-class Romans between the dictatorship of Caesar and AD 19.[62] From that latter year, we have some primary evidence, in the form of a tantalisingly incomplete inscription from

Larinum: a *senatusconsultum* was passed condemning, not for the first time, upper-class participation in such performances, and laying down certain penalties.[63]

In his games of 46 BC Caesar allowed knights, and even the son of a praetor, but no actual senators, to take part in gladiatorial combat.[64] In 38 BC, the senate decreed a ban on senators engaging in such contests (Dio 48.43), and either then or later they and their sons also were excluded from the stage. In 22 BC Augustus extended the ban to their grandsons; Dio (54.2.5) mentions this only at the end of an account of a number of reforms, partly sumptuary and in the interests of economy, but also restricting the opportunities for individual magistrates to win public favour by their munificence, and perhaps showing a concern for public order.[65] The scale and frequency of gladiatorial combats at Rome was strictly regulated: only twice a year, with no more than 120 fighters, and only on authority from the Senate. At some point during Augustus' reign, *equites* also were banned from both stage and arena; this is an inference from Suetonius' statement (*div. Aug.* 43.3) that Augustus himself occasionally used them in such performances, until they were banned by a *senatusconsultum*, which may be the same as the one in 22 BC just mentioned.

Only a few years later, however, L. Domitius Ahenobarbus brought Roman knights and matrons on stage to act in mime, when he was both praetor (19 BC?) and consul (16 BC); his gladiatorial show was marked by such extreme cruelty that Augustus, when private warning was ineffective, was obliged to restrain him by an edict; so says Suetonius (*Nero* 4), characterising the emperor Nero's grandfather as 'haughty, extravagant (*profusus*) and cruel'. He does not say, however, that Augustus attempted to enforce the senatorial decree concerning the appearance on stage of members of the senatorial and equestrian orders. The next breach of the decree mentioned in the sources does not occur for more than a dozen years, and that is at the praetorian games of Quinctius Crispinus in 2 BC, mentioned by Dio, as he says, only because knights and matrons appeared on stage (Dio 55.10.11).

Interestingly, Dio appears to see a connection between this and Augustus' banishment of the disgraced Julia. 'Augustus', he says, 'at first attached no importance to this.' But he flew into a rage on discovering the public debaucheries of his daughter, banished her, put to death one of her lovers (ostensibly as conspiring against himself) and banished the rest. This, says Dio, provoked a spate of accusations against other women, which the emperor was obliged to control by refusing to receive charges concerning conduct before a specified date. Dio does not spell out the connection, but it does seem as though appearance on stage (presumably, since women participated, in mimes and/or balletic performances like that described by Apuleius) is something which he associates with, and regards as a symptom of, loose living and immorality, and specifically sexual immorality, among a section of the Roman upper classes.

This does not necessarily mean, however, that this was in the Augustan period the principal consideration on which the legal penalty of praetorian *infamia* for performers was based. Dio was a contemporary of Ulpian and Callistratus, the two jurists whose editorial comments on the reasons for banning some professional performers were mentioned above. The modern tendency to assume that the praetorian restrictions on actors, beast-fighters, and so on were solely on the grounds of 'immorality' may in fact rest mainly on such late comments; moreover, care is needed in their interpretation. When Arcadius Charisius, for example, in his treatise on witnesses, says (*D*. 22.5.21.2) that where a case compels receipt of evidence from a *harenarius* or 'similar person', their witness is to be believed only if given under torture, this is not to be read simply as an expression of society's contempt for persons of that calling. Torture was already by Arcadius' time in general use against lower-class citizens (de Ste Croix 1981: 459–60 and references there); Arcadius may also be recognising the technical difficulty involved in the fact that fighters in the amphitheatre are *infames* and therefore *intestabiles*.

Again, we are told by Callistratus (*D*. 22.5.3.5), as mentioned above, that the Julian law on assault excluded as witnesses persons condemned in a criminal trial, prisoners, professional beast-fighters and prostitutes. These are, he says, persons who 'are not to be admitted to the giving of evidence to be taken on trust, on account of the stigma and disgrace of their lives' (*propter notam et infamiam vitae suae*), a phrase which by its formulation, using abstract nouns, suggests immoral conduct on their part (rather than its condemnation by others); and that does appear to be how Callistratus takes it, just as Ulpian remarked that beast-fighters, among others, were excluded from postulation as *turpitudine notabiles*. The slide from the technical meaning of *infamis* (i.e. listed in the edict as liable to certain legal disabilities) to the non-technical is present in both comments, though less obvious in Ulpian's formulation. In the edict, however, as quoted by Julian (*D.* 3.2.1), *infamia* is what each of the people listed is branded (*notatur*) with; it is the (legal) *effect* of being listed, not the reason for it. Callistratus' explanation of the unacceptability of convicted criminals and the like as witnesses is (in effect) circular; they are *infames* (in one sense) because they are *infames* (in another). As we saw had happened, by the time of the canonical jurists of the Roman law as preserved to us, in the case of the legal incapacities of women, unquestioned traditional social prejudice was accepted as a sufficient explanation for the imposition or maintenance of the disabilities (despite suggestions to the contrary in the legal texts themselves).

This is basically what, for us, is problematic. 'Augustus', says Dio about the games of Crispinus, 'at first attached no importance to this', and although, as Levick (1983: 107) remarks, he had something better to think about (viz. Julia's lovers), the implication of Dio's remark is not that the emperor would have punished those involved had he not had other more pressing concerns, but quite the contrary: that the mere appearance of knights and *matronae* on stage was not in itself something that he was disposed to regard as particularly worth taking action against.

By AD 11, the senatorial decree was so little regarded that its breaches were simply condoned and the ban was lifted.[66] Permission was given for *equites* to fight as gladiators, and even the emperor himself watched the contests, in the company of the praetors presiding at the games (Dio 56.25.7 ff.). Whether or not a similarly tolerant attitude was shown to stage performances is not reported, but is likely; the two seem sometimes to have been treated together.

Four years later, under a new emperor, Tiberius, and after repeated disturbances particularly involving ballet performers, there was a reaction. Senators were forbidden to enter the houses of ballet-dancers, and knights to be seen with them in public. These measures, however, as Tacitus' account (*Ann.* 1.77) makes clear, were directed against the professional performers, and were an alternative to the flogging by the praetors which some wished to inflict on them.

Professional actors, even those who were citizens (and many were not), were, unlike Roman citizens in general, liable to corporal punishment by magistrates already under the Republic (although Augustus (Suet. *Aug.* 45) limited its exercise to the time of the actual performance), and the reason appears to have been political rather than moral. There are several mentions in literary sources of expulsions of actors for stirring up sedition (Tac. *Ann.* 4.14.4; Dio. 54.17.4; 57.21.3), sometimes coupled with vague accusations of adulterous liaisons (Tac. 4.14.4; Dio 57.21.3 – both concerning AD 23). Pylades, according to Dio (54.17.4), was expelled for *stasis*, sedition; his behaviour, described in more detail by Suetonius (*Aug.* 45) was socially disruptive, involving as it did the public humiliation of a spectator. In the same place, Suetonius recounts two floggings administered to actors (both, like Pylades, with Greek names, so perhaps not citizens); one on the complaint of a magistrate (so presumably because of some violation of public order), the other on the emperor's order, because Augustus learned that he had a Roman matron, dressed in boy's clothes and with her hair cut short, attending him as a servant. The implication of an adulterous liaison is there, but the details given by Suetonius suggest that the gravamen of the matter for the emperor was the open flouting of conventional proprieties of dress and behaviour, and especially of class distinctions. Besides, Augustus did not always stick strictly within legal limits in the infliction of punishments (cf. Suet. *Aug.* 67). Although many actors were slaves, ex-slaves or non-citizens, the infliction on them of corporal punishments and expulsions appears to reflect not so much a general contempt for their calling as unworthy of free citizens, as a reaction to specific occasions on which they appeared to present a danger to public order. Actors were seen as a disruptive force.

After the disturbances of AD 15, Tiberius also imposed limits on actors' salaries, and performances were allowed only in the theatre, that is, they were not allowed to accept private engagements. Nothing is said about upper-class amateurs who participated. We are not told that a ban had been reimposed, but that may not have been necessary; there is something in the suggestion of Levick (1983: 112) that the relaxation had been 'precarious and *ad hoc*' – that is, permission had to be requested each time one of the élite wished to perform, and by implication, in a period of repressiveness and concern for public order, permission would not have been forthcoming. Presumably persistence in appearing in spite of refusal would incur punishment of some sort. We are almost totally uninformed as to what penalties, if any, were imposed at times when such bans were in force.

The inconsistencies of official policy described above are more readily comprehensible on the assumption that more than one type of participation is involved. A distinction should be drawn between upper-class participation on an amateur and occasional basis, and paid appearances on a professional basis. Though the literary sources do not clearly distinguish between the two, the *senatusconsultum* from Larinum uses the language of professional hiring, and legal texts are explicit that it is performance for gain, *quaestus*, that incurs *infamia*.[67] Appearing as amateurs did not automatically render the persons concerned *infames* under the praetor's edict.

In fact, one of the few literary mentions of a penalty in this connection[68] is the passage in which Dio describes the relaxation of AD 11 (56.25.7); the ban on *equites* performing as gladiators was lifted because it was ineffective, since some people were making light of the penalty incurred by performance, which he says was *atimia*, 'loss of rights'.[69] One's suspicions as to how much Dio really knew or understood about the situation are roused when he adds, as further reasons for the removal of the ban (*a*) that the guilty seemed to deserve greater punishment or (*b*) that it was thought that they would be turned aside from such behaviour. How either end would be achieved by permissiveness he does not explain; certainly his following sentence is not to be taken seriously as a description of governmental *intentions* at the time: 'And so they incurred death instead of *atimia*; for they fought none the less, and especially because their contests had an enthusiastic audience, so that even Augustus used to watch them together with the presiding praetors.'

What Dio meant by *atimia* is unclear. There is no other evidence to suggest that loss of senatorial or equestrian status had been a penalty imposed on those who contravened previous bans. He may mean *infamia*; even so, his expression is ambiguous. 'The penalty imposed on such conduct' (*ten atimian ep' auto epikei-menen*) is quite appropriate as a description of the *infamia* already incurred, under the praetor's edict, by all professional performers (not only those of senatorial or equestrian status) in theatre or arena; we cannot deduce from his words that there was (or that he thought there was) some additional penalty imposed on equestrians defying the ban on gladiatorial fighting, still less make any guesses as to its possible nature. It is equally unclear whether Dio was aware of any distinction being made between paid and unpaid performance, or simply assumed – wrongly – that even an amateur appearance as a gladiator or an actor carried *infamia*.[70] That this was not so is clear both from the legal texts and from lines 7–11 of the inscription found at Larinum (see n. 67), which refers specifically to professional engagements.

It is apparent from the wording of the decree that for some time such paid employment had been undertaken by persons of senatorial and equestrian rank. That some may have needed the money is understandable, since the definitions embrace not only those who actually were senators or *equites*, and so possessed of the necessary monetary qualifications, but also a range of kindred who may have been considerably less well-off.[71] At any rate, the prospect of earnings was apparently enough to induce them to risk social disdain (not to mention the risk to life for the arena performers), and also voluntarily to forfeit some of their civil law rights.

The inscription preserves part of the text of the senatorial decree of AD 19, which represents a fresh attempt to impose restraints on such performances. Particular care was to be taken to prevent this happening in future, because in the past, according to the decree (lines 12–14),[72] certain persons, for the sake of *eludendae auctoritatis* ('making mock of the dignity') of that order who had the right to sit in the spectators' seats reserved for *equites*, had deliberately either incurred *p* . . . (possibly *publicam ignominiam*)[73] or got themselves condemned in a *famosum iudicium*, a case in which conviction rendered one *infamis*; and (lines 13–14) 'after they [had become ineligible to sit in the eques]trian places',[74] had pledged themselves (as gladiators) or appeared on stage.

They had done one or other of two things, both of which had in the past apparently had the result of making them ineligible to sit in the fourteen rows. One is quite clearly specified: they had deliberately sought conviction in a lawsuit, which carried the automatic penalty, under the praetor's edict, of being *infamis*. That they were prepared to take this step reinforces the view expressed above, that the practical effects of 'praetorian infamy' on daily life were not very serious or incommoding. The other is left vague (*p[ublicam ignominiam] ut acciperent*, 'to incur public ignominy'), but presumably refers to some other way of becoming *infamis*, for example, by the exercise of one of the professions listed in the edict, or by bankruptcy. The legal penalties have already been described; loss of the symbolic privilege of a seat in the fourteen rows was apparently also a customary consequence.[75]

They had not, however, forfeited their social status. Though the contrary is commonly assumed (on the inadequate basis of this Dio passage and the story of Laberius), and although very little is known about either recruitment to or loss of equestrian and senatorial status in the Principate, there is in fact no evidence that incurring praetorian infamy of itself automatically entailed loss of equestrian or senatorial status.[76]

They had deliberately done something to render themselves technically *infames*; this is presumably the employment of fraudulent evasion (*adhibita fraude*) referred to at the start of the decree. It was not that they automatically lost their privileged status as senatorial or equestrian, nor, I suspect, that they showed themselves indifferent as to whether or not they were degraded from it, both of which would be serious considerations. The text of the decree appears to mention only voluntary forfeiture of one of the incidental privileges of their status: good seats for the show. Such a symbolic, but essentially meaningless, renunciation could very satisfyingly taunt the 'establishment';[77] in itself, however, it is of less moment than the legal rights they have given up by incurring *infamia*. Levick (1983) suggests that there must have been some additional penalty imposed between the relaxation of AD 11 and the Larinum decree of AD 19, possibly in connection with the repressive measures of AD 15, and that that was what they hoped to evade.

If Suetonius' account of measures taken by Tiberius against such dodgers may be associated with the Larinum decree, then, although he mentions no penalty under the senatorial decree, it should perhaps be seen as significant that he links them in the same sentence with matrons who tried to evade penalties under the Julian adultery law by registering as prostitutes (and so also, incidentally, voluntarily becoming *infames*).[78] The effects of being *infamis* were a great deal lighter than the penalties, which as professional prostitutes the women hoped to avoid, for adultery. They achieved nothing; the emperor imposed on all of them the penalty of exile. Tiberius was, in effect, imposing penalties on both groups for their defiance of the standards of behaviour which it had been made clear were expected of them.

The two cases are not, however, entirely parallel. For the women, becoming registered prostitutes rendered them immune from punishment under the Julian adultery law; that is, if they should ever be convicted of adultery. The punishment on conviction was severe. They could expect relegation and loss of one-third of their property and half their dowry. Additionally, because their existing husbands were obliged to divorce them, and because after conviction for adultery they were excluded from marriage to freeborn Romans, upper-class women lost status, since a wife's status followed that of her husband.[79] Incidentally, under another piece of Augustan legislation, the marriage law, wives of senatorial rank, if their status came only from their husbands and not their fathers, presumably automatically lost it on becoming registered prostitutes, since such marriages were invalid; other women, however, could apparently stay married (see above). So, for most of the upper-class women concerned, such loss of status as they might incur was due to the operation of the Augustan laws, not to their becoming *infames* in the terms of the praetor's edict. They had become *infames* precisely in order to avoid any future danger from the much severer penalties of the adultery law, penalties which applied to women of all ranks.

The would-be gladiators and actors, however, had incurred *infamia* by other means in order to be able to pursue professions that carried automatic *infamia*, but no other penalty. Were they trying to evade a much severer penalty than *infamia*? None is mentioned in the surviving portion of the edict (denial of a proper funeral does not seem much of a disincentive to a gladiator), nor elsewhere. Perhaps they were not trying to avoid a penalty, so much as to secure a gain, i.e. the financial rewards for such work – but work which was regarded as unsuitable for persons of their social standing. Persons of lower status incurred no penalty at all for working in the theatre or the arena, other than that of being *infames*.

That was by no means the last that was heard of such senatorial and equestrian performers, nor of performances by amateurs. Notoriously, 'bad' emperors both appeared themselves and obliged upper-class Romans to do likewise, apparently as amateurs, and naturally without incurring penalties other than social disapprobation – covert, no doubt, among their contemporaries, and overt among moralising authors writing in safer times (or even, on the contrary, the sympathy of the latter, when they were represented as participating under compulsion).

Doing it for money – especially sex

In the treatment of the 'shameful professions', various distinctions are observable: between paid professional and amateur activity, and between directly sexual activities and the others. The two sets of distinctions, however, fail to coincide. Although the *lex Julia municipalis* excludes pimps and (male) prostitutes, along with actors and gladiators, from local senates, beast-fighters (and probably originally gladiators) are more severely treated than actors in the praetorian edict. Males who admit homosexual penetration (which would include both amateurs and professionals, i.e. male homosexual prostitutes) are differently treated from pimps and female prostitutes (and probably male heterosexual prostitutes as well).

As we saw, the edict banned from 'postulating' on behalf of anyone else at all any man who *corpore suo muliebria passus est*, whether as an amateur[80] or a professional; pimps could still 'postulate' on behalf of their nearest and dearest, and presumably the same applied to male heterosexual prostitutes.[81] Though women, as we saw, were a special case (being unable to 'postulate' on behalf of others anyway), female prostitutes were excluded, for example, from being witnesses in certain cases. Enthusiastic amateurs, however (i.e. adulteresses), attracted no such praetorian penalty in the Republic. Until Augustus' adultery law, female unchastity was treated as a purely private matter, and so, for that matter, was male extra-marital heterosexual activity, even with other men's wives; after the law, adulterers of both sexes were *infames*, but in consequence of having been convicted in a criminal court.

In the Republic, then, all sex for money was penalised as 'infamous'; so was gratuitous male passive homosexuality.[82] This last received more severe treatment in the praetor's edict than any other variety of 'socially deviant' sex (i.e. any that was extra-marital and not for procreational purposes); not surprisingly, since the pathic's preferred sexual behaviour diverged further than any other from – indeed, was in diametric opposition to – what was needed for the perpetuation of society by successive *patresfamilias*. To what extent the law was actually exercised is another matter. Winkler (1989: 45–70; largely reproduced in Halperin, Winkler and Zeitlin 1990: 171–209) has called in question the frequency of action against male homosexuals in Athens, where, however, the situation differed in two respects: only professional activity incurred prosecution,[83] and more was at stake – actual citizen rights – with death as the penalty for attempts to continue exercising them after conviction. In the Roman context, only commercial sex rendered a man unfit to share in the privilege of running a city as a councillor; but both the amateur and the professional were excluded from intervening in the business of any individual *familia* other than their own. No other penalty is mentioned, though presumably any amateur *qui corpore suo mulieb ria passus est*, as the edict puts it, was identified as the result of a prosecution and conviction under the *lex Sca(n)tinia*; however, we lack information on the content and consequences of this law (see n. 82), or details on the very few prosecutions mentioned in the sources.[84]

Of course, before the edict took its final form, it was possible for praetors to some extent to administer justice with greater or less severity, given their own personal attitudes. There are two anecdotes related by Valerius Maximus; but in 7.7, under the heading 'Wills that were broken', and not under 8.1, 'The causes why certain *infames* when standing trial were condemned or absolved' (though even there *infames* is not used in the technical sense).[85] The urban praetor Q. Metellus refused (7.7.7) to grant possession under the terms of the will of a certain Vibienus to Vecillus, a pimp, simply because he disapproved of Vibienus' choice of beneficiary. In the other example (7.7.6), a consul, Mamercus Aemilius Lepidus, overturned the ruling of the urban praetor Cn. Orestes, who had granted possession under the will of Naevius Anius to a certain Genucius, a Gallus (castrated priest) of the Magna Mater (see n. 2 to Chapter 1, above). Valerius expresses approval of the decision 'not to allow the tribunals of the magistrates to be polluted, under the pretext of obtaining justice, by the obscene presence and polluted voice of Genucius'. Though Mamercus' pretext was that Genucius, having of his own accord castrated himself, could be reckoned neither among men nor among women, it is evident from Valerius' account that the real reason was that the testator, Naevius, had been a freedman, and his patron had appealed to Mamercus against the will. Both of these stories are examples of arbitrary judgments by magistrates, not of the regular operation of the laws.

Female practising prostitutes, if married, were exempt from the operation of the Augustan adultery law; when they retired and gave up the game they became liable for prosecution under that law.[86] It does not seem, however, that they ceased to be 'infamous'. This appears from Ulpian's comment (*D.* 48.5.14(13).2): 'A husband can prosecute for adultery a wife who *has been* a prostitute, although, if she were *vidua* (unmarried, whether widowed or otherwise) *stuprum* with her would be unpenalised.'[87]

Retirement, then, did not suffice to rehabilitate the prostitute. Did it remove the disability from actors, gladiators, beast-fighters, and so on? No text says so; and it is perhaps significant that in references to their activities the verb is generally in the perfect or future perfect tense (as in Ulpian's remark just cited); that is, anyone who *has done* (not 'is doing') these things is, and remains, stigmatised. This interpretation is reinforced by a distinction that appears in the wording of the *Tabula Heracleensis* (lines 122–5): *queive corpore quaestum fecit fecerit; queive lanistaturam artemve ludicram fecit fecerit; queive lenocinium faciet.* Anyone (now or in the future) who *has been* a male prostitute, gladiator or actor is banned. So is anyone who *shall be* a pimp (professional pimps are meant here, not those convicted of *lenocinium* – this text predates the Augustan law on adultery); those who have been pimps (but are not now) are apparently acceptable again, perhaps because they were not themselves directly engaging in disreputable activity, merely profiting from that of others.

Retirement apparently did not restore the status of professional prostitutes, gladiators and actors. On the possibility of rehabilitation envisaged in the edict, see further below.

The conclusion drawn above in the discussion of the inscription from Larinum was that appearances in theatre or arena as amateurs did not automatically render the persons concerned *infames* under the praetor's edict. This is supported by the discussion in *D.* 3.2.6, where a distinction, attributed to ancient authorities (*veteres*), is drawn between those who fought gratis and those who took payment. In his legalistic concern for precision, Ulpian helpfully (from our point of view) labours the point. A beast-fighter who contracts his services (sc. for payment) is liable under the edict, whether he actually fights or not; if he fights without having made a contract, he is not liable. The older authorities, he continues, said that someone giving a display of prowess without wages was not liable, but became so if he then accepted a reward in the arena.[88] He ends with an explanatory comment of his own: 'For I think that they do not escape *nota*'. The point of this last remark, I think, is that Ulpian is trying to pin down and render ineffective the kind of device, familiar to us as 'sponsorship', by which people might contrive to remain technically amateur while nevertheless being paid. This is not an expression of élitist prejudice against paid employment as such; *quaestus* in general did not make all earners of any sort *infames* under the edict. The context is important: it concerns those *in turpitudine notabiles*. The activities in themselves are not approved of, but what actually stirs society to take action against them is the added element of pay. If that was allowed to pass without note, it would be tantamount to a public acknowledgement that such activities were no more morally undesirable than any other kind of lucrative profession – even to an endorsement and encouragement of their pursuit, amateur or otherwise, by Roman citizens.

What was so objectionable about them? I have mentioned above some of the sexually and psychologically disturbing aspects. Also they provided entertainment, but were not productive, so there was perhaps a feeling that such diversions, although providing some relief from the serious business of life, were more properly provided for citizens by non-citizens. Their contribution to society was not seen as essential to the well-being of the community. In a time of severe scarcity of grain, Suetonius tells us (*Aug.* 42), Augustus resorted to large-scale expulsions from the city – slaves in dealers' hands (so not part of any household), all foreigners except doctors and teachers (both useful professions), and gladiatorial *familiae* – all obviously regarded, if not as useless, at any rate as inessential mouths.[89] Someone who voluntarily took on for pay one of these 'shameful professions' could be regarded as openly advertising the fact that they did not intend to make any serious and productive contribution to society.[90] They were therefore not to be allowed to participate in settling legal disputes between individual members of that society, other than those concerning themselves and their near relatives.

Convicted offenders

All criminal convictions,[91] as we saw above, incurred *infamia*; particularly specified are convictions for misuse of one's citizen rights by malicious or collusive prosecution, or for taking bribes to prosecute or give evidence (or to refrain). So did conviction for a number of civil offences, and lists of varying length and completeness are given in several sources (d'Ors 1984).[92] These include delicts (e.g. theft, *dolus* and *iniuria*), that is, mistreatment of another citizen or his property, and breaches of trust in handling the affairs of others (e.g. as partner, guardian or executor of a mandate). To be made *infamis* under the edict is an appropriate penalty. Failure to conduct one's own affairs properly, as a *bonus paterfamilias* should, could also have this result. So bankrupts and undischarged debtors are penalised. Neglect of family mourning and bigamy (or double engagement) also incurred *infamia*;[93] both were matters involving the physical, as well as moral, integrity of the *familia*.

REHABILITATION

Rehabilitation was possible for some *infames*. The edict applied, added the praetor, only to 'any of the above who has not been restored to original status' (*qui in integrum restitutus non erit*, D. 3.1.1.9).[94] To how much of the preceding edict is this sentence meant to apply? Ulpian observed that it could refer in principle, as one would naturally suppose, to *all* the persons already mentioned in the edict; in practice, however, it should normally be taken to refer only to those mentioned in the third edict, that is, those allowed to speak on behalf of a limited specified range of persons. Rehabilitation for those in the previous categories, he remarked, would not be easy to obtain (implying that it was not impossible). This marks another difference in the degree of disapprobation with which actors, compared with professional arena-fighters, were regarded. The latter were not only more restricted in their right of litigation, but had little chance of obtaining a lifting of the ban.

By the time at which Ulpian was writing, rehabilitation, he says (citing Pomponius), was a matter for the emperor or the senate; the praetor's competence was limited to matters within his own jurisdiction, such as the removal of a ban on bringing a case because of the supposed age of an intending litigant.

Remission of *infamia* could be obtained only on appeal or by special grant; otherwise it was permanent. That it did not automatically accompany, for example, the completion of a sentence imposed as a result of a conviction that also carried *infamia* is shown by certain developments under the empire, discussed by Greenidge (1894: 182 ff.). If a heavier penalty were imposed than that required by the law, then the *infamia* would be held to last only until the sentence was complete. Some convictions on grounds not involving *infamia* could have the effect of *infamia*, if the result of the sentence was to make it in practice impossible for the person to do those things barred to the *infamis*; however, they did not make him *infamis*, and so his rights automatically were recovered on completion of the sentence.

CONCLUSIONS

This lengthy discussion has been concerned partly with the nature of the legal incapacity involved in *infamia*, and partly with the behaviour which incurred it. It has been found that, in its practical effects, being *infamis* would have made little impact on the ordinary lives of most citizens. As an index to the conventional attitudes and values of Roman society, it is relevant in that it does carry a connotation of disapproval of certain types of behaviour; however, this disapproval is by no means so highly charged as the rhetorical and moralising use of the non-technical vocabulary of ignominy, infamy and disgrace found in literary sources, nor is it so marked as that expressed in the much heavier penalties imposed by law on certain specific crimes, such as adultery. In criminal convictions, it is an adjunct to the penalty. However, the non-criminal *infamis* is not a complete social pariah; he is merely restrained from exercising his legal capacity in the affairs of any citizen other than himself or a close relative. A woman becoming *infamis* incurs virtually no further handicap; chiefly, the inability to appear as a witness.

Examination of the areas of behaviour incurring *infamia* show that these fall mainly into two kinds, the illegal and the marginal. The former are those who have abused the relation of trust between citizens on which society depends. The latter involve people regarded as frivolous and disreputable, mainly the practitioners of 'shameful professions', who distance themselves from the proper concerns of respectable Roman individuals, which ought to be the perpetuation of their own *familia* through legitimate procreation and the securing of its material well-being, and that of society as a whole, by husbanding and trying to enhance its material resources. The *bonus paterfamilias* is the standard against which they have been found wanting.

6

PARTICIPATION: THE HANDICAPPED CITIZEN

In Roman society, as in others, physical and mental handicap obviously created certain difficulties, both for the sufferers and for those obliged to have dealings with them, in conducting the ordinary business of life. It was on the whole left for these individuals or their families to cope with these problems as best they might; the state took no responsibility for their personal welfare or convenience. Some concern was shown, however, for enabling them to exercise their legal rights (XII T.1.3, and the undertaking given in the praetor's edict to supply speakers, in case of need, to represent the deaf or under-age in court), and some disablements had consequences of which it was found necessary to take account in law. The treatment of the matter in Roman law has certain special features – some of them perhaps surprising to us – stemming from the nature of Roman society itself.

PHYSICAL HANDICAPS

Those handicaps with which the law concerned itself are on the whole not those affecting physical mobility, but those involved in direct personal interaction: sight, hearing, speech. Getting yourself to the right place at the right time was not apparently a matter for which it was felt appropriate that the state should take responsibility. In modern Britain, although there has – at least, within the last few years – been some governmental recognition of the difficulties and needs of the bodily disabled, which has resulted in legislation concerning transport and building design, recent surveys by the Association for Consumer Research (*Which?*, October 1989, 498–502; June 1990, 347–50) show that building regulations still fall far short of what is required, and real improvements to transport are materialising very slowly. Nevertheless, the attitude is that society has an obligation to assist the bodily handicapped. The apparent indifference of ancient Romans is perhaps the more understandable in that not only what we also would regard as private transactions, but most of the dealings of daily life were based on private enterprise, and most litigation as well depended on private initiative.

The emphasis, which in our – late – legal texts is mainly implicit (but see below for some direct statements), is on the performance of transactions directly in the presence of the other party, for example in making contracts based on *stipulatio*. This derives from the circumstances of the physically compact community of early Rome. Even in classical Rome, most transactions occurred between individuals within the same physical area, and legally identical substitutes, such as sons or slaves, could be used for some purposes by those who found it inconvenient to be present in person.[1] Since in the ancient world communicating with anyone at a distance required that some person, even if only a messenger, should physically move to that place, transactions continued to be essentially face-to-face, either between the persons involved or their representatives.[2] Certain procedures, however, did not admit of the use of substitutes or representatives, and these do constitute a legal problem where one of the parties is handicapped.

Blindness

Of the three types of physical handicap mentioned above, blindness appears to raise the fewest problems in Roman law. This is not surprising, given the importance of the spoken, rather than the written, word for most people in Roman society. It was apparently not thought justifiable to provide a *curator* to protect the interests of a blind man. Someone doing business with a person under the age of 25, for example, could insist that the young person have a *curator* for the transaction, to obviate the possibility that he could plead his youth and inexperience to wriggle out of his commitments.[3] Paul, discussing manumissions, is definite (*Sent.* 4.12.9): 'A *curator* cannot be assigned for a blind man, because he himself can appoint a *procurator* for himself.'

That one was helping a blind man was not an acceptable excuse for exemption from public *munera*, according to Papinian (*D.* 50.1.17 pr.), even if the blind man was one's patron. Blind men's disability did not, on the whole, render them incapable of managing their own affairs; the extent to which they might be impeded by their handicap was not thought to justify insisting that special provision be made for them in looking after their own concerns. It was recognised, however, that particular problems might arise. Discussing the question of what constitutes a contract of sale, Ulpian's opinion (*D*. 18.1.11. pr.) is that it can be claimed that there is no agreement if, for instance, the buyer is blind, and so unable to see the nature of the goods. He may be merely making a theoretical point. In real life, one might perhaps expect that persons of the sort likely to think of resorting to legal action if they were dissatisfied with the goods bought would have had slaves to do their shopping for them.

Other practical problems were recognised, but regarded as easily surmountable, and so not constituting any real difficulty. For example, in the making of wills, an unsighted person would not be able to *see* that the necessary witnessing was taking place. In the mancipatory will, apparently only the testator and the 'buyer' spoke (Gaius 2.104: see n. 11 below), but it was necessary for other witnesses to be present. Even for the 'praetorian' written will (Gaius 2.119), it was necessary for seven witnesses to be present and affix their seals. A blind man can make a will, says Paul (*Sent.* 3.4.4), because he can call the witnesses he has invited and *hear* them providing their witness.[4] For the deaf and dumb, however, there was a problem.

Deaf, dumb and blind are occasionally grouped together by the jurists in ways that suggest that the unthinking Roman man in the street was just as prone as his modern counterpart to fail to distinguish between different kinds of handicap, physical or even mental.[5] The dumb, deaf and blind can claim *bonorum possessio*, possession of an estate, 'if they understand what is going on'. They can contract marriages, so they are bound by the rules applying to dowry. As this comes from a work based on decisions made in the imperial court in the time of the Severi, there presumably lies behind it an actual enquiry, by someone with an interest in the dowry in question and a muddled notion that somehow the other party's disability (we are not told which of the three it was – it need not have been all of them) might entail his or her legal incapacity.[6] Ulpian's emphasis (*D*. 1.7.9), *etiam caecus adoptare vel adoptari potest* ('Even a blind man can adopt or be adopted'), bears traces of a similar attitude.

On the whole, however, no doubts are expressed as to whether
the blind are competent to manage matters for themselves. In
addition, the blind were, unlike the dumb or deaf, accepted as
capable of acting as judges and continuing to hold senatorial rank,
according to Ulpian, who cites as an example Appius Claudius
Caecus, though he is doubtful about whether blind men could
exercise magistracies.[7]

It appears, however, to have been recognised that the blind's
inability to see, as well as hear, what was going on could put
others, for whom they attempted to take responsibility, at a disadvantage. They were allowed to be tutors, since they were capable
of giving their authorisation at least, although a tutor who became
blind had the option of giving up his duties, as did one who
became deaf, dumb or chronically ill.[8] Tutorship, however, was
one of the common situations in which a Roman might wish –
or find it necessary – to go to law on behalf of someone else.
The praetor's edict provides accordingly. Blind men are not, unlike
the deaf, among those prohibited from appearing in person in
court to speak even for themselves, but they are not accepted to
plead on behalf of others.

The reasons appear fairly obvious. Appius Claudius might talk
effectively, addressing himself at large to a crowded senate cham-
ber, but in a private court a pleader's rhetoric would lose much
of its impact, and even risk being ridiculous, if not physically
directed towards where the individual addressed happened to be.
Some awareness of this appears to be dimly present in Ulpian's
account of the reasons for the ban, at least as quoted in *D.* 3.1.1.5,
although, as with his version of the reasons for excluding women
from pleading on behalf of others, he seems curiously off the
point.

*Caecum utrisque luminibus orbatum praetor repellit: videlicet
quod insignia magistratus videre et revereri non possit* ('The praetor rejects someone blind in both eyes, clearly because he is unable
to see and show respect to the magistrate's insignia'). As remarked
above (Chapter 5), this alleged reason is irrelevant, since if this
were the reason, then blind men would not be allowed to appear
for themselves either. He continues: *refert etiam Labeo Publilium
Caecum Asprenati Noni patrem aversa sella a Bruto destitutum,
cum vellet postulare* ('Labeo also relates that Publilius Caecus,
father of Nonius Asprenas, was abandoned by Brutus, whose seat
was turned the other way, when he wished to plead'). This could

mean either that Publilius was attempting to plead on behalf of someone else, and Brutus deliberately turned his seat away to indicate that he refused him a hearing; or that Brutus' seat happened to be turned in the opposite direction, so that Publilius (who might, for all we know, have been speaking in his own behalf) was addressing the air. Neither version of the anecdote helps to explain (though, in the former interpretation, it could be held to illustrate) the general prohibition on blind men acting as pleaders for others. The second version could perhaps be held to give the occasion of its first institution (though it is unlikely that it was so late), but it is inadequate as an explanation. Blind men were and continued to be allowed to appear for themselves. However, where only their own interests were affected, it was not apparently thought necessary to try to save them from falling into such a ridiculous contretemps; after all, it was avoidable, since they had always the option of engaging others to speak for them. It was different, however, where the interests of another *familia* might be jeopardised by the deficiencies of its representative.

The deaf and dumb

There were rather more restrictions on what deaf and dumb persons might do, because their physical disabilities often made them incapable of personally carrying out the actions required by law. The two are frequently spoken of together, with or without the words *et, vel, aut* ('and', 'or') but this does not mean that we need always translate (as e.g. Buckland (1908: 595) does) as 'deaf mute'. They are sometimes spoken of separately, and the Romans recognised a difference between those born with these afflictions, and those who came to suffer them later in life.[9]

In the ancient world, those born profoundly deaf were invariably also mute, as remarked by the elder Pliny (*NH* 10.192): *nec sunt naturaliter surdi, ut non iidem sint et muti* ('No people are by nature deaf, who are not also dumb'). The modern techniques of teaching the deaf to communicate in speech seem to go back, like signing, no further than the eighteenth century. The kinds of transaction for which being deaf or dumb creates a legal problem are on the whole those in which verbal interchange is a part of the procedure, and for this it is necessary both to speak and to hear what is said by others. Someone who is incapable of one or the other can be held to be incapable of properly carrying out the transaction.

The point is made more than once. Gaius (3.105):

> It is evident that a dumb man can neither stipulate nor promise (the reciprocal acts required to constitute a contract by *stipulatio*). The same is accepted also in the case of a deaf man, because it is required both that the person stipulating hears the words of the person promising, and that the person promising hears those of the stipulator.[10]

Similarly, Ulpian says (*Reg.* 20.13):

> A dumb man, a deaf, someone mad, someone whose goods are restrained by court order (sc. a *prodigus*, spendthrift), cannot make a will. The dumb man cannot, because he cannot utter the words of the nuncupation; the deaf man, because he cannot hear the words of the *familiae emptor* (nominal buyer of the estate).[11]

The madman is excluded, obviously, on grounds of mental incapacity, and the *prodigus* because he is barred from engaging in any commercial transactions, and so cannot mancipate his estate.[12]

Obviously, deafness and dumbness were disqualifications for acting as a judge (*D.* 5.1.12.2). Other actions requiring some use of speech by the participants were manumission, adoption, mancipations, and possibly being a tutor. Jurists duly have something to say about all of these, and from their comments it is possible to discern how the Romans, at least to a certain extent, managed to accommodate the disabled without sacrificing the basic framework of the legal requirements. It was not generally possible, though, for the disabled to have quite such a range of legal activity open to him as the sound person.

Coping

It was generally agreed that someone who was dumb could not be appointed as a *tutor*, because of the practical obstacle to his giving authorisation, and most authorities, according to Paul, took the view that a deaf man could not either, 'since a tutor is required not only to speak but to hear'. Hermogenianus reports what appears to be an extension of this to *tutores legitimi* (who, of course, were not made by appointment). He does not spell out the consequences, but this would in fact mean that dumb or deaf owners would not have the authority to control their freed-women's disposal of their property (or manumitting fathers that of their emancipated daughters).[13] Application could be made to the praetor for a *tutor* to replace one who was dumb or deaf; Paul does not tell us (*D*. 26.3.17) why it should have been found necessary to have 'many *senatusconsulta*' on this matter. Since, as he says (above), it was generally agreed that they could not be appointed *tutor*, presumably the question of replacements arose whenever someone who was already a *tutor* began to be afflicted. It was even possible, he says (*D*. 3.3.43 pr.), to appoint a deaf or dumb person as *procurator*, at least for administration rather than litigation (*non quidem ad agendum, sed ad administrandum*). The deaf were forbidden in the praetor's edict to litigate even on their own behalf – naturally, the dumb would be unable to plead anyway – and the praetor undertook to provide them with an advocate if it was necessary for them to come to court (*D*. 3.1.1.3–4). References to the appointment of curators for deaf and dumb persons suggest that their disabilities were regarded as possibly a more serious handicap in handling their own affairs than that of blindness.[14]

Formal manumissions in the owner's lifetime appear to have been problematic; so were those by will, since the full-blown mancipatory will was not available to the deaf and dumb (see below). The procedure obviously had difficulties for a deaf person, since a manumitting owner was supposed to be able to hear the collusive claim that the man was free. Someone who was dumb without being deaf, however, one might have expected would be able to manumit, since the essential requirement appears to have been merely to touch the slave with the rod, and no set form of words need be used.[15] Nevertheless, we are told more than once that neither the deaf nor the dumb could manumit *vindicta* in the normal way.[16] The suggestion of Buckland (1966: 73 n. 7)), though not expressly confirmed in the sources, may correctly represent the reasoning behind this view: 'Silence being a sign of assent, a *mutus* or *surdus* could not free in this way.' That is, someone who *cannot* assent because he is constitutionally incapable of speech, or because he cannot hear, being deaf, and understand that his assent is required, cannot be held to be assenting by the mere fact of his being silent.[17] It is worth noting, though, that Paul (*Sent.* 4.12.2), says merely that a dumb man and a deaf cannot manumit *vindicta*. When talking, however, of a *pater* authorising a son or slave to accept an inheritance, he is happy to suggest other ways in which consent can satisfactorily be expressed (*D.* 29.2.93): 'He can instruct him by a nod, so that the benefit of it can lawfully be acquired for him and the situation can easily be dealt with if he knows how to write.'[18] Paul's own view may have been that a handicapped *pater* should not be assisted in depriving himself of any property, but should, on the other hand, be encouraged to find ways of enriching himself; in any case, in the latter instance it is a matter only of his private communication with his son or slave, not of any legal formality.

In the late first century AD, Celsus had taken a more common-sensical view, possibly of an actual case brought to him (*D.* 40.9.1). For the sake of practical convenience (*utilitas*), he thought, a man born deaf ought to be allowed to manumit. Ulpian quotes this opinion, which does not seem, however, to have been generally accepted. Paul has nothing more helpful to say in the text just cited than that the deaf and dumb could, however, manumit infor-mally, and he suggests a fiduciary conveyance of the slaves to a third person to allow them to be properly freed. Otherwise, of course, they would not be citizens. Elsewhere, however, he remarks more sensibly that a *filiusfamilias* can manumit on orders from his father.[19] Women, of course, as he observes, did not have this convenient alternative, since they had no children in their *potestas*.

Lawyers obviously had a great deal of difficulty over the years with the question of how to deal with the wish of deaf or dumb owners to manumit their slaves, and the root of the problem, clearly, is the insistence on direct oral performance, in the presence of other parties, of the necessary legal formalities. By the late third century, the whole problem had been solved. Masters were apparently still expected to be present at manumissions, but all the formalities were carried out by lictors, and the customary words were taken as uttered.[20] This may reflect a high incidence of manumissions in general (rather than of disabled manumitters), requiring a streamlining of procedures. All the same, personal attendance was still a requisite.

Although, as we saw above with reference to mancipatory wills, the deaf and dumb would not be able personally to carry out the necessary exchange of formulae in buying and selling of any prop-erty that was *res mancipi*, buying at least was no problem, since sons and slaves could do it for them.[21] Selling should normally be feasible, too, since sons at least could mancipate with consent.

Testamentary dispositions

The making of wills was another matter. The deaf and the dumb did not have *testamenti factio*; they were unable to make wills that would be legally recognised. Ulpian, as we saw above, gives the reason (*Reg.* 20.13): 'The dumb man cannot, because he cannot utter the words of the nuncupation; the deaf man, because he cannot hear the words of the *familiae emptor*.'

Nevertheless, the deaf and dumb could benefit under wills. Since *testamenti factio* involved two parties, the testator and the eligible beneficiaries, namely, those 'with whom' he had *testamenti factio* (*D.* 28.5.50(49).1), the question appears to have been asked fairly frequently whether the deaf and dumb could benefit by or carry out the instructions in the wills of others. The answer was that, even though they could not make wills themselves, they certainly could be beneficiaries, just as sons and slaves could, even if they were heirs; they could also be liable to the obligations of heirs. This was because there were a number of ways in which heirs could enter upon an estate, without necessarily having to make a formal verbal declaration before the praetor (*cretio*). Even an informal expression of intention to take up the inheritance (*nuda voluntas*) would apparently suffice, though this is mentioned only in Gaius 2.167 and *Inst.* 2.19.7 and still does not appear to have been thought sufficient in the late first century AD[22] (*D.* 29.2.62). To make acceptance, beneficiaries could, possibly from quite early in the Republic, *pro herede gerere*, that is, 'behave as if heir', carrying out acts of administration to do with the estate – such as selling estate property or giving rations to slaves who were part of the estate – or generally making use of the deceased's property.[23]

A formal declaration of willingness to enter upon the estate (*cretio*) was necessary under the empire only if it was expressly required in the will, and it might appear to have been sensible not to do so, if it could be avoided, where the heirs included handicapped people. Under the Republic, it appears that *cretio* had to be made in person.[24] Exception was possibly made for a child under age: cf. *FIRA* iii.59 (Egypt, second century AD), where a mother, with tutor's authorisation, accepts an inheritance from her late husband on behalf of the child whom he instituted as heir. Although Cicero (*ad Att.* 13.46.3, 13.47), while at Tusculum, apparently contemplates sending someone to Puteoli with notice of acceptance of an inheritance, the likelihood is that the person instituted heir was actually Cicero's slave, not Cicero himself.[25]

The deaf and dumb, therefore, would be unable to accept an estate by *cretio*, but they could do so simply by behaving, literally, as if they owned the estate. However, although benefiting under a will was no problem for the deaf and dumb, making a will was. We have no evidence how this was tackled during the Republic, to enable the afflicted to bequeath their property. The only evidence for the Republican period is the discussion by Alfenus Varus and Labeo, reported by Javolenus *D.* 28.1.25 (see n. 9 above), of a response given by Servius to the effect that if a person was struck dumb in the course of making a will, without managing to complete it, the will was not valid. This shows, as Watson (1971a: 26) points out, that under the Republic the rule was that a dumb person could not make a will. Any property left would then go automatically to a man's children, or failing those his nearest agnates, as intestate heirs, and to a woman's agnates or (if she was *in manu*) her husband. This was not an outcome which the Romans would wish to discourage, which may account for the lack of any provision to enable the affliction to be circumvented.

Some limited exceptions appear under the empire (by which time, of course, the rights of heirs, particularly *sui heredes*, had acquired some legal protection: see below, p. 166). Permission could be obtained from the emperor to make a will (*D.* 28.1.7), but how common it was to take advantage of this possibility is not known. Also, soldiers who became deaf or dumb would be dismissed the service on grounds of health (*causaria missio*); while they were awaiting their discharge, soldiers given *causaria missio* were allowed to make wills, but these remained valid for only a year after they left the service.[26] Clearly, the general rule still prevailed, that someone unable to utter the necessary verbal formulae was unable to make a will.

This is the background to a case presented (as real) by Paul (*D.* 28.6.43):

> A man had a son who was adult (*pubes*) but dumb. He asked and obtained the emperor's permission to substitute an alternative heir for his son, and nominated Titius. After

the father's death, the dumb man married and had a son. I
ask: is the will broken?

Paul's answer is that the emperor's intention is to be interpreted
by comparison with the practice provided for in civil law of
pupillary substitution, which ceases to be of effect when the heir
comes of age. 'Pupillary substitution' (Gaius 2.179–81) was used
by fathers making wills while their children were still under age,
to provide against the eventuality that the child inherited and then
died before being able to make a will for himself; this would
prevent the property's then passing by default in some way unacceptable to the father. The emperor was 'imitating the civil law',
in the case of an adult son who was unable to make a will for
himself. Paul goes on to compare the – hypothetical – case of
substitution by imperial privilege to a son who was mad. The
substitution would have to be deemed invalid if the son recovered
his sanity, otherwise the emperor's grant would begin to operate
unfairly, since it deprived a sane man of the power to make a
will. Then he sums up. The substitution no longer held, *not*
because the son had managed to institute an heir (he was still
dumb), but because he now had a *suus heres*, his son. If the
father's will was allowed to stand, that child would be disinherited
at his father's death, since the substitute heir would automatically
succeed. 'And it is not likely (*verisimile*) that either the father or
the emperor had in mind this situation, the disinheritance of a
child born later.'

The sort of will to which this applies is the full-blown mancipatory will, with institution of heirs, and what is apparent from the
evidence just given (and see also n. 11 above) is that during the
Republic this sort of will was not available at all to the deaf and
dumb by birth, or to those who became so before having made
a will. For those who had, the most they could do would be to
alter some of its dispositions by codicil (*D*. 29.7.8.3); they could
not make a completely new will. Under the empire, special permission would have to be obtained from the emperor to make a
will.

As with manumission, so with will-making, procedures were
eventually simplified, and so these problems were overcome (see
n. 25). The change, however, seems in this case to have been
delayed until the fifth century AD. The reason for the apparent
lack of urgency felt by the Romans in this matter is that the

alternative means of disposing of one's estate by bequest which were available to the deaf and dumb tended, as we shall see in a moment, by their very nature to favour disposal to the benefit of the *sui heredes* and so to discourage excessive dispersal of the patrimony.

It has been suggested[27] that by the time of Gaius the actual *mancipatio* at the time of witnessing the tablets may not have been in general use, and may merely have been represented by a formal declaration in the tablets that it had occurred. However, as Buckland remarks cautiously: 'It is probable that, in a somewhat later age [than that of Gaius] the parties were content not to go behind the formal document alleging the *mancipatio*: it is another thing to say that they were compelled by law to accept this.' Whatever the usual practice may have been, and even granted that testators and witnesses customarily colluded in the fiction of a real *nuncupatio* and *mancipatio*, it is clear that the law did not change, and when it was plain that the formulae *could* not have been uttered (because the testator was handicapped), then there could be no will valid in civil law.

What the deaf and dumb could do instead was to make a will of sorts, the so-called 'praetorian will' (Gaius 2.119, 147), that is, a written disposition, sealed with the seals of seven witnesses.[28] This was a more flexible and useful method under the empire than under the Republic, though it still fell short of the powers of the mancipatory will; indeed, it was not a 'will' at all, in terms of Roman civil law.

'Heirs', that is, beneficiaries, could be named in the praetorian will, but they were not heirs, *heredes*, in the civil law sense. If they applied to the praetor for implementation of the will, they would be granted possession (*bonorum possessio*), but unless they were themselves the heirs on intestacy (*sui heredes*) with the best claim, they could lose the lot if the *sui heredes* claimed the inheritance. If they were *sui heredes* there was less of a problem, but the praetorian will was still more vulnerable than the regular civil law (mancipatory) will. Earlier in the Republic, *sui heredes* expressly disinherited in a valid civil law will had no recourse; by the late Republic if disinherited, or left too little, they could sue under a *querela inofficiosi testamenti* or 'complaint of unduteous will' (*D.* 5.2), but without guarantee of success. Against a praetorian will, it was sufficient that they were *sui heredes*. Deaf or dumb testators, therefore, had less freedom in choosing whom to benefit by their wills. They were more or less obliged to make their next of kin their heirs (which most would probably wish to do anyway), but could be less confident that any differentiation in the shares given to their heirs would be respected; the less favoured might decide to contest the matter, and try for the equal shares they would have on intestacy. Other friends and beneficiaries would have to be recognised through legacies.

As far as our evidence goes, it does not look as if the praetorian will could be used to institute tutors (for children or women), or to manumit slaves. If a *pater* was content that the nearest agnate should be tutor, that did not matter. Otherwise, he could perhaps include in the will a request that So-and-So be tutor, and it is at least as likely that the praetor would honour such a request, out of respect for the wishes of a *pater*, as a nomination in a mancipatory will. To manumit slaves, however, the most that could be done via a praetorian will would be to include *fideicommissa*, testamentary requests, to the heirs. Under the Republic, though, beneficiaries were at liberty to ignore such requests. It was only during the reign of Augustus that any means were provided, and then only on an *ad hoc* basis, of seeking their legal enforcement. A regular jurisdiction was not set up until about the middle of the first century AD, but it was progressively reinforced thereafter.[29] Under the empire, therefore, that part at least of a praetorian will was more secure than before.

The limitations on the legal powers of deaf and dumb Romans, then, are a mixture of recognition of the practical impossibility of their carrying out certain functions, and maintenance of the legal rules requiring direct personal participation, especially where to do otherwise would encourage dispersal of the resources of a *familia*.

MENTAL DISORDER

Mental illness is discussed a great deal in legal sources; there are about 280 references in all, conveniently collected, though without much discussion or analysis, in Nardi (1983). The reason for this level of legal interest is obvious. One might paraphrase the famous remark in the preface of Buckland (1908): 'There is scarcely a problem which can present itself in any branch of the law, the solution of which may not be affected by the fact that one of the parties to the transaction is mentally ill.'

The mentally ill person had no legal capacity. A range of words is used – for example, *furiosus, insanus, mente captus, demens* – the two most often used being the first and last, and although there seems to be a conceptual distinction between *furor* on the one hand and *dementia* on the other, its nature is disputed.[30] From the point of view of lawyers, who are concerned with knowing whether a person is legally competent to act, what matters is whether he or she can (*a*) understand what is done and (*b*) will (and so also, consent) that something be done. So, Labeo says that the mentally ill cannot be regarded as properly 'present', any more than children, or (note) the dumb either, since they cannot provide the necessary speech (*D.* 50.16.246 pr.). The mentally ill are compared directly by Gaius with children under age, in that they both lack understanding (G. 3.109). *Furiosi* cannot be said to wish anything – they have no *voluntas* (*D.* 29.2.47, 50.17.40).[31] While ill, they are incapable of any legal act. However, some forms of mental illness are not congenital, or are temporary or subject to remissions, so the lawyers also have to concern themselves not infrequently with establishing the condition of mind of a person at relevant times. Some might become mentally ill only later in life, after marrying, having children, and so on, and problems then arose when their authorisation was needed for certain actions of their families.

The comparison with children legally independent but under age (and therefore not capable of legal action) is also relevant in so far as the mentally ill, like children, can benefit from the acts of others, and this in its turn generates legal problems for their future. One example already touched upon, which also includes the idea of temporary insanity, is that of the receipt of a bequest (Paul in *D.* 28.6.43, above). A father with a son who is mentally ill nevertheless leaves him his estate, but appoints a substitute heir, in case the son dies without recovering sanity and so without the capacity to make a will himself. Temporary insanity was obviously a phenomenon known to the Romans, but given the state of understanding of mental illness in general and the treatments available at the time, recoveries will generally have been spontaneous, rather than the result of medical care, and unpredictable, as well as being relatively much fewer than today.

Determining insanity

Obviously it was frequently important to determine whether and when someone was mentally ill, and there are numerous references in the legal texts to the necessity of making enquiry, or providing some evidence. Schulz (1951: 196–7) rather too sweepingly declares, 'A procedure by which a person might be officially declared insane did not exist'; and, further on, 'the lawyers had no clear conception of mental diseases. Although Greek doctors of classical times already possessed a considerable stock of knowledge and their writings were known in Rome, the lawyers clearly did not pay attention to them.' There is a rather obvious case of argument from silence in these latter remarks. Though lawyers do not discuss expert medical theories in detail, this does not mean that no account was taken of them when magistrates were attempting to determine whether someone was or was not insane, or that doctors were not among those called upon to give evidence. It is clear that it was appreciated that some sort of evidence was needed, even though legal writers seldom discuss in detail what constitutes such evidence.

Moreover, there must have been some procedure for declaring someone insane. The Twelve Tables, as reported by several Roman writers,[32] said, 'if someone is mad, let *potestas* over him and his property belong to the agnates and members of the gens'; that is, a *furiosus* was (like a *pupillus*, with whom *furiosi* are often bracketed) in the control of the nearest agnate, and presumably, as Schulz points out, became free from it when he recovered.

The possibility of temporary or intermittent insanity was certainly recognised. Macer, in a work on criminal law,[33] quotes a reply of Marcus Aurelius and Commodus to an enquiry in the case of someone accused of matricide. The emperors recognise two, or rather, three possibilities: 'If you have clearly established that the accused, Aelius Priscus, was in such a state of madness that his mind was permanently deranged without any understanding, and there is no suspicion that he killed his mother in a pretence of dementia . . .' – that is, Aelius was either permanently deranged; or intermittently, but in a lucid interval and shamming at the time of the killing; or simply shamming all the time.

However, this does not answer the question of how it was decided in the first place that he, or anyone else, was mad. Someone already mad would, of course, be in the *potestas* of his or

her father, who might nominate a *curator* in his will, but although in assigning a *curator* the praetor ought to respect the wishes of the testator as to the person chosen, nevertheless it was the praetor, as a rescript from Marcus Aurelius affirmed, who was responsible for deciding actually to appoint one (*D.* 27.10.16 pr.).[34] Of course, it is possible, and indeed extremely likely, that many people who were born mad or became mad, were never officially declared to be so, simply because the occasion never arose when the question of their sanity became important. This is because, as I have remarked elsewhere,[35] for many people – mainly those with little or no material wealth – the necessity to prove their status and competence may never have arisen. However, when need did arise, some provision would have to be made for someone legally competent to carry out any necessary transactions. For most business to do with property, this would be a *curator*, whose duties and accountability were very similar to those of the *tutor* of a child, and the first person to be approached would be an agnate.[36] If no agnate was available, the praetor or appropriate magistrate in the provinces would appoint a *curator* on application.[37] When doing so, the magistrate would find it necessary, for a number of reasons, to determine whether the person for whom a *curator* was requested really was mad.

Ulpian recommends (*D.* 27.10.6) that particular care be taken with the enquiry, since in his day a pretence of insanity was being used by 'very many' (*plerique*) as a device for escaping civic burdens. Intermittent insanity also created something of a problem, since a *curator* would not be necessary during the lucid intervals. Neither Ulpian's statement (*D.* 27.10.1 pr.) that in those circumstances the person automatically ceases to be in the control of the curators, nor, much later, the attempt by Justinian (*CJ* 5.70.6) at tidying up the whole business by saying that curators are appointed once for all, but activated or inactivated according as the person is currently mad or not, offer any guidance as to how it was determined when either situation actually obtained.

There must have been some criteria, even if, by modern standards, very crude and simplistic ones, which could be applied in deciding whether an individual was at a given time actually insane or not. These criteria, however, are glimpsed only fleetingly in passing references to the sort of behaviour which might typically be regarded as insane; there is no developed discussion in the texts, and probably no official guidelines existed. Most detail about the sort of thing which might be regarded as relevant appears in the legal texts relating to that invaluable and entertaining work – invaluable for the direct insights it affords (like certain sections of the census, for the British) into the daily life of the Romans, and entertaining (like the census) because of the angle and limitations of its gaze – the aedile's edict. Fortunately for us, Vivianus, a jurist of the time of Trajan, whose writing on the praetorian and aedilician edicts was regarded as sufficiently valuable to be cited by later authorities,[38] gave some attention to the question of mental affliction in slaves. That this is mainly ignored in the edict is due to the fact that, when buying slaves, or so it appears from *D*. 21.1, Romans were more interested in their physical than their intellectual fitness. Vivianus, it seems, thought it appropriate to mention it only because some physical illnesses could affect the mind (*D*. 21.1.1.9–11).

Unfortunately, Vivianus' comments, at least as cited, go into detail only on one particular type of behaviour which might or might not be held to indicate mental abnormality, and it is behaviour which, if anything, might be thought more normal in a slave of foreign extraction than in a freeborn Roman; that is, participation in the more extrovert rituals of foreign cults. A slave who on occasion (*non semper*) joins in the head-tossing and 'inspired' utterances of *fanatici* is nevertheless to be regarded as healthy. The rites Vivianus has in mind are not specified, other than by the participle *bacchatus*. If it is a persistent habit with the slave to behave in this way and utter 'as though demented', then that is a mental defect but does not give grounds for invalidating his sale.

Elsewhere (*D*. 21.1.4.1), Vivianus is mentioned as specifying other behaviour which might occasion doubts as to a slave's mental equilibrium (caused, as far as the lawyers' interest goes, by the delirium attending a fever), such as wandering about the streets talking gibberish *more insanorum*, in the manner of the insane. Ordinary conversation (*sermones*) was held to be some index of a person's mental health (*D*. 26.5.12.2).

Disregard of the proper feeling expected between members of families might, it seems, also be held to be a sign of insanity, though we hear of this only in connection with wills. From the late Republic, children who regarded themselves as unfairly treated in a parent's will might bring a *querela inofficiosi testamenti*, a complaint of unduteous will, to try to increase their share. If this was upheld, however, the testator would not be declared to have been actually insane (which would have invalidated the will entirely), but merely, by a legal fiction, 'as if' insane.[39] It is interesting to observe that among the usually far-fetched situations supposed in the Elder Seneca's *Controversiae*, of the half-dozen in which insanity is part of the theme, two present situations conceivable in real life, and both have to do with proper behaviour towards one's children and heirs. In 2.4 a son accuses of insanity his father, who has adopted the illegitimate child born to his other son (disinherited, and now deceased) by a prostitute. Obviously, this spoiled the first son's inheritance prospects. In 2.6, a son, who is himself a rake, accuses of madness a father who has begun to live a life of debauchery, although here, reference to the effect on the son's inheritance prospects of the father's extravagance is made only incidentally, at 2.6.3, 5 and especially 6 *fin.*: Blandus treated the topic 'as if on behalf of a son who had been disinherited'. A line of approach given rather more prominence is the inappropriateness of the old man's behaviour to his age. Eccentricity, behaviour departing from social norms, could be represented as a sign of mental instability.

Modestinus was prepared to entertain a doubt (though no more) as to the sanity of someone who asked in his will that his heir throw his remains into the sea; proper burial was obviously the right thing (*D.* 28.7.27 pr.). That was a borderline case, perhaps, of eccentricity, but someone who tried to leave as legacies property belonging to the emperor, or Roman public places and buildings such as the Campus Martius, the Roman Forum or a temple, was definitely not to be accounted sane (*D.* 30.39.8–9).

Much later, in AD 393, Theodosius grandly declared that someone who insulted the emperor might be either frivolous or insane, or have suffered some injury, and therefore was not to be punished without previous examination by the emperor;[40] this, however, represents an attempt to preserve imperial dignity and the appearance of clemency, rather than a juridical definition of insanity.

From this evidence, scrappy and partial as it is, it nevertheless emerges that there were procedures for enquiring into assertions of someone's insanity, and that magistrates were not expected simply to accept the declarations of doubtless interested parties that this was the case. As for the personal care of the insane, however, apart from the recommendation of restraint or prison for the dangerous (see above), this was left to relatives and friends.[41]

Problems for others

Insanity could create legal problems for other people, particularly in the sphere of personal relationships such as marriage and divorce. *Patria potestas* was not terminated by the onset of madness in the father, nor was a marriage that was already contracted, so that a madman could become a *pater*.[42]

Money and property matters did not present much difficulty for dependants. *Filii*, like slaves, could acquire for a *pater* even without his knowledge. They could have a *peculium*, and the *curator* could grant administration of it (*D.* 15.1.24); and all the actions, such as the *institoria*, available in the ordinary way against *patres* were available also against the insane – even the *actio quod iussu*, since the *curator* could give the necessary authorisation, which was binding upon his charge.[43]

Manumission of slaves, however, was out of the question. Curators could buy, sell and go to law on behalf of their charges, but they could not manumit, since that, according to Pomponius, was not part of the administration of the patrimony. Sons could not manumit either (though those of the deaf and dumb could), presumably because it was impossible for the parent to give consent.[44]

The slaves of the insane, therefore, had to resign themselves to remaining in servitude at least so long as their owner continued mad; except, that is, from the early second century AD, for the lucky few who might have been bequeathed to their current, unfortunately deranged, owner under a *fideicommissum* of emancipation. For their benefit, Octavenus devised a helpful legal fiction (*D.* 40.1.13). If the madman had received a slave by bequest under a *fideicommissum* to manumit, then Octavenus recommended the *traditio* ('handing over') of the slave to a third party, who would then manumit him, so that the *fideicommissum* could be fulfilled. *Traditio* was the normal mode of transferring ownership of property which was not *res mancipi*. From the slave's point of view, this was no doubt better than nothing, since such a manumission at least made him or her a Latin, even if not a citizen (Gaius 1.167). There was not much in it for the madman, since rights of succession and so on went to the bonitary owner, i.e. the manumitter.[45] However, luckily for the slaves concerned, Octavenus was active in the latter part of a period which had seen a long string of measures directed towards the enforcement of *fideicom-missa*, including those of manumission.[46]

Marriage and divorce

Marriage and divorce were also tricky. Legally, as we saw above (Chapter 3, page 54) the consent of a *pater* was required for the marriage of his children, and a *furiosus* was obviously in no condition to give it. Lawyers apparently agreed quite early that nevertheless the daughter of a madman could be allowed to marry. For sons, it was different. Treggiari (1991: 173) quotes, but without comment, a text which indicates that for a long time it was not generally accepted that a son could do so. She is not alone in not commenting; the significance of this passage (*CJ* 5.4.25 Justinian, AD 530), which deserves quoting here, is generally overlooked.

> *Si furiosi parentis liberi, in cuius potestate constituti sunt, nuptias possunt contrahere, apud veteres agitabatur. Et filiam quidem furiosi marito posse copulari omnes paene iuris antiqui conditores admiserunt: sufficere enim putaverunt, si pater non contradicat. In filio autem familias dubitabatur, et Ulpianus quidem rettulit constitutionem imperatoris Marci, quae non de furioso loquitur, sed generaliter de filiis mente capti, sive masculi sive feminae sint qui nuptias contrahunt, ut hoc facere possint etiam non adito principe.*

> It was debated among the ancients whether the children in the power of a mad father can contract marriage. And indeed, as to a daughter, practically all the authorities on ancient law agreed that she could be joined to a husband: for they thought it sufficient if her *pater* did not gainsay it. There was doubt, however, about a *filiusfamilias*. Ulpian however, cites a constitution of the emperor Marcus [Aurelius], which does not speak about a *furiosus* but in general terms about the children of someone mentally afflicted (*mente capti*), whether male or female, who are contracting marriage, that they can do this without approaching the emperor.

The text continues (a part not quoted by Treggiari):

> *et aliam dubitationem ex hoc emergere, si hoc, quod in*

174

demente constitutio induxit, etiam in furiosis obtinendum est, quasi exemplo mente capti et furiosi filios adiuvante.

And another question arose from this, whether what the constitution introduced with reference to the *demens* was to be applied also to cases of *furiosi*, as though the precedent of the mentally afflicted also helped the sons of the *furiosi*.

There are two striking points here. One is the difference of attitude towards sons and daughters, the other is that the text gives no reason for it. The distinction made in the last section is very probably, as Buckland (1966: 114) has it, that between *demens*, perpetually deranged, and *furiosus*, capable of lucid intervals (and so capable from time to time of consenting to marriages). The question was whether Marcus Aurelius' ruling was to be held to apply to both. Justinian's contribution was to declare that it should.

From all this we learn that the marriage of daughters was not felt to constitute a problem, and lawyers soon found a device to make it possible. We are not told why the same was not held of sons, nor *why* the change came when it did. The clue is perhaps to be found in the name of Marcus Aurelius, which gives us a chronological indication, and the reason most probably has to do with inheritance, not only the intestate inheritance from the mad father, but also the inheritance prospects of the sons and daughters from each other.

Until AD 178, children did not have the primary claim to inherit on intestacy from their mothers, while a man's children, of course, were his automatic heirs. A man's marriage, therefore, meant that after his death there could be other direct heirs, his children, with a claim to his property superior to that of his agnates. If he had children, and died before his father, those children were entitled to his share of the intestate inheritance from the grandfather. The consent of the *pater* to a son's marriage, therefore, was not lightly to be dispensed with. A woman's children, however, did not have these inheritance rights before AD 178, and although in classical Rome it was generally accepted as natural and desirable – even a matter of *pietas*[47] – that a mother should be allowed to benefit her children, agnates could still present a claim to have some share in her estate.

A son's marriage, therefore, carried possibilities, which a daughter's did not, for division of the *patrimonium*. After the passing of the *senatusconsultum Orphitianum* in AD 178,[48] this distinction disappeared, since now a woman's children also had priority over all other heirs on intestacy. Even so, marriage was not at first permitted, during the periods of a father's insanity, to the sons of those fathers whose madness admitted of intervals in which their rational consent might be obtained. On the other hand, no such restriction appears to have been introduced on daughters, possibly because of the availability of the *tutela* to exercise some form of control if necessary.

On divorce, the legal evidence is annoyingly incomplete, although what this incompleteness allows us to infer is perhaps debatable. The few texts that we have mainly concern the possibility of divorce of the parties who are actually mad, not that of those who are themselves sane but in the *potestas* of a mad *pater*. Most, as it happens, concern mad wives, though there seems no obvious reason why most of what is said of them should not apply also to husbands.

A wife who was mad could be divorced, acccording to Ulpian (*D*. 24.2.4); her lack of understanding was no bar, because she was 'in the position of someone who does not know' (and, of course, it was unnecessary for the party being divorced to *consent* to be). Divorce could take effect without the other party actually having received notification of it. There was nothing to prevent the sane partner divorcing; the restraints introduced in *D*. 24.3.22.7, on grounds of humanity, that a mad husband or wife ought not to be divorced and could not be divorced 'without fault' unless actually dangerous, may belong to later law. Though the text is attributed to Ulpian, *libro tertio disputationum*, Nardi (1983: 183–4) regards it as an attempt by 'the Byzantines' to find a *media via* between the general ease of dissolution of ancient marriage and the 'programmatic indissolubility' of Christian marriage.

A woman could, personally or through her father, easily secure a divorce from a mad husband, and could then go to law for the recovery of the dowry. Husbands, however, had some incentive (that is, if they were already provided with children as heirs) *not* to divorce insane wives – namely, the dowry, which had to be returned on divorce; either the woman's *pater*, or, presumably, her *curator*, if she were *sui iuris*, could sue for it. Jane Eyre's Mr Rochester retained his mad wife (and, as Charlotte Brontë tells it, had her well looked after) not because of the wealth that came with her but because, despite her unchastity, he was unable to make use even of such cumbersome procedure as the English law before 1857 – or even the civil law before 1937 – allowed, in order to divorce her.[49]

A more sinister story is outlined by Ulpian (*D.* 24.3.22.8), hypothetically, though its reality is all too possible. The situation he imagines is that a wife has gone mad, but her husband is shrewdly determined to keep hold of her dowry and so will not divorce her. To pile on the agony, Ulpian has the husband neglect her. Her father, who could otherwise have intervened and insisted on divorcing the husband,[50] is apparently dead. In such a situation the woman, her *curator* and her relatives are all equally helpless to dissolve the marriage; the best the *curator* and kinsfolk can do is to appeal to the magistrate to oblige the husband to make use of the dowry to provide proper care and maintenance for his wife.

Freedwomen, although *sui iuris*, were unable to divorce their patron-husbands unless the latter consented, and so they were unable to divorce them at all if they became insane (*D.* 23.2.45.5). What was the situation for married children wishing to divorce, if the *pater* was mad? So far as we can tell, in the absence of direct legal evidence, persons *in potestate* could not divorce without the co-operation of the *pater*.[51] According to Ulpian again (*D.*24.3.22.10, 11), after a marriage had been dissolved, if a father is mad (*si pater furiosus sit*) a daughter will be able to recover the dowry through his *curator*, or even by herself, if she gives a *cautio de rato*, that is, an undertaking that if he recovered his sanity he would authorise this (the *cautio* was necessary because of the possibility of the husband retaining some of the dowry). The same applies if the father becomes a prisoner of war. Ulpian does not mention the preceding divorce, but this, of course, could have been initiated by the husband.

There is one text, not cited by Nardi, which might be taken to show the contrary, *D.* 46.3.65 (Pomponius):

> *Si filia furiosi a viro divorterit, dictum est vel adgnato curatori voluntate filiae vel filiae consentiente adgnato solvi dotem.*

If the daughter of a madman shall have divorced, it has been said that the dowry may be paid either to an agnate *curator* at the wish of the daughter, or to the daughter with the consent of the *curator*.

The text is concerned chiefly with the mechanics of recovery of the dowry. Its relevance to the present question rests entirely in the word *divorterit*, which, as observed by Treggiari (1991: 437), is used with great consistency by the jurists to describe the wife's action in separating from her husband. Even here, however, it seems to me, the syntax (i.e. the use of the future *perfect* tense) does not entirely exclude the possibility of parental concurrence at the time of the actual divorce; repayment of dowry came later.

So far as our evidence goes, then, sons and daughters of a mad *pater* were unable to initiate a divorce for themselves, and the law does nothing to help them. This is scarcely surprising, since the Roman law of marriage was much more concerned to secure the contracting and maintaining of marriages than their dissolution and was interested, besides, not in the personal happiness or unhappiness of individual partners, but in promoting the provision of legitimate heirs. Augustan marriage legislation added an extra dimension by rewarding the begetting of children. Natural and adopted children, however, were equally acceptable in the eyes of the law as heirs to a *familia*; impotence was no barrier to legal matrimony.[52]

In this system, the person who came off worst was the son of a mad father, whose own marriage was childless. He could not divorce, to try again with another wife – which he may not have wished to do, in any case; and he could not adopt, to remedy the deficiency. The law was apparently content to let him wait until his father recovered sanity or, as was quite likely in the natural order of things, predeceased him.

Conclusion

To sum up, the provision made by the law for the necessary care of the property of *furiosi*, and for the practical conduct of their lives and those of persons in their power, maintains a respect for the integrity of *patria potestas*, which is breached only (as, for example, to permit the marriage of daughters) when this is not likely to be to the disadvantage of the *familia*.

7

CONCLUSION: THE FACE-TO-FACE SOCIETY

In the preceding chapters, two factors have repeatedly emerged as of primary importance both for the original determination of the peculiar features of the legal powers of the individual Roman, and for their persistence through the subsequent development of Roman society from a small, compact, essentially agrarian community to an empire spread over the greater part of the world known to the peoples living around the Mediterranean. One is the special position of the head of household, the *pater*. The other is the insistence on direct personal presence and participation (usually involving the performance of specified speech acts) for the accomplishment of any action with legal consequences for the persons or property both of the individuals concerned and of others. Both are aspects of the same principle, namely the autonomy of the individual *familia*; an autonomy breached by the state, so far as the conduct of the internal affairs of the *familia* is concerned, only where this may be felt to endanger the stability of other parts of society.

The continuing prominence of the *pater*, I have suggested above, is to be accounted for by the extent to which the individual family 'head' is expected to rely upon self-help and personal initiative in securing the legal rights of his *familia*, i.e. of himself and his dependants, in relation to others, and also by his responsibility to society for the actions of his dependants – and so by the consequent importance of the rôle of the *pater* in Roman society, in supplying elements both of social control and of social bonding between Romans. Reliance was placed on the *pater* to take care of much that in modern society is provided for, or enforced by, the state.

As for the second factor, though direct face-to-face transaction would be the norm in a small-scale, primitive and for a long time mainly, it is to be supposed, illiterate society, literacy or the lack of it does not seem to be a determining factor in the persistence of the preference for personal execution. It is this location, just mentioned, of responsibility in the individual, not the state, rather than the relative levels of literacy or illiteracy in society at large, that is responsible. Recent work on classical Athens[1] has drawn attention to the extent to which, although it began in the fourth century to move towards becoming a literary culture, it remained nevertheless to a very large extent an oral one. The enormously greater amount of written material available from the Roman world, together with the prolixity of much of it (especially, it must be said, of that coming from the lawyers), has tended to blur our perception of the extent to which this was true also of ancient Rome. Those people for whom the developed law of the classical period catered were, *par excellence*, the literate classes. The use of written documents to assist subsequent proof of trans-actions did indeed extend much further down the social scale, as is strikingly illustrated not only by such documents as the wax tablets from Herculaneum and Pompeii, but also, for instance, the 'Transylvanian Tablets', known to us for rather longer than either of these, and affording glimpses of the commercial activities of a mixed community in Dacia in the second century AD.[2] However, the writing and sealing by witnesses of these tablets do not them-selves constitute the transactions, they merely record that they have previously taken place, *viva voce*.

To take a literary example of an orally agreed contract, there is the lively description in Varro (*Res Rusticae* 2.2.5–6) of a sale of sheep. The buyer and seller first work towards an agreed total price for the flock, then carry out the actual sale:

> In buying, we follow the practice prescribed by law. Some introduce more, others fewer provisos (*alii plura, alii pau-ciora excipiunt*) when a price per single sheep has been agreed, as for instance that two late-born lambs should be reckoned as one sheep, and if any sheep have lost their teeth through age, two are to count as one. Otherwise, they usually follow the traditional formula. When the buyer says,

'Are they bought for me at such-and-such a sum (*tanti sunt mi emptae*)?' and the other replies 'They are (*sunt*)', and the buyer has shown he has the money,[3] a stipulation is made in the ancient formula, thus: 'these sheep, which are in question, that they are duly sound, according to the definition of soundness in sheep, without being blind in one eye, deaf or *mina*, that is, bald-bellied, and that they are not from a diseased flock, and that ownership may rightfully pass – do you guarantee that all this is duly so?'

When this has been done, all the same, the flock does not change owner unless the money has been counted out.

Although this is put in the mouth of no less a person than Atticus, the friend and correspondent of Cicero, and himself the owner of cattle farms in Epirus, one can imagine that the scene described, complete with traditional legal formula, was frequently enacted between country people in their local markets, and by people of all sorts, slaves included, who were buying and selling. The various parts of the verbal *stipulatio* not only took the place of something like the modern printed guarantee card, but provided security for the buyer as to the legal validity of the sale. A written, witnessed receipt might be given, like those in the wax tablets mentioned above, and this usually detailed the *stipulatio* in precise terms, but the transaction was already complete without it. What was essential was the personal presence of buyer and seller (or their legal equivalents, such as sons, slaves or other authorised persons) and, desirably in case of possible problems later on, some witnesses.

In the second century AD, Gaius makes the point explicitly (*D.* 22.4.4), with reference both specifically to hypothec (a form of pledge agreement), and to other types of agreement in general, that their validity is not dependent on the presence or absence of a written document. 'Even if an agreement for hypothec is made without writing <and it will be possible to prove it>, the object will be bound by the pledge, for', he says,

> written documents are made for these agreements so that what has been done can more easily be proved by their means; and without these documents what was done is valid <if there is proof of it>, just as is the case with marriages, even though a declaration was made without writing.

The phrases in pointed brackets have been justifiably suspected of being interpolated, since they are redundant. The legal *validity* of a transaction is quite independent of the possibility of bringing proof of its having taken place so that its validity, if challenged, can be established.

In this concluding chapter, I shall first examine the persistence of the preference for personal execution shown in the Roman attitude to matters of proof, and secondly consider a related question: whether, in view of the evident lack of detailed governmental monitoring of the legal status, and so of the legal capacities, of individuals, it can nevertheless be held that the legal distinctions between persons discussed in the previous chapters mattered.

THE PROBLEM OF PROOF

Legal writing under the empire, as represented especially in the *Digest* and the *Codex Justinianus*, not only shows an awareness that it is necessary to state clearly what may be held to constitute sufficient proof, but also, and most strikingly, it does not privilege the provision of documentary evidence, or at least of private documents. Official records, on the other hand, where these exist, have a special status; this was declared by the Senate some time before the mid-second century AD (*D.* 22.3.10). However, these existed and were required for far fewer situations than in the modern world.

Three titles in the *Digest* (22.3–5) and four in the *Codex Justinianus* (4.19–22) are concerned with the matter of proof; there is also one, rather repetitive, chapter in the *Codex Theodosianus* (11.39).[4] The texts in the former two are drawn from a wide variety of legal works and imperial reigns; though the Justinianic compilation lends a deceptive air of unity, they do not in themselves constitute anything resembling a theory of proof. The subjects of the enquiries in *CJ* 4.21, which range in time from Antoninus to Constantine, include debt (alleged to be settled or outstanding), valid sale, gift, claim to ownership of property (against a usufructuary), entitlement to the privileges of veterans, free birth and emancipation. The latter part of the title of the chapter ('On those things which can be done without writing') is particularly significant, in that it is apparently by this time thought necessary to point out that writing is not always required.

The use of written documents as evidence of transactions, independently of confirmation by verbal witness, had perhaps by the early third century (the earliest response in this chapter is dated AD 213) become common. This is the suggestion of Lévy (1987), who associates this development with a change in practice, from the use on documents of seals, which required personal recognition and confirmation by witnesses to the transaction, to that of personal signature. This in itself, of course, did not change the status of the documents, which were created, as Gaius (cited above) insists, merely in order to make it easier to provide proof of the transactions later (and it did not alter the fact that for some of the transactions themselves witnesses were legally required).

There seems, however, to be some confusion in people's minds as to whether these documents are in themselves constitutive, or merely evidential. Enquirers are repeatedly reassured that the loss or unavailability of documents does not affect the legal validity of their claims, and that they can still proceed so long as they can provide proof of some sort.[5] Indeed, some anxious litigants seem to be attaching greater value to documents than to witnesses. There is perhaps a hint of exasperation in Diocletian's response to Leontius (*CJ* 4.21.13), pointing out that it is of no use for proving the truth simply to testify (the word used, *testatio*, may itself refer to the preparation of a written declaration) that there *were* documents but that they have been lost, if the people who are witnesses of the *testatio* are otherwise ignorant of what happened. About forty years later, Constantine's office finds it necessary to tell the *comes* of Spain (*CJ* 4.21.14 = *C.Th.* 11.39.2) that people gain nothing by producing numerous documents to back up their own side of the case, if these are in conflict with each other. In AD 317, Constantine made a formal announcement from Rome (*CJ* 4.21.15 *ad populum*) that for evidential purposes in lawsuits *instrumenta* (here apparently meaning 'documents')[6] and witnesses carried the same weight; this may be seen as merely confirming as law what had long been practice in the courts, but it might not perhaps be going too far to suppose that part of the intention was to discourage the idea that documentary evidence, of whatever sort, was preferable to that of witnesses.[7]

Philippus says (*CJ* 4.19.5: AD 245) that privately prepared documents are not enough on their own, but must be backed by other aids (*adminiculis*); the private nature of the documents is not merely stated, but iterated (*instrumenta domestica seu privata testatio seu adnotatio*).[8] He appears (see below) to be talking about *unwitnessed* documents. However, when emperors want to instruct the praetorian prefect that prosecutors have their case backed by adequate evidence (*CJ* 4.19.25: AD 382), they enumerate that it should be 'supported by suitable witnesses or equipped with the most evident *documenta* or other forms of evidence', an order of words which seems to assign greater importance to witnesses.

A text which appears to state the contrary, in saying that the evidence of witnesses alone is not enough, is *CJ* 4.20.2 (AD 223). There, however, the case (which may call to mind the *soi-disant* Petronia Justa) concerns a claim to free birth, *ingenuitas*.[9] This is not only something for which official documentary evidence might be available, but was obviously a matter in which the state took an interest. The response, however, is one of a number of texts which indicate that all people did not routinely equip themselves, nor were they obliged to, with documentation proving their status. Documents such as marriage certificates and birth certificates were obviously of use not only for private purposes but also in matters of public concern, for which it might be necessary to establish, for example, citizen birth, rank and age; however, they were not compulsory.[10] In their absence, confirmation was sought from fellow members of the community, that is, from witnesses.

In matters of private concern, there is a marked disposition towards insisting, where documents alone, other than officially certified ones, are offered, on the provision of additional evidence, in particular that of witnesses. I have mentioned above a response of Philippus (*CJ* 4.19.5) on 'private' (i.e. unwitnessed) documents. In another response (*CJ* 4.19.6) he states that a mere entry in personal accounts or assertion in a will is not sufficient evidence of the existence of a debt; Gallienus agrees (*CJ* 4.19.7, with a possible glance at official corruption). Although in the late empire *chirographa* (autograph declarations), and even wills, may for a time have been accepted in evidence without the need for further witness, this was a relatively short-lived phase.[11] Eventually Justinian (*CJ* 4.21.20) refused to allow the acceptance of private documents as evidence on a comparison of handwriting, without the attestation of at least three witnesses.

Both witnesses and documents, it is recognised, may be false or unreliable. To ensure so far as possible the reliability of witnesses, Callistratus recommends that particular attention be given to their character, standing and repute, and cites a rescript of Hadrian to the governor of Cilicia to that effect. Attention to social standing alone was not regarded as enough by the emperor Julian, who also required the administration of an oath, but decided finally that even that was insufficient and ordered that more than one witness must be supplied.[12] For documents, on the other hand, the only way of establishing their genuineness is to obtain the evidence of witnesses to that effect. As we have seen in previous chapters, the making of witnessed documents formed a routine part of business transactions between citizens, but the documents were themselves in form merely statements that a transaction had occurred. Even if, as some believe, this statement became no more than a legal fiction, the document itself was nevertheless the product of a direct personal meeting between the various persons (including the witnesses) involved, and they could be called upon to attest to the transaction.

What persists, then, right through the history of classical law, is the principle that the strongest proof of transactions is the direct verbal testimony of witnesses. Earlier (Gardner 1986a: 14) I was content to ascribe the maintenance of this principle to that over-worked and under-examined concept 'Roman conservatism' (which really explains nothing). Modern (to the ancients) technology and modern communications merely mask the extent to which the problem of proof has remained substantially the same. The desire for independent witnesses has withered with such developments as the arrival of printed business stationery, issued by one party to a transaction (and, theoretically at least, available only from them) and, more recently, personally held credit cards. Problems of forgery, however, still arise, as well as of unauthorised use of these documents, and these are to the disadvantage of the complainant, faced with the burden of proof. The modern attempt at solution is not, like Justinian, to revert to demanding witnesses, but to attempt to obviate unauthorised use by refining the technology or by elaborating the security procedures. The latter, since it involves other people, is really just a variant on having witnesses, but these are not witnesses to the actual transaction, rather to the original issue (or reported loss) of the authorised documents used in it. For proof of some transactions, indeed, such as marriage and wills (except holograph wills), and also for example passport applications, not only documents but the signatures of witnesses are still necessary.

It is not, however, simply a matter of the availability of more advanced technology. I have already drawn attention to two important features of Roman society. One is that the entire responsibility for action on behalf of the *familia*, and for prosecutions both civil and criminal, lay with the individual *sui iuris*, who was thus left as an isolated unit in society, and had actively to look for corroboration and support to other members of that society before approaching the forces of law. The other is that, as far as the arrangements within a *familia* are concerned, it was only for a few specific purposes, and with reference to a limited sector of society, that the state had to concern itself with these, and so there was no strong pressure to insist on the fulfilment of legal formalities.

THE LACK OF PROOF

There is, however, considerable evidence, some of which is discussed in some detail in Gardner (1986a), that the lack of any compulsory legal formalities for marriage and birth registration did result in the rules of legal status being breached. Runaway slaves could pass themselves off as free, freed as freeborn, Junians be unrecognised as such; these could in turn, wittingly or unwittingly, 'marry' and produce illegitimate and/or non-citizen children – who were not recognised as such, and so would be going about in Roman society and acting as if they had a status and a private legal capacity to which they were not legally entitled. To these should probably also be added, in view of the evidence put forward by Weaver (1990), the children of Junians for whom no *anniculi probatio* was undertaken, and their descendants, who would technically be *peregrini*.

To rely upon the evidence of witnesses personally acquainted with the persons involved might, for the most part, be safe enough, especially in small communities in which individuals had lived for a long time, but it was by no means foolproof. Neighbours do not know everything. Neighbours' testimony alone does not establish that a baby born in the house is the husband's; they may not know about his chronic impotence, or when he last slept with his wife (*D.* 1.6.6). Friends and acquaintances of the family with which Petronia Justa had grown up gave opposite testimony about her freeborn or manumitted status, either because they had forgotten, or were not directly acquainted with, the circumstances of her mother's manumission a long time ago. Lapse of time compounds the difficulty, especially in larger cities where it is harder to keep track of 'local' genealogies; it is easy to assume that someone whom you have known since childhood was citizen-born like yourself, and to be unaware whether or not his parents originated locally or whether, perhaps, his mother's mother had been an unpromoted Junian and so legally unqualified to marry his grandfather.

Nor does the apparent difficulty disappear with the *constitutio Antoniniana* of AD 212,[13] which made all free inhabitants of the Roman empire Roman citizens. The operation of the Augustan legislation on marriage, adultery and manumission would continue to produce illegitimates, Junians and *dediticii*, and slaves did not stop running away.

Does this mean that the various distinctions of the legal status, and so of the legal capacities, of individuals detailed in our legal texts did not matter? To this question there is not one single answer but different answers, depending upon the particular aspects of Roman society in which one is interested.

From one point of view, found in Jones (1964), de Ste Croix (1981) and Alföldy (1985),[14] by the time of Caracalla being a Roman citizen at all mattered a good deal less than being one of the élite Romans. This response is related mainly to the distinction between *honestiores* and *humiliores*, with regard particularly to its effects in the public sphere and in treatment under criminal law. It is not true, however, of private law, where there were certain differences between *peregrinus* and citizen. These are little discussed in legal texts, since family law (i.e. most of the law of persons and of inheritance) does not concern non-Romans, and they had many of the same capacities as Romans in the law of things (apart from inheritance law) and of actions.

The relations between *peregrini* and Romans in private law are summarised by Buckland (1966: 96–7). Non-Romans had only limited *ius commercii*, that is, property could be transferred between them and Roman citizens and they could make contracts, although they could not, as already mentioned, mancipate and so they could not have full legal ownership of *res mancipi* (Gaius 1.119); a legal fiction also allowed them access to the civil courts (Gaius 4.37). Only exceptionally, however, did they have *conubium*, capacity for lawful marriage, and so most of family law, including the law of inheritance, excluded the possibility of relations between *peregrini* and Romans. Becoming citizens, therefore, would not only affect for them those existing dealings with Romans which were open to foreigners, but would allow them to enter into personal and property relations with Roman citizens which were not previously open to them.

The extent to which it would affect the way they did things amongst themselves in their own communities, however, is more problematic. To a large extent, it would depend on the degree to which their institutions had become Romanised. The ancient Roman lawyers are writing for Romans, and only rarely mention the ways of *peregrini*, with the assumption that these are different.[15] Buckland (1966: 96)[16] says merely: 'Apart from municipalities and the like which here and there received civil or Latin rights, and thus constituted civil enclaves, the provinces were governed by their own private law, little altered by Rome.' Sherwin-White (1973: 392–3) has little of substance to add. Work both on the eastern and the western empire continues, but the extent to which Roman-style institutions were adopted by or imposed upon the provinces cannot yet be fully assessed.

Of particular interest, however, is the recent epigraphic evidence from Spain, especially the *Tabula Contrebiensis* and the *lex Irnitana*.[17] The former shows a Spanish community in the early first century BC still using local law, but already accepting the guidance of the Roman provincial commander in the area and following the pattern of the formulary procedure of the Roman praetor in order to find a mode of settling the dispute. The *lex Irnitana*, issued to a *municipium* in Spain in the first century AD, gives to Irni an entire new legal system. In the law, local judges are at several points (clauses 71, 89, 91) instructed to give judgment following what would apply if the case were being tried at Rome and this means, not as if *peregrini* were on trial at Rome, but, as 91 makes clear, 'as it would be if a praetor of the Roman people had ordered that matter to be judged in the city of Rome between Roman citizens'. Clause 93 goes further:

> for everything else not explicitly covered in this law, concerning the *ius* according to which the citizens of Irni (*municipes municipi [Flavi] Irnitani*) are to deal with each other, they are to do so by the civil law, *ius civile*, which Roman citizens use in dealing with each other.

That is, the inhabitants of Irni are no longer to use local law, but neither is the law which they are to use the Roman law itself.

Rather it is an artificial construct, a mirage of the Roman law.[18] The people of Irni are to behave towards each other *as if* they were all Roman citizens. What was the difference? And what, then, would change for them in AD 212? Answers to these questions may help to shed some light on the questions about status irregularities raised earlier.

The people of Irni were not all Roman citizens. Some already were. For those who were not, adoption of the Roman pattern of law meant becoming acquainted with some new institutions; for their benefit clause 29, for example, details the procedure to be followed and the official to be approached in order to obtain a tutor. Others were not Roman citizens, but might become so (by the exercise of 'Latin rights'). If they did so their change of status, which in Roman law amounted to a *capitis deminutio*, was not to affect legal relationships already existing for them *at Irni* in the new Roman-style system, such as *patria potestas, manus* or *mancipium*, or patronal rights (clauses 21, 86, 97) – naturally, since they also continued to be *municipes* of Irni, and in that respect had not undergone *capitis deminutio*. Some were Latins, that is Junian Latins;[19] their status is mentioned where it is important for defining the special status (in terms of patronal rights) of slaves freed by them (cl. 28), or that of public slaves freed by the municipality (cl. 72); both types of *liberti* are, however, *municipes* of Irni.

The references to Romans and Latins in the *lex* remind us, and the Irnitani, that there is a world outside Irni, and in that world they were (until AD 212) *not* all fellow citizens with rights under the same system of law. The *lex* does not appear to have included any consideration of the legal consequences of other possible trans-status relationships, such as marriages between Roman and non-Roman Irnitani, or formal manumission before Irni magistrates by Roman Irnitani owners – naturally, because such transactions, if any took place, would be valid only within Irni. The marriage would not be valid in Roman law, nor would the manumission create a Roman citizen.

Irni, in other words, could be regarded as a closed system, within which everyone dealt with each other *as if* they were all Romans. Of course, they were not all Romans, and knew that perfectly well, but the legal fiction gave them a perfectly adequate system to live by. Only when they went outside the system did it make any practical difference. If we regard life within the

'closed' Irnitan community as a partial analogue of everyday interaction in Roman society, the failure of the Roman authorities to
monitor in detail and insist on documentary proof of everyone's
personal status becomes more comprehensible. It is only a partial
analogue, since in effect it operates at a different level. (In practice,
of course, Irni would also have its share of invalid marriages,
runaways, and so on, as well as non-Irnitan intruders.) For the
purposes of the argument, I am comparing the Irnitan community
in which everyone collaborates in the fiction of being (in terms
of *civitas* status) 'pretend-Romans' with a Roman community, in
which everyone is *assumed* to have the *personal* status (as freeborn,
freed, *sui iuris*, legitimate, of age, Roman, etc.) which he or she
presents him or herself as having. In both cases, the result is a
modus vivendi, in which the business of life is carried on through
the medium of an agreed set of rules, which is Roman civil law.

Most of the time (that is, while they are in Irni) it does not
matter whether individual Irnitani are in fact Romans or not; if
they go elsewhere, it does. Most of the time, it does not in practice
matter very much whether the individual Roman has or has not
in fact the personal status claimed. As we have seen, various legal
means had been devised to enable daily life to go on, without
sacrificing the basic *pater*-dependent legal structure. For dealings
outside the *familia*, as we have seen above, the system had also
been made elastic enough to accommodate *peregrini* as (almost)
'pretend-Romans'.[20] As we have also seen, a number of the most
important civil law procedures required the participation of witnesses from the citizen community, and witnesses were routinely
sought for others, so that to a large extent the system was self-
policing, between fellow heads of household.

Personal status mattered much more in the sphere of family
and inheritance law, that is for matters within the *familia*, and
these, as we have seen, were usually managed by making sure that
appropriate behaviour was observed by other members of the
community.[21] Certain means of public documentation had also
been made available by the state, for the implementation of a
small number of laws, and those with anything to lose financially
or in public life would take care to avail themselves of these,
because of their usefulness for private purposes.[22] These laws,
however, were primarily aimed at promoting certain public
purposes, not general private convenience; it was not the state's
concern to insist that everyone should provide themselves with

the documents, only those few who might make claims coming under the scope of the laws.

The protection of private interests was left in private hands. The result, no doubt, was that not a few technical illegalities occurred and were not detected. This does not mean, however, either that the rules of personal status did not matter or that they were not thought to matter. The enormous bulk of Roman legal writing, much of it generated by private action, shows that for the Romans they did matter, since they were the basis of a system which, both at a domestic and a community level, maintained stability and order in Roman society.[23]

NOTES

1 THE DISABILITIES OF ROMAN CITIZENS

1 We shall not be concerned with the distinction between 'higher' and 'lower' class citizens, *honesti* and *humiliores*, which appears under the empire. Although it eventually acquires legal force, becoming enshrined in the guidelines which magistrates are expected to follow in, e.g. imposing penalties under criminal law (Garnsey 1970; Millar 1984), in origin it is not a legal distinction but a socio-economic one. It was not part of the classical civil law, nor is it continuous with nor even connected to the patrician–plebeian distinction of the early Republic, the nature of which is not fully understood and is still the subject of debate (see, for example, the essays in Raaflaub 1986), but which appears to have been essentially political.

2 Hermaphrodites were perhaps problematic for the Romans. So were *castrati*, but only so far as marriage (which was assumed to be for the purpose of procreating heirs) was concerned: *D.* 1.7.6.1; 23.3.39.1; 28.2.6; 40.2.14. In other respects, they had the rights of any male citizen, being regarded as a sub-category of *spadones* (impotent men), but unable (unlike *spadones*) to contract lawful marriages (*D.* 23.3.39.1; Dalla (1978) 233–46). According to Valerius Maximus (7.7.6) the consul Mamercus Aemilius Lepidus (77 BC) overturned the award by the urban praetor, Cn. Orestes, of possession of the estate of a freedman, Naevius Anius, to a certain Genucius, who was a Gallus, a castrated priest of the Magna Mater, and had been made heir by Naevius. The grounds Valerius represents Aemilius as giving for his judgment are that Genucius should be regarded as neither male nor female, adding that he had issued a decree that Genucius was not to 'pollute the tribunals of the magistrates by his obscene presence and corrupted voice'; but we may suspect from the narrative that the real reason for the judgment was the influence of Naevius' patron, who was entitled to a half-share anyway (see Chapter 2, page 21), but had appealed. The anecdote does not imply any general ban on appointing *castrati* as heirs, nor on their right to plead in court. They were, after all, biologically normal men, with something subtracted. Hermaphrodites, however, did cross physiological categories, so there could be

doubt whether to classify them as men or women (*D.* 1.5.10) – which could make a real difference to their legal capacities in general. We have no direct evidence, possibly because the problem never arose; the condition is fairly rare. The examples of gender confusion cited by Pliny *NH* 4.36 (repeated in Gell. 9.4.15), one of them a Roman citizen, all concern apparent females who turn out on maturity to be males, and not cases of hermaphroditism.

3 Some of the dangers are pointed out in Kelly (1976) ch. 3, on case statistics and their use, and, to some extent, the more speculative ch. 4.

2 BIRTH: THE FREEDMAN'S CONDITION

1 Philip V: *SIG*³ 543 (214 BC); Chantraine (1972); Sherwin-White (1973) 322; Balsdon (1979) 86. Chantraine 59 n. 2 points out that this inscription is the earliest direct evidence that citizenship normally accompanied manumission.

2 Manumission *vindicta* is traditionally dated to the earliest period of the Republic, and the existence of manumission *testamento* is taken for granted in the Twelve Tables. The institution of the census was traditionally ascribed to Rome's penultimate king; opinions vary on how early manumission *censu* became available. The probable chronological order of the three forms of manumission, and problems about their precise legal nature, have been discussed by a number of scholars; see especially Cosentini (1948) 9–37, Treggiari (1969) 20–31 and Watson (1975) 86–91. For entry by census, see Cic. *de Or.* 1.183; *pro Caecina* 99; Ulp. *Reg.* 1.8; Buckland (1908) 439–41.

3 In 176 BC, the owner was required to be present and take a certain oath to that effect, though the oath at least does not seem to have been normally exacted: Livy 41.9. It was the censors who decided the citizen tribe to which the freedman should be allotted: Livy 45.15.5. This came to be used as a means of limiting the political effectiveness of freedmen *en masse*: Treggiari (1969) 37–52. Slaves manumitted by other methods would also have to await census enrolment before they could exercise their political rights.

4 *Frag. Dosith.* 17 (perhaps early 3rd century AD). Brunt (1971) 701–2 regards this as mechanically copied from an earlier work; his own view is that the practical inconvenience of waiting for the completion of a *lustrum* led to the abandonment of this requirement by the time of Cicero.

5 On the reasons why relatively little military use appears to have been made of freedmen under the Republic, see Sherwin-White (1973) 324–5.

6 Watson (1987) 24, citing Daube (1946) 57 ff. and Fabre (1981) 10 ff.

7 'They were slaves by Quiritary (i.e. Roman) law, but were customarily kept in formal freedom with the assistance of the praetor': Gaius 3.56.

8 Watson (1975) 86–90. Touching with a rod (a symbolic spear) was a regular part of the archaic *legis actio in rem*, the action to assert a claim to ownership of property (Gaius 4.16); in the *causa liberalis*, of course, it was also used to deny that anyone had a claim to own the person.

9 Our historical evidence, of course, does not take us back beyond the period of the Twelve Tables, by which time the procedure of litigation by individuals before a magistrate is already in existence.

10 Gaius 2.101–4; Kaser (1971) 105–9.

11 *Mancipium*: Gaius 1.115, 132, 134, 138–41. The institution and its effects are summarised in Buckland (1966) 133–4. Noxal surrender: Gaius 4.75, 79. Apparently this ceased – how early is not known – to apply to daughters; references in Gardner (1986) 26 n. 9.

12 This is the usual explanation of the origin of the provision of the Twelve Tables (4.2b), 'If a father sells his son three times, let the son be free from his father', cited by Gaius 1.132 in connection with the emancipation procedure; see Watson (1975) 118–19.

13 Buckland (n. 11 above) observes that it is unclear how far the rules about sons in bondage, recorded from a period when the institution survived in a formal sense only, applied in earlier times. There is no obvious reason, however, why they should not; the situations envisaged could equally well have arisen then, and with more serious consequences, since the son's condition was then of longer duration and had more practical reality. How the political rights of sons were originally affected by *mancipium* is not known; but it is not certainly known, either, whether in the very earliest stages of Roman society sons, as well as heads of household, had political rights.

14 This may originally have applied universally. In the rule as stated by Gaius, it was so only for the first two occasions of being *in mancipio*; after the rule of the Twelve Tables, the third mancipation destroyed the *patria potestas*. This created technical problems for Roman lawyers in the late Republic: Gaius 1.135.

15 Sale 'across the Tiber': Steinwenter *TE* xiv. 1010; Schulz (1936) 199; Mayer-Maly (1958). Florentinus (*D.* 1.5.4), who also describes slavery as an *institutio iuris gentium*, seems to regard warfare as originally the sole source of slaves. He produces a fanciful etymology: 'Slaves (*servi*) are so called because commanders customarily sell captives, and so save (*servare*) them instead of killing them; they are called *mancipia* because they are taken by the hand (*manu capiantur*) of the enemy.' Watson (1975) 82–4 gives reasons for believing in the presence of homeborn slaves in Rome at least by the time of the Twelve Tables, though he perhaps exaggerates their relative numbers; see also Bradley (1987) 50 and nn. 38–9. Slaves are unlikely to have been numerous in early Rome, for reasons summarised by Drummond (1989) 125–6; however, he remarks (p. 209), with particular reference to the bondsman, on the 'continuing gulf in status between citizen and slave even where in practice they might be subject to similar physical constraints'. (The same, as illustrated in the text above, applies to sons in bondage.) The rule of the Twelve Tables that insolvent judgment-debtors be sold as slaves 'across the Tiber', he observes, must reflect a desire to avoid having one Roman citizen fall into legal servitude to another.

16 Philip V: *SIG*³ 543 (n. 1 above). Dio: Atkinson (1966) associates military needs with the incentives to marriage and reproduction given to freed slaves in Augustus' legislation on marriage.

NOTES TO PAGES 14–17

17 This view, vigorously argued for in the case of imperial Rome by Alföldy (1972), is now discredited; see Hopkins (1978) 127 n. 63; Harris (1980) 117–40, esp. 118 and 133 ff. nn. 8–9; Wiedemann (1985) 162–75. Though Alföldy remains unrepentant (1986: 329), he has brought no fresh arguments.

18 Sherwin-White (1973) 3–37; Chantraine (1972) 65–6 makes the connection with the enfranchisement of freedmen.

19 The *ius migrationis* is scantily attested. It appears virtually confined in the historical period to Rome and the Latin communities. The right of Latins to become citizens by moving to Rome disappears by the time of the Social War. See Sherwin-White (1973) 34, 103–4, 107, 110. On admission of foreigners to early Rome, see Drummond (1989) 261. Livy's account also has several examples of individuals moving to other cities and settling as citizens there.

20 In later law, *postliminium* is explained, with reference to Romans, as the recovery of rights and status, which were suspended during foreign captivity, by those who returned (Gaius 1.129).

21 Watson (1967) 94 agrees, using an assumed change in the status of freedmen to account for the adoption of a slave no longer being possible:

> A *libertinus* (freedman) adopted by an *ingenuus* became an *ingenuus* only so long as it was accepted that the position in the state of an adopted person was that of the adopter. Also so long as this was the position, a slave adopted by a Roman citizen automatically became a Roman citizen. But once it was decided that status in the state was not altered by adoption (and for this change we have evidence in respect of *libertini*) a slave could not be adopted, because a non-Roman could not be a *filius in potestate* to a *civis Romanus*.

Watson's argument is not entirely lucid here; it does not seem at all relevant to the status of the adoptee that the adopter was or was not freeborn; freedmen were also perfectly capable of adopting, and sons born to freedmen were *ingenui*, although their fathers were not.

22 For what follows, see also Gardner (1989) 238–42 (where, however, a rather different argument was presented, since it was assumed that *vernae* were a relatively later development).

23 For the technical definition, Gaius 1.11: '*Ingenui* are those who were born free; *libertini*, those who were manumitted from lawful slavery'. Gaius specifies 'lawful slavery', since a citizen proved by a *causa liberalis* to be freeborn and therefore wrongfully enslaved recovered his status. For the other sense, see e.g. Cicero *Brutus* 67, *ingenuum fastidium*; *Fin.* 5.48, *ingenuis studiis atque artibus delectari*; Juvenal 11.154, *ingenui vultus puer ingenuique pudoris*.

24 One should not attach too much weight to the suggestion, made by Watson (1975) 86 and repeated by others, that

> it is in the highest degree significant for social attitudes that in the Twelve Tables serious injuries to slaves were assimilated with

195

those to free citizens, whereas centuries later under chapter 3 of the *lex Aquilia* the same injuries to slaves were equated with those to animals.

The Twelve Tables specified that the penalty for breaking the bone of a slave was half that of a free man. Watson takes both the preceding and the following clauses (8.1 and 3) on physical damage (*si membrum rupsit*) and assault (*iniuria*) to apply equally to slaves and free men, though slaves are not mentioned in either clause. Cato in the *Origines* (Prisc. *Gramm.* 6.13.69) said that the nearest cognate avenged both damage and broken bones on the principle of *talio*. None of this rules out the possibility that the penalty for all three under the Twelve Tables was half, if the victim was a slave. As for injury to animals, our surviving fragments of the Tables do not happen to tell us what the going rate was.

25 Details, and the legal procedures involved are discussed by Crook (1976).

26 Not, of course, for *operae* (see below), and the previous owners' inheritance rights over Junians were greater than over citizen freedmen (Sirks 1983). The supposition in the text above is borne out by the careful provision made in the *lex Irnitana* (see Gonzalez 1986) for preservation of patronal rights where either the patron or the freedman undergoes a change of status. The whole subject of Junian Latins needs further investigation; Weaver (1990) raises the important question of the status of the children of those Junian Latins who never succeeded in becoming citizens.

27 Senatorial marriages: these had previously attracted social disapproval, perhaps going so far as censorial stigma upon the freeborn upper-class partner, but were not legally banned before Augustus: Treggiari (1969) 81 ff. Civil rights: Ulpian (*D.* 48.18.1.9) implies that freedmen could be tortured to give evidence, in cases where the accused was someone other than their patron; he is, however, stating an exception, benefiting the freedman, to what was by the time of Marcus Aurelius the general practice of examining lower-class witnesses under torture (*CJ* 9.41.11).

28 'Patronal rights' are summarised by Watson (1987) 35–43; more comprehensively by Buckland (1966) 88–90.

29 Compare the heading to *D.* 37.15, *De obsequiis parentibus et patronis praestandis*, ('On the obedience due to parents and patrons').

30 Cosentini (1948) 39–44. Inheritance rights, and also the guardianship (*tutela*) of freedmen under puberty (*impuberes*) and of freedwomen, were granted to patrons by the law of the Twelve Tables; by an interpretation of the law it was accepted that this was a *tutela legitima* (i.e. equivalent to that of agnates), since the Twelve Tables provided that agnates, who were called to inherit, should also be tutors (Gaius 1.165–6). It was, Gaius says, on the analogy of the *tutela* of patrons that it was accepted that manumitting parents should have *tutela legitima*. If Gaius and Ulpian are right in making the situation regarding freed slaves the model for that concerning emancipated children, rather than

vice versa, this may indicate that the former was already in the 5th century BC the commoner occurrence.

31 The explanation appended in the *Digest* text, that praetors thought patrons should be allowed a kind of *societas* ('partnership') in the estate, like that which they had customarily had in the freedman's property during his life, may be disregarded, as the mention of *societas* patently derives from the last clause of 38.2.1.1, *videlicet si hoc pepigisset, ut, nisi ei obsequium praestaret libertus in societatem admitteretur patronus* ('that is, if he had made a formal agreement that, if the freedman did not render him due obedience, the patron would be admitted to partnership'), which looks like an attempt by compilators to explain something which had long ceased to exist. The practice of imposing as a condition of freedom a contractual obligation of partnership (*societas*) in all future acquisitions had been made unactionable by the time of Labeo, i.e. by the end of the Republic (*D.* 38.1.36). Cosentini (1948) 190 ff. interprets this provision of the edict as intended to 'establish the subjection of the freedman to the patron'; his view is that the various obligations of freedmen towards their patrons were evolved by the ruling classes through the centuries as a deliberate policy of subjection; this does not account for its later disappearance. Waldstein (1986) 149 ff. regards it as part of a recoil against the concessions made to freedmen by the edict of the praetor Rutilius.

32 As the *senatusconsultum Gaetulicianum* (*P. Berol.* 11753: *FIRA* ii.427) indicates, a similar device was resorted to in attempts to evade the inheritance restrictions of Augustan marriage legislation: Noy (1988).

33 Social stratification: summarised in Garnsey and Saller (1987) 107–18.

34 There were, probably by the end of the Republic, certain circumstances in which a parent could claim against the will of an emancipated son, but these appear to be based on the *querela inofficiosi testamenti*, 'complaint of unduteous will', and the *lex Falcidia* (Buckland (1966) 328–9, 342–3). Not only could an emancipated son's will in favour of an unsavoury person, such as a prostitute, be entirely set aside in favour of a parent, but the parent passed over in a child's will could claim a certain portion (a quarter) of the estate against other (sc. external) heirs; nor could he be obliged to give up any of 'his portion, which is owed to him' for the fulfilment of testamentary requests, *fideicommissa* (*D.* 37.12.3: Paul, citing Paconius).

35 See n. 36, and also the discussions of Treggiari and Watson.

36 Gaius 1.165–6; *D.* 37.12 and 15. That emancipated children had to obtain praetorian permission to prosecute parents is shown by *CJ* 2.2.3 (AD 287).

37 Garnsey (1970); Millar (1984); Rilinger (1988).

38 e.g. Lambert (1934) esp. 34 ff., 73 ff.; Duff (1958) 36–43. A similarly wide-ranging concept seems to underly the dramatic but imprecise language used by Veyne (1961; 1987). For a detailed examination of the meaning of *obsequium* in the sources, see Waldstein (1986) 51–68. Treggiari (1969) 69–73 and Watson (1975) 104–8 demonstrate that it cannot be proved that under the Republic *obsequium* was backed by any special patronal rights or powers.

39 (pr.) *Hoc edictum a praetore propositum est honoris, quem liberti patronis habere debent, moderandi gratia. Namque ut Servius scribit, antea soliti fuerunt a libertis durissimas res exigere, scilicet ad remunerandum tam grande beneficium, quod in libertos confertur, cum ex servitute ad civitatem Romanam perducuntur.*

(1) Et quidem primus praetor Rutilius edixit se amplius non daturum patrono quam operarum et societatis actionem, videlicet si hoc pepigisset, ut, nisi ei obsequium praestaret libertus, in societatem admitteretur patronus.

(2) Posteriores praetores certae partis bonorum possessionem pollicebantur: videlicet enim imago societatis induxit eiusdem partis praestationem, ut, quod vivus solebat societatis nomine praestare, id post mortem praestaret.

40 Watson (1967) 231–4; Treggiari (1969) 78–9. Watson, who takes the favourable view that Rutilius' edict was protective of freedmen, wants to date the inheritance restrictions fairly soon afterwards, before freedmen got used to their rights and became defensive about them. Waldstein (1986) 149 ff. also sees the restrictions as part of a recoil against concessions made to freedmen in Rutilius' edict.

41 Masi Doria (1989) arbitrarily interprets *obsequium* as an obligation (which she believes existed) on the freedman to stay with the patron, and suggests that the pact of *societas* was an alternative invented by Rutilius to give the freedman the option, either of staying or of giving the patron a half share in anything he acquired.

42 *D.* 38.1.36; 44.5.1.7.

43 Another symptom of hardening attitudes of the freeborn towards freedmen in this period may be the *lex Aemilia* of 115 BC (*de vir. ill.* 72) on freedmen's suffrage: Treggiari (1969) 47–9.

44 For examples from Delphi and elsewhere, see Hopkins (1978) ch. 3.

45 *D.* 38.1.6; 38.1.9; 12.6.26.12. Cosentini (1948) 125–77 reviews earlier theories on the distinction, which for him is entirely post-classical.

46 *D.* 38.1.18 (Paul), 19 (Gaius), 21 (Javolenus).

47 *D.* 38.1.16 (Paul), 38 (Callistratus).

48 So, I think correctly, Crook (1967) 192; Crook himself has a fine sense of humour.

49 Frier (1980) ch. 2 shows that in the urban rental system of Rome arrears of rent were possible only for the relatively expensive lets, not for the accommodation affordable only by the poorest.

50 Details in Champlin (1991) 131–6, 175–80.

51 Treggiari (1969) 259–64.

52 Zosimus: *ILS* 1949. Will of 'Dasumius': *CIL* VI. 10229 and *FIRA* iii.48; see also Eck (1978) and Champlin (1986). Canto (1991) identifies the testator as L. Licinius Sura.

53 *ILS* 1984: *D. Otacilius Felix fecit sibi et / Otaciliae Hilarae collibertae, / D. Otacilio Hilaro l., / D. Otacilio Eudoxo l.,* < *in consilio manumisso*>, */ Luriae Musae uxori, / ceteris libertis libertabusque meis omnibus posterisque eorum, praeter / quos testamento meo praeteriero.* Otacilia is described as 'fellow freedwoman' of Felix. Hilarus and Eudoxus were probably her sons, born in slavery and subsequently bought and

manumitted by Felix. The words 'manumitted before a tribunal' have been added later in smaller letters; Eudoxus was evidently under the age required by the *lex Aelia Sentia*, so 'good cause' had to be shown for the manumission; Felix specifies this so that there shall be no doubt of Eudoxus' citizen status.

54 Treggiari (1979) 71–2.

55 Bove (1984a); an appendix, pp. 167–74, gives a list with bibliographical details up to *TP* 89. Texts of these and other tablets are most easily accessible in successive volumes of *AE*.

56 The significance of filiation is perhaps ambiguous. What, for example, is to be made of a text such as *AE* 1986.167 (= *TP* 98)? In this list of nine witnesses to the sale by *emptio–venditio* of a slave in AD 38, one has filiation and tribe, one filiation only, and the remaining seven no indication of status at all. We might perhaps conclude that those without any indication of status are freedmen (as, probably, those in *AE* 1987.119; see above), though the nomenclature alone does not reveal whether they are citizens or Junian Latins. The presence or absence of tribal affiliation in the designation of the freeborn witnesses could be linked with the decay of the census and the voting assemblies in this period; mention of tribe soon ceases to be customary. The man named by filiation alone could, theoretically, be freeborn but not citizen. He could, for example, be the son of a Junian Latin freedman who had not achieved citizenship; nevertheless he could engage in transactions such as *emptio–venditio*. However, the buyer would acquire full Quiritary ownership, that is, ownership with full legal title (Buckland (1966) 186 ff.), only by going through the further procedure of *mancipatio*, witnesses to which at that time had to be Roman citizens. Gaius 1.119 stresses that *mancipatio* is an institution peculiar to Roman citizens; Ulp. *Reg.* 19.3 and 20.8, according to which Junian Latins also could be witnesses, must reflect a later development. Since it is unlikely that the buyer would go to the trouble of assembling a separate group of citizen witnesses to that procedure, we ought perhaps to suppose all nine witnesses in this text to be Roman citizens.

57 For example, the fragmentary album of *Augustales* from Herculaneum (*AE* 1978.119, discussed above), which contains a dozen or so names known from wax tablets, *tabulae ceratae*, from the area, lists two C. Petronii, S . . . and Stephanus. C. Petronius Stephanus is mentioned in a number of tablets from Herculaneum as the former owner of the mother of Petronia Justa, the protagonist in a well-known suit concerning status (*Tab. Herc.* 13–30). In one tablet found with the dossier (30), a fragment of a triptych with a list of ten names, the name appears twice, once with the addition *pater*, 'father'.

58 *TP* 21.22, 25: *AE* 1984.208, 233.

59 References in Buckland (1908) 636–40; see also Michel (1962) 157–67. The rules for compelling the fiduciary owners to grant freedom were first formulated in a rescript of Marcus Aurelius and Verus (*D.* 40.1.4 pr.).

60 Buckland (1908) 640. He cannot require *operae*, nor can he sue the freed slave for ingratitude (under the *actio* established by the *lex Aelia*

Sentia; see below); and he has rights of intestate inheritance, but cannot claim contrary to a will. However, he is protected against prosecution by the freedman.

61 The prosecution and conviction in 54 BC of Gabinius Antiochus (Cic. *Att.* 4.18.4) under the *lex Papia* of 65 BC against foreigners falsely presenting themselves as Roman citizens (*ne quis peregrinus se pro cive gereret*) is puzzling. If Gabinius was a properly manumitted freedman, he was a citizen; if not, at that period, he was not a *peregrinus* but still a slave, whose *de facto* liberty was, however, protected by the praetor. Possibly the law included a clause covering such slaves.

62 Senators: Dio 54.16, 56.7.2; see also *D.* 23.2.23 and 44; Ulp. *Reg.* 13.1. Adulteresses: Ulp. *Reg.* 13.2; *D.* 23.2.43.13.

63 Gaius 1.13-21, 25-6, 36-41.

64 Gaius 1.22-4, 28-35; 3.56. On the *lex*, and its chronological relationship to the *lex Aelia Sentia*, see Balestri Fumagalli (1985), Gardner (1991), spec. n. 23.

65 The reasons why, nevertheless, the law was drafted so as to apply to all testamentary manumissions are discussed in Gardner (1991) 37 ff.

66 Crook (1967) 94 defined *officium* as 'mutual serviceableness between status equals', but it is also used of deferential and obliging behaviour by someone lower in social standing to someone higher (e.g. Fronto *ad Verum* 2.7); see also Saller (1982) index s.v.

67 Buckland (1908) 422-7; de Francisci (1926) 297-303; Cosentini (1948) 206-12. Though de Francisci and also Treggiari (1969) 74 take Tac. *Ann.* 13.26 as evidence for the penalty originally imposed, this is scarcely sufficient on its own. As Manning (1986) points out, the theoretical discussion in the third book of Seneca's *de beneficiis* of the undesirability of an action for 'ingratitude' in general (not just on the part of freedmen) may contain echoes of a continuing debate on the best means of regulating the behaviour of ex-slaves.

68 Kunkel (1973) 64, 69 ff.

69 It is not even clear that Claudius' judgment arose from an *actio* under this law. The perceived connection arises from the wording of Suetonius' reference to the incident (*Claud.* 25): *ingratos et de quibus patroni quererentur revocavit in servitutem advocatisque eorum negavit se adversus libertos ipsorum ius dicturum.* ('He re-enslaved freedmen who were ungrateful and about whom their patrons complained, and told their advocates that he would not entertain a suit against their (i.e. the advocates') freedmen').

70 *D.* 37.14.19 (Paul); 37.15.11 (Papinian).

71 *Iniuria*: Buckland (1966) 589-94; Frier (1989) 177-200, with bibliography at 259-60.

72 Tacitus' allusion (*Ann.* 13.26) to taking legal action *aequo iure* is unspecific and in a tendentious context (besides relating to a rather later period, AD 56), and so does not help in determining the extent and nature of the use of legal process by patrons against freedmen.

73 As the next sentence shows, the words that follow here in the text, *cum in manu nostra sint*, cannot be correct. Editors either omit the phrase, or insert *non*. They are missing from *Inst.* 4.4.2, where, how-

ever, the remark *id enim magis praevaluit* indicates that the inclusion of wives was held to arise from legal interpretation, which would be unnecessary of wives in *manus*.

74 *Warning*: the Penguin Classics translation of this text by Kolbert (1979) 167 produces nonsense by mistranslating *conlibertus* as 'a freedman' and *cessaret* (*sic*) as 'should be granted'. The relevant sentence reads: *si autem conliberto nupta esset, diceremus omnino iniuriarum marito adversus patronum cessare actionem, et ita multi sentiunt.*

75 Buckland (1908) 423–4.

76 De Francisci (1926) 308 convincingly argues that, in the context, *in potestate patronorum redigi* does not mean re-enslavement to the former owner. The statement of Buckland (1908) 424 that Severus in AD 205 treats the power of re-enslavement as existing is not supported by the text he cites (*CJ* 3.6.2), which has to do with someone *suis nummis emptus* (see text above), and merely says that the intended fiduciary manumitter cannot either make him his slave, or require *operae* from him (sc. as a condition of manumission). De Francisci's interpretation of subsequent texts, particularly *CJ* 6.3.12 (Diocletian), is more detailed and on the whole more careful than that of Buckland (1908) 424.

77 *CJ* 6.7.2. *Si quadam iactantia aut contumacia cervices adversus eum erexerit aut levis offensae contraxerit culpam* ('If he shall have lifted up his neck against [his patron] with a certain vaingloriousness or stubbornness, or shall have incurred the fault of a slight offence'). Those who had originally been manumitted before the imperial *concilium*, Constantine says, may recover their liberty once they have shown themselves duly penitent, but only if their patrons support the request.

78 Buckland (1966) 589 and references at nn. 10, 11.

79 Buckland (1966) 88; Watson (1967) 40.

3 DEPENDENCE: THE ADULT CHILD

1 According to Gaius *Inst.* 1.95, those who become citizens, along with their children, by Latin right, that is, after completion of a magisterial office in their local community, automatically (in contrast to other peregrines, who require a special imperial grant) acquire *potestas* – which might seem to imply that they did not have it before. However, a point already noted by Sherwin-White (1973) 378–9, and made quite clear by the recent addition to the text of the Flavian municipal law with the publication of the copy from Irni in Spain (Gonzalez 1986), is that among the *municipes* of some communities with Latin rights there did exist the institution of *patria potestas*, as well as *manus*, *mancipium*, *tutela* and patronal rights; for *potestas*, see especially clauses 21, 22 and 86. It is commonly assumed that under the empire the *municipes* in these communities who were not Roman citizens were Latins. On the other hand, Millar (1977) 630–5 argued strongly that there was no evidence for the existence of communities of freeborn provincial Latins in the imperial period, or of a general category of *Latini coloniarii*; this left Junian Latins as the only known category. According to Gonzalez (1986) 148, from the new evidence of the Irni

text 'it becomes clearer than ever that it was a mistake to argue that there was no such thing as a *civis Latinus*, naturally by virtue of his membership of a community of Latin rights'. However, neither his arguments nor those of Humbert (1981), to whom he refers, seem to me to be conclusive. In support of Millar's view, see now Fear (1990).

2 Saller (1986; 1987); Saller estimates that as few as 20 per cent of fathers (25 per cent among aristocrats) were still alive to see their sons married, and fewer than 50 per cent outside the aristocracy saw their daughters married. These conclusions are dependent upon extrapolation from those funerary inscriptions which happen to mention age at death, and in which the relationship of the commemorator (especially parent or spouse) to the deceased is stated or can be deduced. However, recent unpublished work by Hanne Sigismund Nielsen on *CIL* VI shows the inadequacy of a model which excludes inscriptions which mention no term of relationship (43 per cent of her sample) or do not name a dedicator (40 per cent).

3 Dio 54.16.7; *D.* 23.1.9; Gaius 1.196.

4 For the former view, see Daube (1969) 75–91; for the latter, Watson (1977) 23–30.

5 Summary, and references, in Buckland (1966) 103–4; see also Rabello (1979).

6 Cicero's acquiescence (*ad Fam.* 8.6.2; *ad Att.* 6.6.1) in the choice of a third husband made by his daughter, along with her mother, may be contrasted with Cato Minor's rejection of the marital offers made on behalf of himself and his son by Pompey, which were welcomed by Cato's womenfolk (Plutarch, *Cato Min.* 30; *Pompey* 44).

7 *D.* 23.2.19. To allow wilful paternal opposition would not have assisted the operation of Augustan legislation to encourage marriage. M. Aurelius and divorce: Paul *Sent.* 5.6.15.

8 Rabello (1979) 14 ff.; Voci (1980) 50–66; Harris (1986).

9 Voci (1980) 51–2, 74–5. Voci suggests that, since the Twelve Tables contained a clause (4.1) allowing the killing of a child born deformed (Cic. *de leg.* 3.8.19), this text represents a later interpretation of the implication that the killing required some justification. He points out that Romulus was credited with having introduced some restrictions on the right of killing the newborn (Dion. Hal. 2.15).

10 'Suppose the head of the family was ninety, his two sons seventy-five and seventy, their sons beteen sixty and fifty-five, the sons of these in their forties and thirties and the great-grandsons in their twenties', Daube (1969) 75.

11 Young Marcus wanted to go to Spain to serve with Caesar (the Munda campaign); in the end, he did as his father wished and went to Athens to study.

12 *ad Att.* 14.16.4, 17.5; 15.15.4, 17.1, 20.4; 16.1.5.

13 *ad Att.* 16.1.5 (*fin.*), with 15.29.2.

14 See especially *D.* 14 and 15; Kirschenbaum (1987) ch. 2; Watson (1987) ch. 6.

15 Suetonius *Vesp.* 11; *D.* 14.6.

16 For these, besides Kirschenbaum (1987) (chs 2–3) and Watson (n. 14

above), see Buckland (1966) 533–6 and his detailed legal exposition, (1908) 207–49.

17 *D.* 15.1.46 (Paul) *qui peculii administrationem concedit, videtur permittere generaliter, quod et specialiter permissurus est* ('Someone who authorises administration of the *peculium* appears to give permission in general, for what he is also going to permit in an individual instance'). Compare *D.* 6.4.1 (Ulpian *septimo ad edictum*). Kirschenbaum (1987) 40–3 lists a range of transactions covered by administration of a *peculium* and attested in legal texts; these would give the son a good deal of practical independence.

18 Buckland (1966) 520 ff. and 554 ff. on assignment or transfer of obligation; see also Crook (1967) 241–3.

19 Buckland (1966) 169 ff.

20 Though a public slave of the Puteoli town treasury acknowledges a loan in *TP* 26 (= *AE* 1973.147).

21 *TP* 7 (= *AE* 1973.147, cf. 1984.239) as re-edited by Wolf and Crook (1989) no. 3.

22 Discussed in several recent publications; see especially Bove 1984 (a and b) and Serrao (1984).

23 *TP* 15 (= *AE* 1972.86); Wolf and Crook (1989) no. 1.

24 *TP* 16 (= *AE* 1972.87); Wolf and Crook (1989) no. 2.

25 On landlords' liabilities, see Frier (1980).

26 *Peculium castrense*: Buckland (1966) 280–1. For later extensions, see *CJ* 12.30.1; 1.51.7; 2.7.4; 1.3.33(34); 12.16.5 pr.; 3.28.37.1.

27 Daube (1969) 88–90; Veyne (1987) 29–30. Thomas (1981) is on the whole more cautious, but see 688–9 and 715.

28 Details and numerous references are conveniently assembled in Rice Holmes (1928) I.73–4. The advantage allegedly taken of the proscriptions by Oppianicus, Catiline and the relatives of Roscius of Ameria was aimed not at contriving the death of a *pater*, but at removing relatives who were rivals to inheritance from a third party. It should be noted also that the law on 'parricide', the *lex Pompeia* (*D.* 48.9.1), actually covered crimes not only against fathers but against *parentes* generally, a whole range of relatives, both direct and collateral. Although the date of this law is unknown, Cloud (1971) 57 ff. suggests 55 or 52 rather than 70 BC, and Thomas (1981) 713 considers it at least plausible that some of the excesses of the triumviral period may have prompted its passage.

29 *Tormenta quaestionum poenasque parricidarum repraesentabat exigebatque coram.* The imperfect tenses are perhaps significant, though here, as elsewhere (Chapter 2, n. 69 above), Suetonius may be generalising on the basis of one incident. He also relates that Vitellius was suspected of killing his own son (whom he had already emancipated), alleging attempted parricide (Suet. *Vit.* 6), but clearly does not expect Vitellius' accusation to be believed.

30 *Cum inter ceteras sceleris causas Macedo, quas illi natura administrabat, etiam aes alienum adhibuisset, et saepe materiam peccandi malis moribus praestaret, qui pecuniam, ne quid amplius diceretur, incertis*

nominibus crederet: placere, ne cui, qui filio familias mutuam pecuniam dedisset, etiam post mortem parentis eius, cuius in potestate fuisset, actio petitioque daretur, ut scirent, qui pessimo exemplo faenerarent, nullius posse filii familias bonum nomen expectata patris morte fieri.

The translation of the Watson–Kruger–Mommsen edition of the *Digest* also misrepresents Macedo as a *filiusfamilias*: 'Whereas Macedo's borrowings gave him an added incentive to commit a crime to which he was naturally predisposed and whereas those who lend money on terms which are dubious to say the least, often provide evil men with the means of wrongdoing'. The crucial words are *aes alienum*, a phrase which means literally '(bronze) money belonging to another', and is admittedly usually used with reference to the person who has it (i.e. the debtor). In the text, however, *aes alienum adhibuisset* is explained as *materiam peccandi praestaret* – *materiam peccandi* being virtually a synonym for *causa sceleris*. The 'persons of evil disposition' to whom Macedo supplies this 'cause of wrongdoing' are the borrowers; the Watson–Kruger–Mommsen version identifies them as the money-lenders, by dint of translating *crederent* instead of the *crederet* of the text. 'Doubtful terms' for *incertis nominibus* has perhaps some support in Quint. 11.38: *tibi, ut ais, certis nominibus grandem pecuniam debuit* ('he owed you a large sum on good security'); my translation 'unreliable debtors', on the other hand, may be compared with Cic. *ad fam.* 5.6.2, *bonum nomen existimer* ('I may be considered a good payer').

31 The origins and intention of the procedure are uncertain. Watson (1975) 118–19 plausibly suggests that the rule of the Twelve Tables (4.2b), 'If a father sells his son three times, let the son be free of his father', originally concerned *nexum*, the practice by which a father put his son temporarily into bondage to another person as security for a debt (see Chapter 2 above, at n. 12). The Twelve Tables restricted the number of times this was permissible, to curtail what was felt to be an indignity for a freeborn son. An early interpretation of the rule, possibly by the pontiffs (Watson (1977) 24 and nn. 3–5), introduced its use as a general means of ending *potestas*.

32 *D.* 37.6 and 7; Schulz (1951) 229–33; Buckland (1966) 324–6. For additional examples, see *CJ* 6.20. Emancipated children claiming *bonorum possessio*, without mention of *collatio*: *CJ* 4.5.5, 6.14.1, 6.19.1, 6.19.4, 6.57.2 (claims on a mother's estate), 6.59.1.

33 There are indications in the *Digest* that attempts were made to exploit emancipation to enable a woman's dowry to remain with her husband and children at her death: *D.* 24.2.5; 24.3.59; Gardner (1986) 106. Lawyers supported the interests of her *pater*.

34 There are well-known literary examples, e.g. Pliny *Ep.* 4.2, 8.18; Suet. *Vit.* 6; and numerous examples in legal sources: *D.* 5.3.58; 26.5.21.1; 28.5.47; 28.7.18.1; 29.4.27.1; 29.7.6 pr.; 32.50 pr.; 35.1.70, 77 pr.; 37.4.16; 45.1.107; *CJ* 3.28.25; 6.42.15; 6.25.3; 8.54.5, and by implication also 2.20(21).5; 5.16.16. With the unhappy marital, or ex-marital, situations apparently underlying many of these testamentary conditions in

the wills of mothers, may be contrasted the more harmonious relationship between a certain Julius Phoebus and his first wife, as reported by Paul in the early 3rd century AD (*D.* 36.1.83); that is, well before the provision of Constantine reported in the text above. Phoebus in his will left his two children by his first wife, and another, still a minor, by his second wife, as equal heirs. He was careful to specify that his own testamentary requests to the older children were not to be held to apply to anything received from their mother or grandparents. Phoebus' first wife appears to have left some property by will to her children, but to have been quite content that it should, while he was still alive, belong to their *pater*. His will showed that her trust was justified.

35 Gardner (1986) 198–200, (1987) 52–4. All fathers had to do was refuse the condition of emancipation; the will was then broken and the children, still in power, had first claim as heirs on the intestate estate; otherwise, if the mother had nominated substitute heirs, the estate would pass to someone else.

36 Arjava (forthcoming). His original description was 'partial emancipation', but, regarding this as an unhappy choice of words, he subsequently modified it to the more appropriate phrase in the text above. I am grateful to Dr Arjava for allowing me to see portions of his work in progress.

37 This was subsequently extended by later emperors to bequests from more distant ascendants (*C.Th.* 8.18.7). In AD 426, Theodosius and Valentinian intervened on behalf of fathers whose sons had been emancipated before their mothers' death. Since this meant that the father lost all benefit from the mother's property, he was to be assigned the usufruct of a share of the property, proportional to the number of his sons. The point about waiting until the children reached majority would presumably be that then they could conduct their own legal business; otherwise, the *parens manumissor* would merely be complicating the administration of what was in the first place his own property.

38 *D.* 25.3.5; see also *CJ* 5.25.

39 e.g. *CJ* 3.29.2; 4.13.1; 4.26.8(9); 6.46.5; 8.53(54).11; 10.62(60).3.

40 See n. 34 above; among the rescripts cited there, a condition of emancipation in a mother's will, or as a condition of gift from a mother, is mentioned in *CJ* 3.28.25, 6.25.3 (AD 216) and 8.54(55).5 and implied in 2.20(21).5, 5.16.16, and 8.55 (56).3. Possibly one should add also *CJ* 5.62.19, in which a man asks to be released from being *tutor* to his daughter, because of the possibility of litigation with her mother.

41 *CJ* 7.71.3, 10.52(51).4, and perhaps 4.13.2. Care had to be taken, however, since forming a separate *familia* could actually create a liability to *munera*: 10.50(49).2, 10.62(60).3.

42 And 'parricide' in the terms of the *lex Pompeia*, could in fact involve members of other *familiae*.

43 Half the amount granted a patron: Gaius 4.46.

44 Crook (1967) 206–11 and (less entertainingly) Nicholas (1969) 167–71. Watson (1977) 15–17 gets very cross with the 'irrationality and . . . absence of careful consideration of the needs of logical development' of the Romans for creating a separate type of contract when, he says,

mandatum would have done the job perfectly well. Gaius 3.90 does not bother to mention *depositum* or *commodatum* under real contracts; *D.* 13.6 and 16.3 cover a multitude of contingencies, for which see also Buckland (1966) 467–73.

45 *D.* 43.24; Buckland (1966) 731; Crook (1967) 167; Nicholas (1969) 108–10.

46 Murecine: Crook (1978), Bove (1979). Petronia Justa: Arangio Ruiz (1948; 1959).

47 A *stipulatio* was a promissory agreement, made verbally, which created a contractual obligation which could be pursued at law (Gaius 3.92–3).

48 *TP* 18 (= *AE* 1973.138); Wolf and Crook (1989) no. 5. Eunus' spelling is very poor:

> C. Novius Eunus scrips <s> i me debere Hesuco C. Cessaris Augusti Germanic(o) ser(vo) Eueniano stertertios mil(l)e ducentos qui(n)quaginta nummos reliquos ratione om <i> ni putata quos ab eo mut(u)os accepi quem sum(m)a(m) iuratus promis <s> i me aut ipsi Hesuco aut C. Sulpicio Fausto red(di)turum K(alendis) No(v)embribus primis . . . quotsi ea die non solvero me non <t> solum peiurio teneri set etiam peone (for poenae) nomine in d(i)e si(n)gulos sestertios vigienos nummo obligatum iri.

49 Macqueron (1984).

50 For a general outline, with some examples from the Republican period, see Shatzman (1975) 75–9, 136–8, together with much detail under individual entries in his catalogue. Hallett (1984) and Dixon (1988) have both drawn attention to the influence that mothers and other female relatives (*sui iuris*) might exercise. Pliny's letters also provide some evidence of financial accommodation between friends, e.g. 2.4, 3.11, 6.32, 7.11, 7.14.

51 For a selection of relevant recent bibliography, see Garnsey and Saller (1987) 48 n. 7.

52 And possibly also daughters, though they would have been under some inconvenience because of the restriction on their ability to make contracts (see excursus at end of chapter).

53 These aspects of the emperor's work are discussed in detail in Millar (1977) chs. 5 and 8, to which should be added the remarks in Millar (1990).

54 For instance, this is true also of the *tutela* of women, which was not abolished until AD 410 (see excursus). Dixon (1984) has demonstrated how, the original purpose of the institution having been obscured by development in practice, jurists in later classical law resorted to alternative explanations (in terms of women's supposed weakness and need for protection) to explain its retention. However, since her account rather underestimates the power that still resided in magisterial discretion to refuse women's requests for overruling of tutorial decisions, I would not agree that the retention of *tutela* represents simply the Romans' 'reluctance to tamper with venerable institutions'. *Tutela*, like *patria potestas*, still had powerful teeth, which need not be constantly

in use but could be used at need. See further on *tutela* in the following chapter.

55 *D*. 1.6.9.1: *filius familias in publicis causis loco patri familias habetur, veluti ut magistratum gerat, ut tutor detur.* Ulpian remarks (*D*. 50.4.2): 'With regard to offices (*honores*), even a man in his father's power is considered to have a son in his power.' Presumably he has in mind the accelerated promotion to office which Augustan legislation on marriage accorded to fathers of legitimate children.

56 See Jones (1964) 749; he points out (1309 n. 87) that even these lists are not quite exhaustive. On the history of the system, and the stresses that developed from the conflicting demands of the imperial government and the local communities, Millar (1983) is fundamental.

57 *D*. 50.2.1; 50.4.3.5. Ulpian remarks (*D*. 50.4.3.3) that women were prevented by their very sex from participating in *munera* involving corporal activity (they were excluded from the personal *munus* of *tutela* except, in late law and under certain conditions, that of their own children); however, Diocletian and Maximian said that they were liable for patrimonial *munera* (*CJ* 10.42(41).9). The studies by van Bremen (1983) and Rogers (1992) document much activity of benefaction by women in the Greek provinces of the Roman empire, even with some magisterial titles, though, as van Bremen's account makes clear, the offices themselves were essentially titular, being really only liturgical. Roman law did not allow women to hold public office. Women still *filiaefamilias* were perhaps less likely to be in a financial position to undertake *munera*.

58 Usually, that is – though Antoninus Pius, against most legal opinion, thought a son might appropriately be appointed *curator* for his insane father (*D*. 26.5.12.1; 27.10.1.1).

59 Cicero, *de inv*. 2.52, uses the same incident, without comment on the legal and personal issues involved, to illustrate methods of arguing a case that turns on the definition of an action. The father, he says, was charged with *maiestas* for interfering with tribunician authority. He can deny the charge, on the plea 'I used the *potestas* I had over my son'. This can be countered, he says, with 'One who uses *patria potestas*, which is a private authority, to lessen *tribunicia potestas*, which is a power of the people, does commit *maiestas*.' Consistency is not always to be expected, however, from an author making a moral point. For instance, Dionysius of Halicarnassus 2.26.4–5 cites this story (using plurals, and without names) as an example of the power Romulus the lawgiver gave fathers over sons, contrasting the allegedly beneficial effects of such severity with the mildness of the laws of early Greek lawgivers: 'and accordingly among the Greeks many unseemly deeds are committed by children against their parents'. At 6.89.3, however, he makes much of the religious import of tribunician sanctity and the stern sanctions imposed by the Romans upon its violators. See also n. 62 below.

60 Both versions are in Livy (2.41), and also in Dionysius of Halicarnassus (8.79 ff.), who has the senate condemn him, but on the denunciation of his father, who then executes his punishment privately. Dionysius

is sceptical, however, about the father's involvement, pointing out that had Cassius' father been alive, the destruction of Cassius' house, and confiscation of his property, could not have happened, since a son in power could not own such things. Livy carefully uses *peculium* in the version involving the father, but prefers the story that he was accused by the quaestors and condemned by the people – typically, giving no reason for his preference.

61 A variation in the theme is the story in which a father in office either uses his official authority, or his paternal, in despite of *pietas* (the natural affection he might be expected to feel towards his offspring), to maintain the security or discipline of the state. The best-known examples are Junius Brutus – the story is told by numerous ancient authors – expeller of the last Roman king, putting to death his own sons who conspired to restore the monarchy; and another Manlius Torquatus, consul in 340 BC, who put to death his son after a foray by the latter against the enemy which, though successful, had been made in breach of orders (Livy 8.7).

Valerius Maximus uses the story of Manlius several times. In 2.7.6 it is an example of military discipline: Manlius acted 'thinking it better that a father be wanting a brave son than the fatherland military discipline'. In 5.8.3 (*fin.*) it demonstrates paternal severity, whose memory is a model to the later Manlius (see text above). In 6.9.1 it is one of the correctly motivated and/or public-spirited actions by which Manlius senior redeemed himself after a youth distinguished only by the dullness and stupidity which made his father send him to the countryside. It makes its most curious appearance under the heading 'On anger and hate' (9.3.4); Valerius says that while the older generation gave Manlius senior a joyful reception on his victorious return to Rome, the younger ones boycotted the welcome because of his excessively harsh punishment of his son. 'I do not defend their behaviour,' says Valerius, 'I merely indicate the strength of anger, which can divide the generations and the emotions within a single state.'

62 Mitchell (1990) 215. Mitchell thinks that the tribunician sacrosanctity indicates that tribunes were freed from *patria potestas*, like Vestals and certain priests, although he admits that, unlike these latter, they did not form legally separate households. He is anxious to deny any real authority to *patria potestas*, arguing elsewhere (250 ff.) that the declaration in the census of children in *potestas* was merely a record of their hereditary succession rights. He describes *patria potestas* as being 'unreliable and nearly unworkable as a concept' with 'little relevance to public or private life', notions the falsity of which the foregoing pages have, I hope, amply demonstrated.

63 e.g. Cicero, *de rep.* 2.39–40; Livy 1.42–3.

64 For example, as mentioned above, to protect the interest of *sui heredes* in at least a portion of their patrimonial inheritance. However, an important point is that the rights of inheritance between mothers and children established by the *senatusconsultum Orphitianum* are not symmetrical; convergence upon the children of both paternal and maternal property is encouraged, while the possibility of the patrimony passing

through children to mother and being dispersed is limited (see Gardner (1986) 196–200).

65 For policing and maintenance of public order, at least in the larger urban centres, see Stambaugh (1988) 124–7 and references there.

66 This is borne out by the nature of the intervention by the state in the lives of certain categories of productive citizens in the late Empire. The relationship was essentially one-sided. Individuals' freedom of movement, both physically (i.e. in change of location) and to change status or occupation, was placed under tight regulation, to facilitate the fulfilment of the demands made by the state. The internal structure of the family and its property rights were, however, scarcely touched. See Jones (1964) chs 20, 21; (1974) chs 14, 18 and 21.

4 GENDER: THE INDEPENDENT WOMAN

1 *D.* 22.6.9 (Paul), 49.14.2 (Callistratus); van Warmelo (1954), spec. pp. 26–7. Also regarded, at least in later law, as in need of special indulgence were the young (*adulescentes*), peasants and soldiers (the two last because, respectively, of their *rusticitas* and *simplicitas*). Their sex alone, however, did not suffice to excuse women in all instances (Warmelo, ibid.).

2 *D.* 50.17.2.

3 This is to be understood in a broader sense than in Nicolet (1980) 334–41. He rightly draws attention to the intimate involvement of criminal justice in the political in-fighting of the late Republic. However, he exaggerates in saying (p. 336), 'criminal justice was largely a political matter and affected a small number of men in public life, not the man in the street in his ordinary affairs'. Cicero's works provide evidence to the contrary.

4 On *infamia*, see Greenidge (1894), Pommeray (1937), Kaser (1956), d'Ors (1984) and Chapter 5 below.

5 The consequences included inability both to appoint a representative for oneself in lawsuits and to act as a representative for others; see further Chapter 5 below.

6 Bankers: *D.* 2.13,12 (Callistratus). *Sctum Velleianum*: *D.* 16.1; Crook (1986); Gardner (1986) 75–6, 234–5.

7 This is one of four meanings of *familia* (the other three are: property unit; group of persons under the *potestas* of one person; household complement of slaves) given by Ulpian (*D.* 50.16.195, *xlvi ad edictum*). He gives both a wider and a narrower sense, the narrower being the agnates, i.e. all those who *had* been in the *potestas* of one person, the wider spanning an indefinite number of generations, 'those deriving from the same ultimate ancestor (as, for example, we talk of the Julian family), as though from some source of memory'.

8 Ulpian: *mulier autem familiae suae et caput et finis est* (*D.* 50.16.195.5).

9 *D.* 50.17.2 (*libro primo ad Sabinum*): *feminae ab omnibus officiis civilibus vel publicis remotae sunt et ideo nec iudices esse possunt nec magistratum gerere nec postulare nec pro alio intervenire nec procuratores existere. Item impubes omnibus officiis civilibus debet abstinere.* 'Ought'

in the last sentence may indicate that the erosion of the principle that minors were excluded from public offices and responsibilities had already made some progress (see Wiedemann 1989, ch. 4).

10 *Virile officium*: *D.* 26.1.16 (Gaius), *CJ* 2.12.18 (Diocletian and Maximian, AD 294); *munus masculorum*: *D.* 26.1.18 (Neratius); *virile munus*: *CJ* 5.35.3 (Alexander, AD 224). Of the two imperial responses, Alexander's adds the conventional excuse of women's weakness ('such an undertaking is beyond a sex of female weakness', *femineae infirmitatis*), while Diocletian alludes to it ('acknowledged to be beyond the female sex').

11 Gardner (1986) 147–52.

12 Beaucamp (1976) has argued strongly, against Solazzi (1930), that expressions such as *infirmitas sexus* in the jurists were classical and not, as Solazzi thought, Byzantine interpolations. She believes she detects a shift in attitude, from the 3rd-century use of *infirmitas* to justify the exclusion of women from certain activities, to the Justinianic use of the idea of *fragilitas* as a justification for what were represented as protective measures towards women. However, although ideas of feminine weakness and unreliability seem to be common currency among Roman (male) authors before the end of the Republic – see Schulz (1951) 181–4 on *tutela*, with the critique of Dixon (1984) – they do not, as noted in the text above, in themselves serve to explain the origin of these restrictions on women.

13 On *tutela* and its historical development, see Gardner (1986) 14–22, where, however, the basic purpose of the institution is insufficiently clearly brought out.

14 Dixon (1984) 343, with references at n. 4. Unfortunately, the completion of her sentence misrepresents both the legal situation, and legal historians' perception of it, for she continues, 'and was designed to safeguard *male rights* (my italics) rather than to protect women'. The rights protected were originally those of the nearest agnates, who, as Roman legal historians were well aware, included the sisters as well as brothers of the deceased who were still within the *familia*. It could even happen that the nearest agnate for the purpose of inheritance was a woman (e.g. the deceased's sister), though the *tutela* of his children devolved upon another relative, since it had to be fulfilled by a man: *D.* 26.4.1.1.

15 *C.Th.* 4.20.1 (AD 379), where the grounds on which debtors, both private and those owing the *fiscus*, may be excused are *dilapidatio* of their property in consequence of robbery, shipwreck, fire or some other major calamity.

16 See Dixon (1984) 351 ff. Dixon, however (pp. 343, 351), is not prepared to regard it as evidence for the general estimation of feminine capability among Cicero's contemporaries.

17 Recounted in detail in Evans (1991) 11–13 and, given the general lateness, and anecdotal and largely rhetorical nature of the sources, perhaps taken too literally as factual accounts of what was common and accepted in the behaviour and outlook of men in early Rome. Pliny *NH* 124.89 claims Fabius Pictor (end of 3rd century BC) as a source for his anecdote about a matron allegedly starved to death by her kin for having broken

into the chest containing the keys to the wine cellar; but Egnatius Mecenius, who is said to have put his wife to death for drinking wine, he represents as contemporary with Romulus. This story is also told by Valerius Maximus (6.3.9), who, despite his own moralising on the evils to which immoderate drinking by women can lead, lists this under examples of severity, but 'for a lesser cause by far' than others already cited. Dionysius of Halicarnassus' 'law of Romulus' (2.25.6), listing drinking among the causes for which a wife *in manu* could be put to death, is historical fiction. In Aulus Gellius 10.23, the elder Cato (in a speech on dowries) says that a divorcing husband could 'fine' his wife for wine-drinking (not 'condemn', as in Kunkel (1966) 233–41, cited by Evans p. 39. n. 42) – an obvious reference to the action *de moribus* (Gardner (1986) 89–90). Fabius Pictor and Cato take us a long way from the historical origin of *tutela*.

18 *Lessum*, a word whose meaning was lost long before Cicero's day. Some of the old interpreters (*veteres interpretes*), Cicero tells us, thought it might mean some kind of mourning garment. Cicero prefers Lucius Aelius' suggestion 'sorrowful wailing', since this is forbidden in a law of Solon (he assumes that Solon's laws were the model for the Twelve Tables).

19 Contrast the clear appreciation of Paul that different categories of people may be liable to the same exclusion for different reasons (*D.* 5.1.12.2, quoted in my main text). Women were also, as remarked above, liable to many of the legal disabilities imposed upon those declared, for criminal or other moral shortcomings, *infames*. The praetor's edict, according to Ulpian (*D.* 3.1.1.5), specified three *distinct* grounds on which persons might be forbidden to bring suit on behalf of others: sex, physical handicap and moral turpitude; cf. also *D.* 49.14.18 (Marcianus).

20 Even under the Twelve Tables, in the absence of other procedures a wife automatically came into *manus* after a year had elapsed by 'use' (*usus*), unless active steps were taken to arrange for her to be absent from the matrimonial home for three days. This latter device presumably reflects a later introduction, rather than a primitive institution. The other two methods of entry into *manus*, by *confarreatio* and *coemptio*, appear normally to have been undertaken at the time of entry into marriage, pre-empting the operation of *usus*: Gardner (1986) 11–14; Treggiari (1991) 16–21, 33–4. Treggiari (p. 33) raises the theoretical possibility that *usus* itself might be an innovation, but with the mistaken inference that previously use of *confarreatio/coemptio* was not universal: 'the creation of *manus* by *usus* (which might logically have grown out of *coemptio*) could be much later than the type of marriage in which the wife was never intended to come into *manus*.' Rather, *usus* developed as an additional (but delayed-action) means of bringing a wife into *manus*, the previous situation surely being that all marriages were accompanied as a matter of course either by *confarreatio* (the patrician method) or *coemptio* (the plebeian?). Transferring responsibility for a wife to the family into which she married was obviously

desirable in the relatively insecure conditions of primitive society, before the development of effective procedures for obtaining justice.

21 According to Gaius 2.101, 'Originally there were two kinds of wills: for they used to make them either in the *comitia calata*, an assembly held twice a year for the purpose of making wills, or *in procinctu*, that is, when they were taking arms for battle.' Since women played no part either in the political assemblies or in the armed forces, neither method, obviously, was available to them; however, the third kind of will, added later according to Gaius, was the will *per aes et libram* (ancestor of the historical Roman will), which took the form of a notional sale.

22 Of course, it would have been possible in theory for a woman simply to enter any marriage of her choice (and *manus*) without constituting a dowry; her whole property would then automatically be absorbed in that of the husband. It is hard to believe, however, that Roman male society in general ever encouraged such a practice, since it would not be in their long-term interests either financially or indeed socially, since it would forfeit them the power to control the manufacture of social alliances in the interest of their kin-group.

23 Buckland (1966) 147–8; Evans (1991) 28–9.

24 Champlin remarks (1991: 49) that 'for women, even more than for men, inheritance must have been the major means of acquiring property'. This is not necessarily true, however, of upper-class women in the late Republic and the empire, nor of urban women owning or operating businesses.

25 The epigraphic and legal evidence does not permit confident assertion of statistics: Frier (1982); Gardner (1986) 38–40; Shaw (1987); Treggiari (1991) 398–403. Wives, married with *manus*, predeceasing their husbands could not testate either.

26 Champlin (1991) 114–25 discusses the evidence for bequests to daughters and wives.

27 Livy 39.19.5; see also Watson (1971) 20 n. 1.

28 Thomas (1980); Treggiari (1991) 107–19 is mainly concerned with the imperial period, and relationships through both males and females (*adfinitates*).

29 Adoption was also used in classical Athens, where a will bequeathing an entire estate could be made only if a man had no natural sons (MacDowell (1978) 99–101).

30 See references in n. 6 above.

31 *quod ad fideiussiones et mutui dationes pro aliis, quibus intercesserint feminae, pertinet, tametsi ante videtur ita ius dictum esse, ne eo nomine ab his petitio neve in eas actio detur, cum eas virilibus officiis fungi et eius generis obligationibus obstringi non sit aequum, arbitrari senatum recte atque ordine facturos ad quos de ea re in iure aditum erit, si dederint operam, ut in ea re senatus voluntas servetur.*

32 Buckland (1966) 169–72, 721–2; Watson (1971) 42.

33 *D.* 2.13.12 (Callistratus); banking is, we are told, *opera virilis*, men's work.

34 Compare also *TP* 27 (= *AE* 1973.148 (1984.238)), with the explanation of Macqueron (1984) 195–6. *A. [Cas]tric[ius Onesimus] scripsi me pr[o]-*

m[is]isse C. Sulpici[o Fa]usto quanta pecunia ex auctione P. Servili Narcissi in stipulatum meum meorumque veniet venerit diducto mercede ('I Aulus Castricius Onesimus have written that I have promised to pay C. Sulpicius Faustus the amount realised from the auction of (the goods of) P. Servilius Narcissus, according to my stipulation (with the buyer), less my fee'). See also Chapter 3 above, p. 76.

35 *CJ* 4.18.2 pr. and 1; *Inst.* 4.6.8; Lenel³ (1927) 132–5. The *actio recepticia* applied to all kinds of property, not merely to 'fungibles' (i.e. items, including money, which could be weighed, measured or counted), and the banker was liable even though the original debt was non-existent.

36 These suits included not only cases involving delicts such as theft, robbery with violence, deception (*dolus*) and outrage (*iniuria*) but also, for example, partnership, trust (*fiducia*), guardianship, mandate and deposit: Gaius 4.182 (omitting deception), who summarises the penalties; Schulz (1951) 45.

37 Gardner (1986) 262 and nn. 10, 12. They could, for example, pursue the murder of a parent, child or patron. Exception was made, under the empire, for cases concerning the *annona* (food supply) as this was regarded as being in the public interest; Marcianus (*D.* 48.2.13) attributes the ruling to Severus and Antoninus. Women are, however, among the long list of categories of those forbidden to bring accusation concerning the *fiscus* (*D.* 49.14.18).

38 Gaius 4.97–8, 101; Buckland (1966) 708–10, 714. See further in Chapter 5 below.

39 The section ends (*h.t.* 6 *fin.*) with a statement that those contravening this ban will not only be refused permission to prosecute but will be fined. Lenel³ (1927) 76 rejects this sentence as an interpolation, but accepts the likelihood that there was a penalty (superfluous to mention) of a fine. Some doubt may be occasioned as to how efficiently praetors and other magistrates themselves implemented the edict by the strange statement of Marcianus (*D.* 48.16.1.10):

> Papinian gave the opinion that a woman barred from bringing accusation of forgery because she was not seeking redress for a wrong done to herself or a close relative was not liable to be penalised on withdrawal under the Turpilian decree of the senate [which penalised withdrawal from an accusation without obtaining the consent of the magistrate].

It is difficult to see why the question should have arisen at all, unless a magistrate had mistakenly allowed the woman to start proceedings in the first place.

40 *et ratio quidem prohibendi, ne contra pudicitiam sexui congruentem alienis causis se immisceant, ne virilibus officiis fungantur mulieres: origo vero introducta est a Carfania improbissima femina, quae inverecunde postulans et magistratum inquietans causam dedit edicto.*

41 Val. Max. 9.1.3; cf. Livy 34.3–4.

42 Cf. the laudatory epitaphs of Claudia, *CIL* I. 1007 (2nd century BC): *Suom mareitum corde deilexit souo . . . domum servavit, lanam fecit* ('She loved her husband whole-heartedly . . . she stayed at home, she

worked at her wool'), and of Amymone: *lanifica pia frugi casta domi-seda* ('Wool-working, devoted, modest, thrifty, chaste, stay-at-home').

43 A third text, Tacitus *Ann.* 3.34, is added by Dixon to improve the linking. Tacitus does borrow some of the arguments of Livy's *lex Oppia* debate for his own account of a senatorial debate, in AD 30, on a proposal to forbid governors to be accompanied to provinces by their wives. The subject, however, is too remote fom the other contexts, and the situation of the women concerned too untypical, to justify taking the three passages together in this way.

44 Papinian, cited by Marcianus, and Marcianus himself, on the other hand, simply mention 'weakness of the sex' (*sexus infirmitatem*), without attempting further explanation, as a reason for refusing suit to a woman not personally involved: *D.* 48.16.1.10; 49.14.18.

45 For conjectures as to the nature and circumstances of Maesia's trial, see Marshall (1990).

46 Gardner (1986) 117–18. Ovid *Ars Amatoria* I presents itself as a guide to men on picking up girls in public places.

47 *Quo matronale decus verecundiae munimento tutius esset, in ius vocanti matronam corpus eius adtingere non permiserunt, ut inviolata manus alienae tactus relinqueretur* (2.1.5). In late imperial law, when the idea of female frailty and need for protection is taken as given, Constantine (*CJ* 1.48.1 = *C.Th.*1.22.1, AD 316) forbids *iudices* on pain of death to compel matrons to appear personally in court. Valerius cites this among other examples of the proverbially austere morality of the good old days, such as women's sitting, not reclining, at meals; the honour paid to *univirae* (women married once only); the absence of divorce in early Rome; the settling of matrimonial quarrels (by implication, in the husband's favour) at the shrine of *Venus Viriplaca*; and the oft-quoted *vini usus olim Romanis feminis ignotum fuit* ('once upon a time, Roman women were unacquainted with the use of wine'). The indulgence of their husbands, however (he says), let them make themselves attractive with gold and purple, and they dyed their hair – since no one, of course, contemplated adultery in those days.

48 See the texts cited above (n. 44) and also *CJ* 10.32.44 (AD 393): 'No one is to be bound to serve as a decurion (a hereditary and financially onerous office) because of descent in the maternal blood-line alone, because the weakness of women never renders other liable to those functions from which it is itself exempt.' Elsewhere, as in Ulpian's comments on the *senatusconsultum Velleianum*, women's presumed lack of experience of the business and legal world of the forum seems to be regarded as a relevant factor.

49 Maine (1861) 123–4:

> The foundation of Agnation is not the marriage of Father and Mother, but the authority of the Father. . . . In the primitive view, relationship is exactly limited by Patria Potestas. . . . It is obvious that the organisation of primitive societies would have been confounded, if men had called themselves relatives of their mother's relatives. The inference would have been that a person

might be subject to two distinct Patriae Potestates; but distinct Patriae Potestates implied distinct jurisdictions, so that anybody amenable to two of them at the same time would have lived under two different dispensations.

50 As said above (n. 20), Treggiari (1991) 33–4 mentions, but only as a theoretical and unprovable possibility, that marriage without the creation of *manus* at all may have predated the creation of *manus* by *usus*.

51 Though my comments on Sacks (1974) in the text above may seem negative, I would refer the reader to her admirable resumé (pp. 221–2) of a study of 17th-century England. Sacks is fully alive to the fact that women then (and later) have been employed as labourers, and that the social cost to the family was (is?) something of no interest to exploitative employers.

5 BEHAVIOUR: DISGRACE AND DISREPUTE

1 As Crook (1967) 83 remarks, 'The subject is complicated and much has been written about it.' Of the bibliography he gives (303 n. 77), Greenidge (1894) and Kaser (1956) will be found most useful; to these may be added d'Ors (1984). Pommeray (1937) is detailed, but rests on a rather dubious central theory.

2 As a juristic term, applied to the restrictions in the praetor's edict, this noun appears only in *D*. 3.1.9; in the surviving portion of the edict (*D*. 3.2.1) and elsewhere the adjective *infamis* is normally used, while Gaius (*Inst.* 4.182) prefers the noun *ignominia* to describe the effects of 'praetorian infamy'. For the commoner non-technical uses of *infamia*, and cognate words, see Kaser (1956).

3 See especially Kaser (1956) 220–2, 227–35. The rest of his discussion, however, is concerned only with categorising the types of disability according to their juristic origins.

4 Greenidge (1894) 61 conjectures that the censors in early Rome were concerned mainly with behaviour affecting the security and soundness, both moral and financial, of the *familia*; however, his reconstruction of the censorial edict of later times is modelled essentially on the praetor's edict and the *lex Julia municipalis*. Our knowledge is fragmentary. The census itself was only irregularly held in the 1st century BC and disappeared during the Principate; and as Kaser (1956) 227 points out, a censorial *nota* in itself did not necessarily produce any effect on the individual's exercise of his rights. For these reasons 'censorial *infamia*' will not be considered here.

5 This assumption appears to underlie, for example, the attempt in Tyrrell and Purser's edition of Cicero's *Letters*, vol. IV p. 419, on *ad Fam.* 6.18.1, to explain the exclusion of *praecones* from the municipal senate in the *lex Julia municipalis*. 'The reason . . . would appear to be that they were regarded with detestation, like pawnbrokers and usurers with us, as trading on the misfortunes of others' – an aspect of their calling which Cicero frequently mentions. On the *praecones*, see further below,

and for recent discussion of their financial and political standing, Rauh (1989) with bibliography. On the point of interest to the present study, he makes at 457 n. 27 what I believe to be substantially the correct suggestion, though see my comments below, n. 49.

6 Greenidge (1894) 154 ff.; Kaser (1956) sections 4, 6.

7 Nor, apparently, in criminal courts: *D.* 48.2.11 (Macer). According to Ulpian (*D.* 4.3.11), it was the opinion of Labeo that prodigals and spendthrifts (*luxuriosi* and *prodigi*) *ought* not to be allowed to bring suits for *dolus malus* (deceit), since condemnation incurred *infamia.* This wording, however, suggests that exception could be made, as also for freedmen against patrons (also mentioned in this text), if the offence was serious (cf. *D.* 2.4.10.2). We would not be justified in deducing from this qualified restriction a penal ban on bringing *all* defaming actions (a possibility mentioned, but not defended, by Greenidge (1894) 164–5).

8 Lenel (1971) 76 ff., 86 ff. Representing others: *D.* 3.1.1; Paul *Sent.* 1.2.1; being represented: Gaius 4.124; *Vat. Frag.* 322–4.

9 *D.* 3.1.6; Gaius 4.124; *Inst.*4.13.11. Pommeray (1937) 138–9 observes the unavailability to the praetor of a list of the disqualified and the consequent need for vigilance. On the possibility of magisterial error or incompetence, see also ch. 4 n. 39.

10 So the Watson–Kruger–Mommsen edition's rendering, despite the awkwardness of taking *suae dignitatis* in two constructions, as a genitive dependent upon *habendae rationis* and as forming a gerundive phrase with *tuendae.* Mommsen's suggested textual emendation (*decoris sui suaeque dignitatis tuendae causa*) yields a more straightforward sense: 'for the sake of taking account of his dignity and protecting his position'.

11 Greenidge (1901) 147, while accepting Ulpian's reason as applying to these also, betrays a slight uneasiness: '[This partial disqualification] was clearly based, *even* in the first two cases [i.e. women and blind persons], on a desire to protect the dignity of the court' (my italics).

12 Greenidge (1901) 235–43; Kaser (1966) 114 ff.; Watson (1971) 127 n. 4, 161 ff.

13 Originally and in Cicero's time at least; by the latter part of the 2nd century AD (Gaius 4.84) procurators might be appointed also to deal with specific lawsuits: Greenidge (1901) 237–8. In later law, *cognitor* and *procurator* were largely assimilated, and texts do not always clearly distinguish the two.

14 For these distinctions, see Greenidge (1901) 146. According to Ps.-Ascon. *in div.* 4.11, a distinction was drawn between the *patronus*, who actually pleaded in court in support of the litigant, and the *advocatus*, who gave legal advice, or sometimes did no more than show solidarity by being present in court. By the early empire, the two terms have come to be used indiscriminately (Tac. *Dial.* 1.1); so, as we have seen, the praetor's edict speaks of assigning an 'advocate' to represent those incapable of representing themselves.

15 Gardner (1986) 32, 60 n. 8, 129, 136 n. 42.

16 This is suggested by Ulpian's phrase (*D.* 3.1.1.6) *aequissimum est.*

17 Buckland (1966) 151–2, presumably by inference from *D.* 26.3. A man freeing a slave child with 'good cause' shown under the provisions of the *lex Aelia Sentia* would, as patron, be the child's *tutor legitimus.*

18 Greenidge (1894) 166 ff. This is attested both as a provision for procedure created by a criminal law, and also as a penalty inflicted by such a law (*D.* 22.5.3.5; 28.1.20.6; 48.11.6). Ulpian twice mentions it as a penalty resulting from condemnation for libellous compositions, instituted either by a *senatusconsultum* (*D.* 28.1.18.1) or by a law (*D.* 47.10.5.9). The word *intestabilis* was used, according to Aulus Gellius 15.13.11, as early as the Twelve Tables, in which it was declared that someone who had allowed himself to be a witness or had been a scales-balancer (i.e. had assisted at a mancipation or the making of a mancipatory will) and then had refused to give testimony, was deemed *improbus* and *intestabilis.* No particular legal significance can be attached to the former word.

19 And apparently not necessarily remunerative; Champlin (1991) 80. Wills: *D.* 22.5.15; 28.1.18, 26. As the earlier form of will, *testamentum per aes et libram*, on which the praetorian will's requirement of sealing by seven witnesses was based, was in form a property conveyance (*mancipatio*), one may presume that the ban applied also to witnessing mancipations.

20 *Inst.* 2.10.6. Greenidge (1894) 169 mistakenly takes Papinian in *D.* 22.5.14 to be saying that later interpretation was that such people could not receive under a will; what is actually said, however, is that a will which was witnessed by such a person was not valid either in civil or in praetorian law, and a result it could not be implemented: *ut neque hereditas adiri neque bonorum possessio dari possit* ('so that entry cannot be made upon the inheritance, nor possession of property granted').

21 Champlin (1991) 24–5, 87–102. At 201–2, he gives a list of references to *captatio* and related improprieties; there are twenty-seven in Martial alone.

22 Pugliese Carratelli (1948) 170; Arangio Ruiz (1959) 229. For the probable function of the person concerned, see Arangio Ruiz (1948) 134.

23 Garnsey (1970); Jones (1972) ch. 3; Millar (1984).

24 It is a penalty under two Julian criminal laws, the law on adultery, and that on *repetundae* (as a penalty for accepting bribes to give or not give evidence under the law): *D.* 28.1.20.6; 48.11.6. Certain categories of people already stigmatised for other reasons are, according to Callistratus, not to be prosecution witnesses in cases under the Julian law on assault: *D.* 22.5.3.5.

25 Nor to bring a charge (*postulare*), nor judge a case (*D.* 48.11.6).

26 So Lintott (1968) 107 ff., cited by Brunt (1971) 556 n. 6.

27 Deduction from Gaius 1.119.

28 Though the law was aimed primarily at conniving husbands, persons (of either sex) abetting the adultery were also liable: Gardner (1986) 132.

29 The so-called 'Rules of Ulpian' (*Ulpiani liber singularis regularum*; also known as *Epitome Ulpiani*); see Schulz (1946) 180–2 for discussion of its authenticity and authorship.

30 That such women were not mentioned specifically in the clause of the *lex Julia* relating to senatorial marriages appears to be borne out by Paul's citation from the law (*D.* 23.2.44 pr.). This quotation from the law (*D.* 23.2.44 pr. and 1), probably in the form it took after Marcus Aurelius (cf. *D.* 23.2.16), mentions only freedwomen and those *qui ars ludicra fecit fecerit* – that is, performers at the games, actors or entertainers. However, this does not appear to be an exhaustive list, but merely an excerpt from the law, sufficient for the purposes of his commentary. Prostitution is one of the disgraceful activities (the other is engaging in *ars ludicra*) which, along with condemnation in a public trial, lost a senator's daughter her status (*D.* 23.2.47, from the second book of Paul's commentary on the *lex Julia et Papia*).

31 Notoriously, Mommsen and others believed that no marriage between freeborn and freed was valid until the Augustan legislation, a mistake based principally on the misleading formulations of Dio and Celsus: Treggiari (1969) 82 ff. There does not seem to be any basis for the suggestion of Demougin (see n. 71 below) that the Augustan marriage legislation also imposed some restraints on the marriage of equestrians.

32 *FIRA* i².13. For the problem of dating, see Brunt (1971) Appendix 2.

33 Kaser (1956) 223–7 draws a firm distinction between the general regulation of the moral and political life of citizens by the 'so-called' censorian *infamia*, and the citizens' legal rights, with which it had nothing to do. He would therefore presumably not accept Greenidge's view that both the praetorian rules and the *lex Julia municipalis* represent adaptations of 'the censorian infamia' (Greenidge (1894) 117).

34 The *Fragmentum Atestinum*, from Ateste in Cisalpine Gaul, the *lex Coloniae Genetivae Juliae* and, above all, the *lex Irnitana*, from Irni (*Municipium Flavium Irnitanum*) in southern Spain, which has added greatly to our knowledge of the content of the Flavian municipal law (see Gonzalez 1986).

35 However, both gladiators and *bestiarii* are listed in a citation from Paul already mentioned, *Coll.* 4.3.2. Though the juristic texts used in this work, the *Collatio legum Mosaicarum et Romanarum*, show signs of post-classical revision (Schulz (1946) 312), the revision may have been less thorough than that of the compilers of the *Digest*.

36 Jones (1964) 1398 n. 87. Constantine instructed (*C.Th.* 15.12.1) that convicted criminals who would otherwise have been sentenced to fight as gladiators in the arena were instead to be sent to the mines. Why the alternative, that they fight as *bestiarii*, was unacceptable, is not clear; expressly what was found objectionable was not bloodshed in itself, but men killing each other; the text as we have it begins 'bloody spectacles are not wanted in times of domestic peace and quiet' (*cruenta spectacula in otio civili et domestica quiete non placet*).

37 The latter point is also demonstrated by d'Ors (1984), with reference to the introduction of the various *actiones* mentioned.

38 Not in the inscription.

39 References in Rauh (1989) 460 n. 40. This is the aspect on which most emphasis is placed by Hinard (1976).

40 For a description of their typical employments, see Rauh (1989) 452–4; their services both as criers and as auctioneers would be called upon.

41 Purcell (1983) 147 n. 128.

42 The Augustan law forbade persons of senatorial rank marriage with actors and actors' children (*D*. 23.3.44 pr. Paul). The Puteolan councillor and his father: *ILS* 1934.

43 Festus s.v. *Quiris*, p. 304 L., Varro, *L.L.* 7.42; cf. Ter. *Phorm*. 1026. These funerals, as Hinard (1976) 735 remarks, were presumably those of the more eminent citizens, though this does not mean that the *praecones* were not engaged privately; even Hinard, for whom *praecones* are public officials only incidentally and occasionally engaging in the provision of private services, can describe their rôle as no more than 'quasiment officiel'.

44 As it is by Saumagne (1965) 31–6, criticised by Hinard (1976) 730 ff.

45 A view necessarily rejected by Saumagne, who wishes to dissociate this text from the law. His view is that the *praecones* in the law are not the same as those spoken of by Cicero. The former he thinks are employed privately to assist at funerals, while Cicero is referring to those *praecones* who had a public rôle as *apparitores*, attendants on magistrates.

46 Hopkins (1983) 209–10.

47 *AE* 1971.88, edited and discussed by Bove (1967).

48 Hinard (1976) insists that all *praecones* were 'public'; and, pointing out (correctly) that no evidence *explicitly* identifies any as 'private', suggests that the textual evidence for some occasions on which manifestly private tasks are being carried out concerns merely incidental activity from which they derived some complementary income during the periods when they were not required for service by a magistrate. Rauh (1989) spec. 454 n. 12, mainly because the wealth and apparent social eminence of a few individuals leads him to exaggerate the general significance of membership of the *ordo* at Rome, is inclined to believe in the existence of two distinct groups: *praecones publici*, who were members of the *ordo*, and others. The matter is, on existing evidence insoluble; nevertheless, one doubts whether the social disparity between individual *praecones* in Italian towns can have been so great; besides, on the theory of the existence of two categories of *praecones*, some qualification, such as *publicum*, would be expected in the Julian law. The evidence for the organisation and selection of the apparitorial service does not allow us to determine whether such official posts constituted a permanent career or merely temporary employment (Purcell (1983) 131); however, the regulations for their recruitment at Urso in Spain (*lex Coloniae Genetivae Ursonensis*) clearly provide for *apparitores* serving only for a portion of the year (Bruns[7] 28, LXIII).

49 Rauh (1989) 457 n. 27 grasps the significance for the *praeco*, in that his earnings 'depended to some degree upon the proceeds of public auctions'. However, he goes wide of the mark when he says, 'Any senator, municipal or Roman, who derived his living *from wage earnings, that is, anyone who lacked independence of means* (my italics), could not be trusted to act impartially on matters of public concern.' An employee working for wages is a modern concept. We should not confuse this

with a self-employed person contracting to provide his services, or those of his workforce, for a fee. For the latter, see, for example, the Puteoli inscription; an example of the former is Aulus Castricius Onesimus, who in *TP* 43 contracts to pay Gaius Sulpicius Faustus, from the proceeds of the auction sale of the goods of Publius Servilius Narcissus, an agreed amount, less his fee. In modern local government, a clear distinction is made between the use of direct and contracted labour for such things as refuse clearance and maintenance of council property. The misunderstanding by Hinard, mentioned in the text above, echoes that of Greenidge (1894) 12, who not only assumed 'a general rule at Rome that anyone who exercised a trade or profession for payment should not be eligible for the magistracy', on the basis of an incident in 304 BC in which a magistrate's clerk was rejected as a candidate for office until he gave up this work, but went on to claim that this supposed rule 'was based on the consideration that it was beneath the dignity of a Roman magistrate to be engaged in such an occupation'.

50 Edwards (forthcoming). I am very grateful to Dr Edwards for allowing me to see a text of this paper in advance of publication.

51 'It is rather another manifestation of the struggle on the part of those laying claim to moral and legal authority to marginalise these threatening persons', Edwards, *op. cit.*

52 Paul, cited in *Coll.* 4.2.2; see Gardner (1986) 121–3.

53 This, apparently, is what causes the infatuation of the senatorial lady Eppia (Juv. 6.103 ff.); Juvenal emphasises that the appearance of her gladiator lover is, by conventional standards of attractiveness, repellent.

54 She contrasts chariot-drivers, who are not among the lists of *infames*, and the backstage trainers and service workers, about whom jurists were doubtful. This doubtfulness, however, somewhat weakens the argument, and chariot-driving had, as she admits, prestigious connections with Rome's historic past.

55 I have not had access to a copy of this book, but have heard a portion as a paper, and had valuable discussion with Dr Wiedemann.

56 Moreau (1983) 44, followed by Lebek (1990) 76, explains *summa rudis* and similar expressions as either a trainer or umpire; though, as Moreau notes, Ville (1981) 370 n. 55 was doubtful because a stele from Telmessos with the inscription of a *secunda rudis* was accompanied by a mutilated relief possibly representing a gladiator.

57 *primo palo*: see Ville (1981) 324 n. 17.

58 *In Cat.* 2.23, *pro Murena* 13; cf. *In Pis.* 2, *In Verr.* 2.3.23.

59 That is to say, stage performers in general (but not the Atellani) were, already under the Republic, excluded from two of the major functions of a citizen – voting, and serving as soldiers – though, since most of those who were Roman citizens will have been freedmen, they were ineligible for the legions anyway and for much of the Republic their voting rights were restricted. Jory (1970) has a different interpretation. According to him, Livy's explanation that the non-exemption from military service of the Atellanes was because of their amateur status is simply invalid. The real reason, he believes, is that the religious import-

ance of dramatic performances in the period of which Livy speaks made the presence of all participants in what amounted to religious rites – and so, of the actors – essential. Hence the exemption of actors in general (most of whom were not Roman citizens, so not liable anyway) from military service. The Atellane players, however, besides being Italian (and therefore normally liable to military service), were not, he says, introduced to festivals until much later, when the sense of their religious importance was much weaker. This does not, however, account for Livy's express statement that actors were excluded from the tribes also.

60 *Spintriae* (Suet. *Gaius* 16; cf. *Tib.*43).

61 Suet. *div. Jul.* 39; *div. Aug.* 43–5; Dio 43.23.5; 54.2.5.

62 Summarised in Levick (1983) 105 ff.; Lebek (1990) 50 ff.

63 The text has recently been re-edited by Lebek (1990), who cites the main earlier bibliography (pp. 38 ff.); see especially Levick (1983) and Moreau (1983).

64 Dio 43.23.5. Suetonius *div.Jul.* 39 adds a *former* senator.

65 Between the restrictions on public banquets and games, and the ban on performances by senators' grandsons, Dio mentions the transfer of the fire-fighting service to the curule aediles, with a staff of public slaves.

66 Although, as we learn from the inscription from Larinum (lines 17 ff.), either as part of the decree lifting the ban, or as a separate pronouncement in the same year AD 11, it was declared that no freeborn women under the age of 20, and no freeborn men under 25, were to pledge themselves (as gladiators) or hire out their services – the text is deficient at this point, but has been restored to read *in scaenam turpesve ad res alias* ('for the stage or other base purposes') – except those who (according to Lebek's reconstruction), after a hearing before Augustus or Tiberius, have been assigned as judgment-debtors to creditors who have allowed them to hire out their services in this way. (As convicted debtors, they would already be *infames*.)

67 *senatusconsultum* lines 7–11:

> *[Pla]cere, ne quis senatoris filium filiam, nepotem neptem, pronepotem pronepteam, neue que[m, cui ipsi cuiusve patri aut avo v]el paterno vel materno aut fratri, neue quam, cuius viro aut patri aut avo <vel> paterno ve[l materno aut fratri ius] / fuisset unquam spectandi in equestribus locis, in scaenam produceret auctoramentove rog[aret, neue, ut feras confice] / ret aut ut pinnas gladiatorum raperet aut ut rudem tolleret alioue quod eius rei simile min[isterium praestante operam] / praeberet, conduceret; neue quis eorum se locaret.*

Lebek (1990) 60, 72–9. Legal sources: *D.* 3.1.1.6 (*bestiarii*); 3.2.2.5 (stage performers).

68 The grounds on which Augustus punished some knights with *ignominia* are not specified by Suetonius (*div. Aug.* 39); it was one of a range of penalties of varying severity that he imposed, and clearly was not the same as *infamia* under the praetor's edict.

69 Unhelpfully translated in both the Loeb and Penguin Classics editions as 'disfranchisement', but certainly not to be taken to mean loss of citizenship: Levick (1983) 108 n. 27.

70 The case of Decimus Laberius, who performed in one of his own mimes at Caesar's triumphal games, does not, as is often assumed, prove the contrary. Levick (1983) 109, for example, following Shackleton Bailey on *ad Fam.* 12.18.2, says Laberius 'was forced to play in one of his own mimes and lost his status as an *eques* until it was restored to him by Caesar, who returned him to his place in the fourteen rows and gave him half a million HS'. This interpretation, however, does not rest on Suetonius (*div. Jul.* 39.2), who says only, 'At the games Decimus Laberius, a Roman knight, performed his own mime and after being given 500,000 HS and a gold ring passed from the stage through the orchestra to a seat in the fourteen rows.' Immediately before, Suetonius mentions the participation in the gladiatorial contests of two men of senatorial rank, with no hint that they suffered any loss of status in consequence. The reluctance of the occupants of the seats to allow him room (Sen. *Controv.* 7.3.9) is to be seen merely as their personal expression of disapproval; Cicero made a joke of it. As Wiseman (1987) 61–6 makes clear, the gold ring and possession of 400,000 (not 500,000) HS were only *unofficially* regarded as qualifications for equestrian status until the reign of Tiberius. The story about the disgrace and rehabilitation of Laberius depends on the late evidence of Macrobius (2.7.3), who, however, represents the 500,000 HS as a *fee* offered by Caesar in advance (so making Laberius' appearance as an actor professional), and quotes, as from Laberius' prologue: *ego bis tricenis annis actis sine nota / eques Romanus e lare egressus meo / domum revertar mimus* ('I these sixty years past without *nota*, having gone out as a Roman knight shall return home a mime') – words, given the context of their utterance, obviously intended merely as a humorous mock-apology for his appearance in person. Without the new significance put on the money by Macrobius, there is little justification for assuming *nota* to refer to any official degradation from status.

71 As pointed out by e.g. Moreau (1983) 36 n. 3, and Demougin (1988) 555 ff., the range of 'parenté sénatoriale', senatorial kin, resembles that of the *lex Julia de maritandis ordinibus* (D. 23.2.44 pr.; cf. 50.1.22.5) – four generations down in the agnatic line from a senator. For 'parenté équestre', however, the decree provides completely new and unparalleled evidence. Kinship is reckoned both for men and women, and not confined to agnates, and it is not the descendants of *ego*, but his/her *ascendants* and collaterals who are specified (Demougin draws attention, p. 576, to the requirement for entitlement to the *anulus aureus*, the golden ring signifying equestrian status, mentioned in Pliny *NH* 33.32, of free birth for three generations): 'Anyone (m.) who himself, or whose father, paternal or maternal grandfather, or brother, or anyone (f.) whose husband, father, paternal or maternal grandfather, or brother ever had the right of watching from the equestrian seats'. It is, however, straining the evidence to suggest, as Demougin does, on the basis of Dio 54.2.5, that these definitions were fixed in 22 BC; the further

suggestion that the Julian marriage law also contained a clause, less restrictive than that for senators, allowing knights and their kin to marry freedwomen but not *probrosae*, lacks evidence.

72 *eludendae auctoritatis eius ordinis gratia quibus sedendi in equestribus locis ius erat aut p[ublicam ignominiam] / ut acciperent aut ut famoso iudicio condemnarentur dederant operam et postea quam ei des[?civer- ant sua sponte ex] / [equ]estribus locis, auctoraverunt se aut in scaenam prodierant.*

73 For *ignominiosus*, rather than *infamis*, of the effects of 'praetorian infamy', see n. 2 above.

74 So Lebek: *et, posteaquam ei des[ierant posse sedere in eques] /* vvvv *tribus locis.* The reading is not entirely satisfactory, since four letter-spaces remain unaccounted for.

75 This is not stated in any source, but rests essentially on an inference from Cic. *Phil.* 2.18 (and not on the story of Laberius; see n. 70 above). The meaning is not that bankrupts (*decoctores*) were assigned a special section in the theatre, but that any of the privileged occupants of the fourteen rows who became bankrupt lost that privilege, since bankrupts were *infames*.

76 Statuses to which Augustus himself had given some definition, and assigned formal qualifications to the rank of *senator* and *eques*, though these did not become fully definitive until the reign of Tiberius. On recruitment and expulsion, see Millar (1977) 279–300. As for loss of status because of *infamia*, the evidence listed in *RE* VI.1, 296 ff. is quite inconclusive.

77 Whose pique does appear visible in the tone of the decree: these people have behaved 'in a manner unbecoming their rank' (2: *contra dignitatem ordinis sui*) 'in order to mock its dignity' (14: *eludendae auctoritatis eius ordinis gratia*). What penalties the decree wished to impose hence-forth is not known; the surviving text mentions only denial of a proper funeral.

78 Suet. *Tib.* 35; see also Tacitus *Ann.* 2.85. The women concerned, if senatorial through marriage, would also lose their status, but that would not be in consequence of the *infamia*, but of the provisions of the Augustan marriage legislation.

79 Gardner (1986) 78 n. 1; see also the Larinum decree, line 8.

80 Voluntarily, that is; Pomponius, according to Ulpian, was of the opinion that someone raped by 'bandits or enemies' should not be penalised. Lawyers' hesitation no doubt arose from the difficulty of establishing, in many cases, the absence of volition. Defence of one's male chastity was an acceptable defence against some charges of murder. On the importance attached to male honour, see Dalla (1987) 51–62, spec. 59 ff. However, Dalla is incorrect in drawing the inference from *D.* 3.2.24 that, till Severus, being a male prostitute while in slavery still entailed *infamia* once a man was freed. The rescript as quoted by Ulpian says merely *non offuisse mulieri famae quaestum eius* (*sic* S; al. *eius quaestum*) *in servitute factum* ('the woman's *fama* is not impaired by her earning while a slave'). The kind of *quaestus* is not specified, and need not have been *corpore*. More importantly, there is no reason

to assume a significant distinction between the sexes; a woman is mentioned presumably because it was about a particular woman that the question had been raised.

81 According to Paul (*Sent.* 2.26.4) on the Julian adultery law, those taken in adultery whom a wronged husband might kill were *infames et eos qui corpore quaestum faciunt* ('the "infamous" and those who earn from their body'); this need not be taken to mean that no male prostitutes were *infames* (since *infamia* would not apply to those prostitutes who were also, as a matter of fact, slaves).

82 As for active homosexuals, a law of uncertain date, the *lex Sca(n)tinia* (Dalla (1987) 82 ff.), appears to have made them liable to prosecution, but in what terms and with what penalties, if any, is unknown. If, as Dalla thinks (p. 91), it was made the subject of a *publicum iudicium*, those convicted would be *infames*. They are not specifically mentioned in the lists of offences in legal sources and the *lex Julia municipalis*. Their absence from the former is explicable by the fact that their offence was subsumed under *stuprum* in the Augustan adultery law (*D.* 47.11.1.2). As for the *Tabula Heracleensis*, if, as Kunkel (1962) 122–3 believes, adultery and *stuprum* were treated under the Republic as capital charges, convicted offenders would obviously be unavailable as potential council candidates; alternatively, and more probably, one might suppose that they were prosecuted for *iniuria*, which was a defaming action.

83 Cohen (1991) 176–7 suggests very plausibly that, in the case of homosexual relations between an Athenian man and a free boy without the use of force or payment, it was open to the boy's family to prosecute the man for *hubris*, outrage. We have no evidence, however, for any penalty for the passive partner, whether boy or adult.

84 Dalla (1987) 82 ff. summarises the evidence.

85 The only examples involving sex are the following. *Acquittal*: (5) the legend of the Vestal virgin Tuccia, accused of unchastity, who proved her innocence by fetching water in a sieve; (12) Calidius, accused of adultery after being found hiding in a married man's bedroom at night, who was acquitted after explaining his presence as due to his lust for a boy slave of the owner. *Condemnation*: (8) an unnamed man who subdued and killed an ox to satisfy the gourmet whim of his boy slave with whom he was infatuated ('He was innocent', remarks Valerius, 'had he not lived in such primitive times'). Under 'Absolved' (7), Valerius mentions, but omits to specify the charge, the trial in 329 BC of Q. Flavius (Livy 8.22.3) *stupratae matris familiae*, for violation, or seduction, of a married woman.

86 Paul *Sent.* 2.26.11; Gardner (1986) 133. Their husbands were probably also similarly exempt from prosecution for *lenocinium*. Sex with an unmarried female prostitute did not count as *stuprum*.

87 *Sed et in ea uxore potest maritus adulterium vindicare, quae volgaris fuerit, quamvis, si vidua esset, impune in ea stuprum committeretur.*

88 *ergo qui locavit solus notatur, sive depugnaverit sive non; quod si depugnaverit, cum non locasset operas suas, non tenebitur: non enim qui cum bestiis depugnavit, tenebitur, sed qui operas suas in hoc locavit.*

*denique eos, qui virtutis ostendendae causa hoc faciunt sine mercede,
non teneri aiunt veteres, nisi in harena passi sunt se honorari.*

89 Suetonius adds *partimque servitiorum*; it is unclear whether he refers
to slaves in the larger private households or only in the staff of the
emperor himself – more probably the latter.

90 Cicero, in a well-known passage (*de Officiis* 1.150–1), draws a snobbish
distinction between (socially) 'demeaning' activities, and those fit for
the upper classes. Within the former category, he singles out as least
worthy of approval those trades that minister to the pleasures.

91 Criminal convictions rendered a man unacceptable to undertake the
military defence of his fellow citizens, according to Arrius Menander
(*D.* 49.16.4.7); correspondingly, anyone dishonourably discharged
from the army was regarded neither as fit to govern his fellow citizens
(*lex Julia municipalis*) nor to litigate or give evidence in their behalf
(*D.* 3.2.1.1).

92 See also the list of actions excluded from the competence of a municipal
magistrate in ch. 84 of the *lex Irnitana* and the commentary of Gonzalez
(1986) 228.

93 Gardner (1986) 51 ff. and 91–3.

94 On rehabilitation, see Greenidge (1894) ch. 8, who discusses also developments such as temporary *infamia*, for the duration only of a sentence,
or substitution of a heavier sentence without *infamia* for a lighter one
with.

6 PARTICIPATION: THE HANDICAPPED CITIZEN

1 Or, with more sophistication, independent mandatories or procurators,
for whom legal procedures were duly developed: see Watson (1961),
and above on *institores* and agents.

2 Gardner (1986a).

3 At first this was an *ad hoc* arrangement. It took a surprisingly long
time for it to be regularised. In the reign of Marcus Aurelius it became
possible for a minor to apply for a *curator* to act for the whole of the
period until he or she reached the age of 25 (Buckland 1966: 169–72).

4 Much later, the procedure to be followed in making wills is carefully
detailed in an imperial instruction, *CJ* 6.22.8 (AD 521), where it is
suggested that a professional scribe or an eighth witness should be
engaged to write down the terms of the will, which should then be
read out to the testator and the witnesses, and that all the witnesses,
and the writer, should then affix their seals to the document. This is
in contrast to what, by the time of Gaius at least (2.103), had become
normal practice among sighted testators; the contents of the will were
not read out to the witnesses, and the *nuncupatio* by the testator
amounted only to an affirmation that he gave and bequeathed according
as it was written in the tablets (see n. 11 below). However, the enactment of AD 521 is intended as a variation not to this procedure but to
that of the 'tripartite will' in use by that time – see n. 25 below.

5 The title of a BBC radio magazine programme for the physically disabled is 'Does He Take Sugar?', from the regularity with which this

question is asked of the pushers of wheelchairs, rather than their occupants.

6 *D.* 37.3.2 (Ulpian); 23.3.73 pr. (Paul) = *Sent.* 21B.1a.

7 *D.* 3.1.1.5; 5.1.6. On Appius Claudius, who acquired the *cognomen* Caecus, 'the blind', see Münzer in *RE* 3.2.2681 ff., who produces evidence that Appius became blind only in later life.

8 *D.* 26.8.16; 27.1.40: *Vat. Frag.* 238.

9 Born: *D.* 29.2.5; becoming afflicted: *D.* 28.1.6.1, 28.1.25 – likely to be a theoretical argument:

> Varus, in the first book of his *Digest*, has written that Servius gave the response that where a person who was making a will became dumb after he had made declaration of the first heirs, but before specifying the second, he had begun to make a will, rather than made one; therefore, the first-named heirs would not be heirs under that will. Labeo's view is that this is true, if it were established that the testator had wished to nominate further heirs; I do not think that Servius meant anything else.

10 Cf. Ulpian, *D.* 45.1.1 pr.:

> A stipulation can be effected only when both parties can speak, and therefore neither a dumb nor a deaf person nor an *infans* (one not yet capable of speech) can make a contract by stipulation; nor, indeed, can someone who is not present, since both parties should be able to hear each other. If, therefore, one of these persons wishes to take a stipulation, he should do it through a slave who is present, and may acquire for him an action on stipulation.

11 The verbal declaration and response was essential. Gaius 2.104 gives the formulae. First the testator formally conveys his estate to the notional buyer, who strikes a bronze piece on a pair of scales in token of symbolic purchase, after saying, in a formula suitably flavoured with archaic language: *familiam pecuniamque tuam endo mandatela tua custodelaque mea <esse aio, eaque>, quo tu iure testamentum facere possis secundum legem publicam, hoc aere aeneaque libro esto mihi empta* ('I declare that your *familia* and money are under your direction and in my care, and let them be bought to me with this bronze piece and this scale, so that you may be able to make a will rightly according to the public law'). The testator, holding in the classical period the tablets on which his will is already written out (this would not originally have been necessary before the development of specific bequests and legacies), responds with the nuncupation: *haec, ita ut in his tabulis cerisque scripta sunt, ita do, ita lego, ita testor, itaque vos quirites testimonium mihi perhibetote* ('According as it is written in these tablets and wax, so I give, so I bequeath, so I call to witness, and so, Quirites, do you bear me witness'). What was, and remained essential for the mancipatory will was not the writing of the contents in tablets (a later development) but the oral affirmations and the subsequent confirmation by witnesses. The emperor Gordian's rescript of AD 242 (misrepresented

by Schulz (1951) 243 and Buckland (1966) 286 n. 10) does not make new law, but restates the old, in declaring that even if there were no written tablets, an orally delivered will, subsequently attested to by seven witnesses, is valid in civil law, in contrast to the 'praetorian' will (see above, p. 166) since it was deemed to have fulfilled the necessary conditions for a *nuncupatio*.

12 This is one of the few instances in which a (male) *pater* does not have full control over the internal management of his *familia*. In the Twelve Tables, this intervention was provided for, in the case of intestate heirs, in the interests of the agnates. Later it was extended to freedmen, clearly to protect the patron's inheritance prospects, and to freeborn *sui heredes* inheriting by will – saving them from themselves. Other cases were added by Antoninus Pius: Schulz (1951) 200–1.

13 *D.* 26.1.1.2–3 (Paul); *D.* 26.4.10 (Hermogenianus).

14 *D.* 26.5.8; 27.1.45.

15 See the references cited by Buckland (1908) 451 n. 3, esp. *CJ* 2.30.2, where an *impubes* girl is said to have manumitted before a *consilium*.

16 Paul *Sent.* 4.12.2; assumed also in *D.* 40.2.10 (Marcianus).

17 A parallel to this form of reasoning may be found in the apparent exception to the rule that *postliminium* did not apply to marriages, in the case of a marriage between freedwoman and patron: see Gardner (1986) 228 and n. 65.

18 Callistratus (*D.* 1.7.29) similarly remarked that a dumb father's consent to give his son in adoption could be expressed otherwise than in speech. Whether the deaf and dumb could adopt is not stated in our texts.

19 Paul *Sent.* 1.13a.2; cf. *D.* 40.2.10 (Marcianus).

20 *D.* 40.2.23 (Hermogenianus).

21 Buckland (1966) 235–8. Ulp. *Reg.* 19.4.18.

22 This is an inference drawn by Buckland (1966) 313 from *D.* 29.2.62, where Javolenus expresses disagreement with Labeo as to whether a clause in a will, 'Let him be heir if he shall have sworn', takes effect once the oath is sworn (his own view, and that of Proculus), or only after the nominee *pro herede gesserit* (Labeo's view). *Nuda voluntas*, i.e. without the sworn declaration, is not mentioned.

23 Gaius 2.164–73, and see Zulueta's commentary *ad loc.*; Ulp. *Reg.* 22.25 –32; *D.* 28.1.16; *D.* 29.2.5. For examples of *cretio*, see Cic. *ad Att.* 11.2.1, 11.12.4 and 13.46.3, and *FIRA* iii nos. 59 and 60 (60 is translated by Crook (1967) 125). The heirs of 'Dasumius' (*FIRA* iii.48; Eck (1978)) are required to make *cretio* within 100 days. Gaius 2.166 gives the formula to be used. On the availability of *pro herede gestio* under the Republic, Watson (1971a) 188 n. 6.

24 Watson (1971a) 188–93.

25 Watson (1971a) 192–3.

26 Permission from the emperor: *D.* 28.1.7; *causaria missio*: *D.* 3.2.2.2; 29.1.4; 29.1.26.

27 e.g. Schulz (1951) 243; Buckland (1966) 285, followed by Gardner (1986a) 14.

28 Gaius 2.119, 147; Buckland (1966) 285–6, 383–98. In AD 439, the

praetorian and civil law wills were effectively replaced by a single form of will, sealed and signed by seven witnesses: *CJ* 6.23.21.

29 Impallomeni (1963) ch. 3.

30 Renier (1950).

31 Neither, according to Pomponius in the second example, do those *cui bonis interdictum sit*, i.e. prodigals who are banned from independent management of their property. In their case, however, this is surely to be understood differently; *prodigi* are not mentally incapable, but their *voluntas* has been nullified by the legal restraint placed upon them.

32 Quoted: Cic. *de Inv.* 2.50.148; *Auct. ad Herenn.* 1.13.25. Alluded to: Cic. *de Rep.* 3.33.43; Varro *RR* 1.2.8; Cic. *Tusc.* 3.5.11, etc.; Nardi (1983) 67-9.

33 *D.* 1.18.14, Macer *libro secundo de iudiciis publicis*. The title of *Digest* 1.18 is *De Officio Praesidis*, 'On the duties of a magistrate'.

34 See the remarks of de Visscher, quoted in Nardi (1983) 102 n. 15.

35 Gardner (1986) 149; (1986a), 6.

36 On the range of operations which might be carried out by a *curator*, and the extent of the latter's responsibility, see the texts cited in Nardi (1983), 117-64. Texts (e.g. *D.* 26.7.3 pr.; 27.10.7.3; 41.3.4.11; *CJ* 5.70.3) envisage the possibility of there being more than one *curator*, possibly because of the relatively greater burden involved (than in, say, the *tutela* of a child or a woman) of looking after, for an indefinite time, all the affairs of someone who might be an adult *paterfamilias* with dependants.

37 Nardi (1983) 98-116. Even a son could be appointed, after Antoninus Pius, to manage the affairs of his mad father (see above Chapter 3, n. 58), but this was not thought appropriate for a father who was merely prodigal. A mother (presumably widowed) should be put in the care of her son, Ulpian thought (*D.* 27.10.4), on grounds of *pietas*.

38 Vivianus is not included directly in any legal sources, appearing only in citation: Schulz (1946) 190, 214.

39 *D.* 5.2.2. Marcianus says *recte quidem fecit testamentum, sed non ex officio pietatis* ('he made the will correctly, but without due regard to family feeling').

40 *CJ* 9.7.1 pr.

41 *D.* 24.3.22.8: the *curator* (who is, apparently, *not* the husband) and relatives of a madwoman can appeal to the praetor to compel a husband to maintain her.

42 *D.* 1.6.8; *D.* 23.2.16.2; Paul *Sent.* 2.19.7.

43 *D.* 15.4.1.9; Nardi (1983) 253 ff.

44 *D.* 12.2.17.2; 40.1.12,13; 40.2.10. Pomponius (40.1.13) actually says that an agnate who is *curator* could not manumit a slave. The specific elements in this ('agnate' and 'slave') are not to be taken as limiting, but probably come from a judgment in an actual case; presumably no *curator* could alienate or otherwise dispose of any *res mancipi*.

45 Buckland (1966) 94 and references there.

46 Impallomeni (1963) ch. 3.

47 Val. Max. 7.8.2; though Valerius does not use the word, he says that

the mother's will was *plenae furoris*, 'full of madness', obviously with
the *querela inofficiosi testamenti* in mind.
48 Gardner (1986) 198–200.
49 Cretney (1984) 99–101.
50 *D.* 24.2.4, 24.3.22.9.
51 Gardner (1986) 11 and 86, against Corbett (1930) 242. I am less inclined
now to accept Corbett's view (p. 241) that a *filiusfamilias* could divorce
independently in classical law. As for the text which he cites, *CJ* 5.17.12,
to show that the law for some time before Justinian had permitted
children to divorce against the will of their parents, this in fact shows
precisely the opposite.
52 *D.* 23.3.39.1; Dalla (1978) 233–46.

7 CONCLUSION: THE FACE-TO-FACE SOCIETY

1 See especially Thomas (1989) 15–94; Hansen (1991) 311–12.
2 Texts of the Transylvanian Tablets may be most conveniently consulted
in *FIRA* iii, nos 87–90, 120, 122–3, 125, 150 and 157. Some are translated
and discussed in Crook (1967); see his index s.v.
3 So Tilly (1973) 241.
4 *D.* 22.3, *de probationibus et praesumptionibus* ('On proofs and pre-
sumptions'); 4, *de fide instrumentorum et amissione eorum* ('On the
reliance to be placed upon documents, and on their loss'); 5, *de testibus*
('On witnesses'); *CJ* 4.19, *de probationibus* ('On proofs'); 20, *de testibus*
('On witnesses'); 21, *de fide instrumentorum et amissione eorum et
antapochis faciendis et de his quae sine scriptura fieri possunt* ('On the
reliance to be placed upon documents and their loss, and the making
of written statements (that a debt has been paid) and on those things
which can be done without writing'); 22, *plus valere quod agitur quam
quod simulate concipitur* ('Action, rather than a pretence of action, is
what counts'). *Apocha* was a written receipt from a creditor (*D.*
12.6.67.3 (Scaevola); 46.4.19 (Julian); 47.2.27 (Ulpian)), confirming that
payment had been received, *antapocha* a corresponding document from
the other party, confirming that payment had been made. Justinian in
AD 529 (*CJ* 4.21.19) writes to the praetorian prefect of the East that,
to avoid subsequent disputes, creditors should be at liberty to require
that their debtors either sign a copy of the receipt given them, or supply
an *antapocha*, though failure to do so should not be to the creditors'
prejudice. The same was to apply also in cases of *coloni* claiming
freedom from claims alleged by their *domini*. This text is most readily
comprehensible if we assume that it refers to payments made, or alleged
to be made, in partial, rather than final, settlement of an obligation.
Despite its rubric, the single title in the Theodosian Code (11.39), *de
fide testium et instrumentorum* ('On the reliability of witnesses and
documents'), is mainly concerned with the question of where the
burden of proof should lie.
5 See Gardner (1986a) and Watson (1973–4). In *CJ* 5.4.9, discussed by
Watson, a similar answer is given by Probus to a certain Fortunatus,
who is worried about the lack of documentary evidence for his marriage

and the legitimate birth of his daughter. Gardner p. 12 n. 66 explicitly disagrees with Kaser (1971) 231, who held that written evidence was in general merely declaratory, but was constitutive when specifically required, as for contracts and wills.

6 Paul (*D.* 22.4.1) adopts a different usage. Everything, he says, which can back up a case is to be accepted as *instrumenta*, and this applies, he says, both to *testimonia* and to *personae*. Here *testimonia* seems to mean documentary attestation, in contrast to *personae*, direct personal witness.

7 Even in post-classical law, although we find Justinian insisting (*CJ* 4.21.17) that documents (which may be either privately prepared and signed by the parties, or prepared by official scribes, *tabelliones*) be produced for certain contractual agreements to have any force, within two years (*CJ* 4.21.20) he has retreated to acknowledging the necessity of what is almost classical practice, that is having the documents witnessed initially (three witnesses are apparently regarded as enough), and then calling upon these witnesses personally to acknowledge their hands (or else having their handwriting independently vouched for by comparison with other writing of theirs). This is to treat other documents like wills, for which Roman law continued to insist on witnesses, and also usually on writing (though writing might exceptionally be dispensed with: *CJ* 6.23.21.4, AD 439).

8 By a 'private' *testatio* he apparently means an unwitnessed written declaration.

9 The defendant is told to use *instrumenta* and *argumenta*.

10 See especially the texts cited in Gardner (1986a) pp. 4, 7–8.

11 Lévy (1987) spec. 479 ff.

12 Callistratus: *D.* 22.5.3, a text already mentioned above in the discussion of *infamia*. Julian: *C.Th.* 11.39.3.

13 Whether or not one believes in the continuing exclusion from citizenship of certain communities within the empire, as *dediticii*: see Sherwin-White (1973) 279–87, 380–93.

14 Jones (1964) 16–18; de Ste Croix (1981) 454–62; Alföldy (1985) 176–85.

15 e.g. Gaius 1.55, 2.40, 3.93.

16 But effectively no later than 1932.

17 *Tabula Contrebiensis*: Richardson (1983); Birks, Rodger and Richardson (1984). *Lex Irnitana*: Gonzalez (1986).

18 This was the description used by Professor Richardson (previous note) in 'The reception of Roman law in Spain: the evidence of recent epigraphic discoveries', unpublished seminar paper delivered at Institute of Classical Studies, London, March 1992.

19 In this I agree with Millar (1977) 485–6, 630–5, and Fear (1990).

20 It is worth bearing in mind that, at least until the late 2nd century AD (Chapter 2, n. 56 above), no fewer than seven Roman citizens would have to be mistaken or perjured as to the status of a *peregrinus* before he could successfully complete a *mancipatio* (Gaius 1.119).

21 Besides those already mentioned, one might cite e.g. the praetorian rules of *c.* AD 130 requiring numerous witnesses to the pregnancy and

parturition of a divorcée or widow, if her child's claim to its alleged
father's estate was to be recognised: *D*. 25.3 and 4; Gardner (1984).
22 Gardner (1986a) 2–4.
23 A concern for stability and the avoidance of unecessary disruption may
been seen in the introduction by Hadrian of a 'statute of limitations',
forbidding enquiry into status once five years had elapsed after the
death of the person in question (*D*. 40.15; *CJ* 7.21).

BIBLIOGRAPHY

Alföldy, G. (1972) 'Die Freilassung von Sklaven und die Struktur der Sklaverei in der römischen Kaiserzeit', *RSA* 2, 97–129 = Alföldy (1986) 286–331 (with additional discussion).
—— (1985) *The Social History of Rome*, London.
—— (1986) *Die römische Gesellschaft*, Stuttgart.
Amirante, L. (1981) 'Sulla schiavitù nella Roma antica', *Labeo* 27, 26–33.
Andreau, J. (1974) *Les Affaires de Monsieur Jucundus*, Rome.
—— (1987) *La Vie financière dans le monde romain: les métiers de manieurs d'argent*, Rome.
Arangio Ruiz, L. (1948) 'Il processo di Giusta', *PdP* 8, 129–51.
—— (1959) 'Testi e documenti IV – Tavolette Ercolanesi (il processo de Giusta)', *BIDR* 62, 223–5.
Arjava, A. (forthcoming) *Women and Law in Late Antiquity*.
Atkinson, K. M. T. (1966) 'The purpose of the manumission laws of Augustus', *Irish Jurist* n.s. 1, 356–74.
Balestri Fumagalli, M. (1985) *Lex Julia de Manumissionibus*, Milan.
Balsdon, J. P. V. D. (1979) *Romans and Aliens*, London.
Beaucamp, J. (1976) 'Le vocabulaire de la faiblesse féminine dans les textes juridiques romains du IIIᵉ au VIᵉ siècle', *RHD* 54, 485–509.
Birks, P., Rodger, A. and Richardson, J. S. (1984) 'Further aspects of the *Tabula Contrebiensis*', *JRS* 74, 45–73.
Bove, L. (1967) 'Due iscrizioni da Pozzuoli e Cuma', *Labeo* 13, 22–48.
—— (1979) *Documenti Processuali dalle Tabulae Pompeianae di Murecine*, Naples.
—— (1984a) *Documenti di operazioni finanzarie dall' archivio dei Sulpici*, Naples.
—— (1984b) 'Les Tabulae Pompeianae di Murecine', *RHDFE* 62, 537–52.
Bradley, K. R. (1987) 'On the Roman slave supply and slavebreeding', in M. I. Finley (ed.) *Classical Slavery*, London.
—— (1991) 'Remarriage and the structure of the upper-class Roman family', in B. Rawson, (ed.) *Marriage, Divorce and Children in Ancient Rome*, Oxford, 79–98.
Broughton, T. R. S. (1951) *The Magistrates of the Roman Republic*, New York.

BIBLIOGRAPHY

Brunt, P. A. (1971) *Italian Manpower*, Oxford.
—— (1988) *The Fall of the Roman Republic*, Oxford.
Buckland, W. W. (1908) *The Roman Law of Slavery*, Cambridge.
—— (1966) *A Text-book of Roman Law*, Cambridge.
Camodeca, G. (1983–4) 'Per una riedizione dell' archivio Puteolano dei Sulpicii', *Puteoli vii-viii*, 3–69.
—— (1985–6) 'Per una riedizione dell' archivio Puteolano dei Sulpicii', *Puteoli ix-x*, 3–40.
Canto, A. M. (1991) '*CIL* VI 10229. ¿El testamento de Licinio Sura?', *Chiron* 21, 277–324.
Champlin, E. (1986) '*Miscellanea Testamentaria*', *ZPE* 62, 247–55.
—— (1991) *Final Judgments: Duty and Emotion in Roman Wills 200 BC-AD 250*, Berkeley.
Chantraine, H. (1972) 'Zur Entstehung der Freilassung mit Bürgerrechtserwerb in Rom', *ANRW* I.2, 59–67.
Cloud, J. D. (1971) '*Parricidium*: from the *lex Numae* to the *lex Pompeia de parricidiis*', *ZSS* 101, 1–66.
Cohen, D. (1991) *Law, Sexuality and Society: The Enforcement of Morals in Classical Athens*, Cambridge.
Corbett, P.E. (1930) *The Roman Law of Marriage*, Oxford.
Cosentini, C. (1948) *Studi su Liberti*, vol. i, Catania.
Cretney, S. M. (1984) *Principles of Family Law*, 4th edn, London.
Crook, J. A. (1967) *Law and Life of Rome*, London.
—— (1976) '*Sponsione provocare*: its place in Roman litigation', *JRS* 66, 132–8.
—— (1978) 'Working notes on some of the new Pompeii tablets', *ZPE* 29, 229–39.
—— (1986) 'Feminine inadequacy and the Senatusconsultum Velleianum', in B. Rawson (ed.) *The Family in Ancient Rome*, London, 83–92.
—— (1989) = Wolf, J. G., and Crook, J. A. (1989) *Rechtsurkunden in Vulgarlatein aus den Jahren 37–39 n. Chr.*, Heidelberg.
Dalla, D. (1978) *L'incapacità sessuale in diritto romano*, Milan.
—— (1987) '*Ubi Venus mutatur*': omosessualità e diritto nel mondo romano, Milan.
Daube, D. (1946) 'Two early patterns of manumission'. *JRS* 36, 57–75.
—— (1969) *Roman Law: Linguistic, Social and Philosophical Aspects*, Edinburgh.
de Francisci, P. (1926) '*Revocatio in servitutem*', in *Mélanges P. Cornil*, Paris, 295–323.
de Martino, F. (1974) 'Intorno all' origine della schiavitù a Roma', *Labeo* 20, 163–93 (= *Diritto e Società nell' antica Roma*, Rome 1961, 130–61).
Demougin, S. (1988) *L'Ordre équestre sous les Julio-Claudiens*, Rome.
de Ste Croix, G. E. M. (1981) *The Class Struggle in the Ancient Greek World*, London.
Dixon, S. (1984) '*Infirmitas sexus*: womanly weakness in Roman law', *TRG* 52, 343–71.
—— (1988) *The Roman Mother*, London.
d'Ors, A. (1984) 'Un nueva lista de acciones infamantes', *Sodalitas* (Scritti Guarino) 6, 2575–90.

233

Drummond, A. (1989) 'Rome in the fifth century I: the economic frame-
work', and 'Rome in the fifth century II: the citizen community', in
F. W. Walbank, A. E. Astin, M. W. Frederiksen, R. M. Ogilvie (eds)
The Cambridge Ancient History, VII.2, 2nd edn, Cambridge, 113–71,
172–242.
Duff, A. M. (1958) *Freedmen in the Early Roman Empire*, Cambridge.
Dumont, J. C. (1987) *Servus: Rome et l'esclavage sous la république*,
Rome.
Eck, W. (1978) 'Zum neuen Fragment des sogenannten *testamentum
Dasumii*', *ZPE* 30, 277–95.
Edwards, C. (forthcoming) 'Unspeakable professions: public performance
and prostitution in ancient Rome'.
Engels, F. (1891) *The Origin of the Family, Private Property and the
State*, 4th edn, Moscow.
Evans, J. K. (1991) *War, Women and Children in Ancient Rome*, London.
Eyben, E. (1991) 'Fathers and sons', in B. Rawson, (ed.) *Marriage, Div-
orce and Children in Ancient Rome*, Oxford, 114–43.
Fabre, G. (1981) *Libertus: recherches sur les rapports patron–affranchi à
la fin de la république romaine*, Rome.
Fear, A. T. (1990) '*Cives Latini, servi publici* and the *lex Irnitana*', *RIDA*
37, 149–66.
Frier, B. (1980) *Landlords and Tenants in Imperial Rome*, Princeton.
—— (1982) 'Roman life expectancy: Ulpian's evidence', *HSCP* 86, 1–13.
—— (1983) 'Roman life expectancy: the Pannonian evidence', *Phoenix*
37, 328–44.
—— (1989) *A Casebook on the Roman Law of Delict*, Atlanta.
Gardner, J. F. (1984) 'A family and an inheritance: the problems of the
widow Petronilla', *LCM* 9, 132–3.
—— (1986) *Women in Roman Law and Society*, London.
—— (1986a) 'Proofs of status in the Roman world', *BICS* 33, 1–14.
—— (1987) 'Another family and an inheritance: Claudius Brasidas and
his ex-wife's will', *LCM* 12.4, 52–4.
—— (1989) 'The adoption of Roman freedmen', *Phoenix* 43, 236–57.
—— (1991) 'The purpose of the lex Fufia Caninia', *EMC/Classical Views*,
34 (n.s. 10), 21–39.
Garnsey, P. D. (1970) *Social Status and Legal Privilege in the Roman
Empire*, Oxford.
—— (1981) 'Independent freedmen and the economy of Roman Italy
under the principate', *Klio* 63, 359–71.
—— and Saller, R. (1987) *The Roman Empire: Economy, Society and
Culture*, London.
Genovese, E. (1976) *Roll, Jordan, Roll*, New York.
Girard, P. F. (1911) *Manuel élémentaire de droit romain*, Paris.
Gonzalez, J. (1986) 'The *Lex Irnitana*: a new copy of the Flavian munici-
pal law', *JRS* 76, 147–243.
Greenidge, A. J. H. (1894) *Infamia: Its Place in Roman Public and
Private Law*, Oxford.
—— (1901) *The Legal Procedure of Cicero's Time*, Oxford.

Guadagno, G. (1977) 'Frammenti inediti di albi degli Augustali', *Cronache Ercolanesi* 7, 114–23.

Hallett, J. P. (1984) *Fathers and Daughters in Roman Society: Women and the Elite Family*, Princeton.

Halperin, D. M., Winkler, J. J., and Zeitlin, F. (1990) *Before Sexuality: The Construction of Erotic Experience in the Ancient Greek World*, Princeton.

Hansen, M. H. (1991) *The Athenian Democracy in the Age of Demosthenes*, Oxford.

Harris, W. V. (1980) 'Towards a study of the Roman slave trade', in J.H. D'Arms and E.C. Kopff (eds) *The Seaborne Commerce of Ancient Rome*, *MAAR* XXXVI, Rome, 117–40.

—— (1986) 'The Roman father's power of life and death', in R. S. Bagnall and W. V. Harris, *Studies in Roman Law in Memory of A. Arthur Schiller*, Leiden, 81–95.

Hinard, F. (1976) 'Remarques sur les *praecones* et le *praeconium* dans la Rome de la fin de la République', *Latomus* 35, 730–46.

—— (1990) 'Solidarités familiales et ruptures à l'époque des guerres civiles et de la proscription', in J. Andreau and H. Bruhns (eds) *Parenté et stratégies familiales dans l'antiquité romaine*, Paris and Rome, 555–70.

Hopkins, K. (1978) *Conquerors and Slaves*, Cambridge.

—— (1983) *Death and Renewal*, Cambridge.

Humbert, M. (1972) *Le Remariage à Rome*, Milan.

—— (1981) 'Le droit latin impérial: cités latines ou citoyenneté latine?', *Ktema* 6, 207–26.

Impallomeni, G. (1963) *Le manomissioni mortis causa*, Padua.

Jones, A. H. M. (1964) *The Later Roman Empire 284–602*, Oxford.

—— (1972) *The Criminal Courts of the Roman Republic and Principate*, Oxford.

—— (1974) *The Roman Economy*, Oxford.

Jory, E. J. (1970) 'Associations of actors in Rome', *Hermes* 98, 223–36.

Kaser, M. (1956) 'Infamia und Ignominia in den römischen Rechtsquellen', *ZSS* 73, 220–78.

—— (1966) *Das römische Zivilprozessrecht*, Munich.

—— (1971) *Das römische Privatrecht*, 2nd edn, Munich.

Kelly, J. M. (1971) *Roman Litigation*, Oxford.

—— (1976) *Studies in the Civil Judicature of the Roman Republic*, Oxford.

Kirschenbaum, A. (1987) *Sons, Slaves and Freedmen in Roman Commerce*, Jerusalem and Washington.

Kolbert, C. F. (1979) *Justinian: The Digest of Roman Law: Theft, Rapine, Damage and Insult*, Penguin Classics, Harmondsworth.

Kunkel, W. (1962) *Untersuchungen zur Entwicklung des römischen Kriminalverfahrens im vorsullanischer Zeit*, Munich.

—— (1966) 'Das Konsilium im Hausgericht', *ZSS* 83, 219–51.

—— (1973) *An Introduction to Roman Legal and Constitutional History* (tr. J. M. Kelly), 2nd edn, Oxford.

Lacey, W. K. (1986) '*Patria potestas*', in B. Rawson (ed.) *The Family in Ancient Rome*, London, 145–69.

BEING A ROMAN CITIZEN

Lambert, J. (1934) Les operae liberti: *contribution à l'histoire des droits de patronat* (diss.), Paris.
Landi, A. (1980) 'Richerche sull' onomastica delle tabelle dell' agro Mure- cine: contributo all' onomastica di Puteoli in età imperiale', *Atti dell' Accademia Pontaniana* 29, 175–98.
Lebek, W. D. (1990) 'Standeswürde und Berufsverbot unter Tiberius: das SC der Tabula Larinas', *ZPE* 81, 37–96.
Lenel, O. (1927) *Das Edictum Perpetuum*, 3rd edn, Leipzig.
Levick, B. (1983) 'The *Senatus Consultum* from Larinum', *JRS* 73, 97–115.
Lévy, J.-Ph. (1987) 'Coup d'oeil d'ensemble sur l'histoire de la preuve littérale', *Index* 15, 473–501.
Lintott, A. W. (1968) *Violence in Republican Rome*, Oxford.
MacDowell, D. M. (1978) *The Law in Classical Athens*, London.
MacMullen, R. (1974) *Roman Social Relations*, New Haven and London.
Macqueron, J. (1984) 'En relisant les quittances de Pompeii', *Sodalitas* (Scritti Guarino) 7, 3593–3603.
Maine, H. S. (1861, repr. 1986) *Ancient Law*, New York.
Manning, C. (1986) '*Actio ingrati* (Seneca *De Benef*. 3.6–17: a contri- bution to contemporary debate?)', *SDHI* 52, 61–72.
Marshall, A. J. (1990) 'Roman ladies on trial: the case of Maesia of Sentinum', *Phoenix* 44, 46–60.
Masi Doria, C. (1989) 'Die *Societas Rutiliana* und die Ursprünge der prätorischen Erbfolge der Freigelassenen', *ZSS* 106, 358–403.
Mayer-Maly, Th. (1958) 'Das Notsverkaufrecht des Hausvaters', *ZSS* 75, 116–25.
Michel, J.-H. (1962) *La Gratuité en droit romain*, Brussels.
Millar, F. G. B. (1977) *The Emperor in the Roman World*, London.
—— (1983) 'Empire and city, Augustus to Julian: obligations, excuses and status', *JRS* 73, 76–96.
—— (1984) 'Condemnation to hard labour in the Roman empire', *PBSR* 39, 124–47.
—— (1990) 'L'empereur romain comme décideur', in C. Nicolet (ed.) *Du pouvoir dans l'antiquité: mots et réalités* (Cahiers du Centre Glotz I), Geneva, 207–20.
Mitchell, R. E. (1990) *Patricians and Plebeians: The Origins of the Roman State*, Ithaca and London.
Moreau, P. (1983) 'À propos du sénatus-consulte épigraphique de Lari- num', *REL* 61, 36–48.
Nardi, E. (1983) *Squilibrio e deficienza mentale in diritto romano*, Milan.
Nicholas, B. (1969) *An Introduction to Roman Law*, 3rd edn, Oxford.
Nicolet, C. (1980) *The World of the Citizen in Republican Rome* (tr. P. S. Falla), London.
Noy, D. (1988) 'The *Senatusconsultum Gaetulicianum*: manus and inheri- tance', *TRG* 56, 299
Pommeray, L. (1937) *Études sur l'infamie en droit romain*, Paris.
Pugliese Carratelli, G. (1948) 'Testi e documenti: Tabulae Herculanenses II', *PdP* 8, 164–84.
Purcell, N. (1983) 'The *apparitores*: a study in social mobility', *PBSR* 51, 125–73.

BIBLIOGRAPHY

Raaflaub, K. A. (ed.) (1986) *Social Struggles in Archaic Rome*, California.

Rabello, A. M. (1979) *Effetti personali della patria potestas I: dalle origini al periodo degli Antonini*, Milan.

Rauh, N. K. (1989) 'Auctioneers and the Roman economy', *Historia* 38, 451–71.

Renier, E. (1950) 'Observations sur la terminologie de l'aliénation mentale', *RIDA* 3 (= *Mélanges de Visscher* IV) 429–55.

Rice Holmes, T. (1928) *The Architect of the Roman Empire*, Oxford.

Richardson, J. S. (1983) 'The *Tabula Contrebiensis*: Roman law in Spain in the early first century BC', *JRS* 73, 33–41.

Rilinger, R. (1988) *Humiliores–Honestiores: zu einer sozialen Dichotomie im Strafrecht der römischen Kaiserzeit*, Munich.

Rogers, G. M. (1992) 'The constructions of women at Ephesos', *ZPE* 90, 215–23.

Sacks, K.(1974) 'Engels revisited: women, the organisation of production and private property', in M. Z. Rosaldo and L. Lamphere, *Woman, Culture and Society*, Stanford, 207–22.

Saller, R. (1982) *Personal Patronage under the early Empire*, Cambridge.

—— (1986) '*Patria Potestas* and the stereotype of the Roman family', *Continuity and Change* 1, 7–22.

—— (1987) 'Men's age at marriage and its consequences in the Roman family', *C. Phil.* 82, 21–34.

—— (1991) 'Corporal punishment, authority and obedience in the Roman household', in B. Rawson (ed.) *Marriage, Divorce and Children in Ancient Rome*, Oxford, 144–65.

Saumagne, C. (1965) *Le Droit latin et les cités romaines sous l'empire*, Paris.

Schulz, F. (1936) *Principles of Roman Law*, Oxford.

—— (1946) *History of Roman Legal Science*, Oxford.

—— (1951) *Classical Roman Law*, Oxford.

Serrao, F. (1984) 'Minima di Diogneto et Hesicho: gli affari de due schiavi a Pozzuoli negli anni 30 d.C.', *Sodalitas* (Scritti Guarino) 7, 3605–18.

Shatzman, I. (1975) *Senatorial Wealth and Roman Politics*, Brussels.

Shaw, B. (1987) 'The age of Roman girls at marriage: some reconsiderations', *JRS* 77, 30–46.

Sherwin-White, A. N. (1973) *The Roman Citizenship*, 2nd edn, Oxford.

Sirks, A. J. B. (1983) 'The *lex Junia* and the effects of informal manumission and iteration', *RIDA* 30, 211–92.

Solazzi, S. (1930) '*Infirmitas aetatis e infirmitas sexus*', *Archivio Giuridico* 104, 3–33.

Stambaugh, J. E. (1988) *The Ancient Roman City*, Baltimore.

Thomas, R. (1989) *Oral Tradition and Written Record in Classical Athens*, Cambridge.

Thomas, Y. (1981) 'Parricidium I: le père, la famille et la cité', *MEFRA* 93, 643–713.

—— (1982) 'Droit domestique et droit politique à Rome: remarques sur le pécule et les *honores* des fils de famille', *MEFRA* 94, 527–80.

Tilly, B. (1973) *Varro the Farmer: A Selection from the Res Rusticae*, London.

Treggiari, S. M. (1969) *Roman Freedmen during the Late Republic*, Oxford.

—— (1979) 'Lower class women in the Roman economy', *Florilegium* 1, 65–86.

—— (1991) *Roman Marriage: Iusti Coniuges from the Time of Cicero to the Time of Ulpian*, Oxford.

van Bremen, R. (1983) 'Women and wealth', in A. Cameron and A. Kuhrt (eds) *Images of Women in Antiquity*, London, 223–42.

van Warmelo, P. (1954) *'Ignorantia iuris'*, *TRG* 22, 1–32.

Veyne, P. (1961) 'Vie de Trimalchio', *Annales ESC* 16, 213–47.

—— (1978) 'La famille et l'amour sous le Haut-Empire romain', *Annales ESC* 33, 35–63.

—— (1987) 'The household and its freed slaves', in P. Veyne (ed.) *A History of Private Life, I: From Pagan Rome to Byzantium* (tr. A. Goldhammer), Cambridge, Mass., 71–95.

Ville, G. (1981) *La Gladiature en occident des origines à la mort de Domitien*, Paris.

Voci, P. (1980) 'Storia della *patria potestas* da Augusto a Diocleziano', *Iura* 31, 37–100.

Waldstein, W. (1986) Operae Libertorum: *Untersuchungen zur Dienstpflicht freigelassener Sklaven*, Stuttgart.

Wallace-Hadrill, A. F. (1989) 'Patronage in Roman society: from republic to empire', in A. F. Wallace-Hadrill (ed.) *Patronage in Ancient Society*, Oxford, 63–87.

Watson, A. (1961) *The Contract of Mandate in Roman Law*, Oxford.

—— (1967) *The Roman Law of Persons*, Oxford.

—— (1971) *Roman Private Law around 200 BC*, Edinburgh.

—— (1971a) *The Law of Succession in the Later Roman Republic*, Oxford.

—— (1973) 'Private law in the rescripts of Carus, Carinus and Numerianus', *TRG* 41, 19–34.

—— (1973–4) 'The rescripts of the emperor Probus 276–282 AD', *Tulane Law Review* 48, 1122–8.

—— (1974) *'Enuptio gentis'*, in A. Watson (ed.) *Daube Noster*, Edinburgh, 331–41.

—— (1975) *Rome of the XII Tables: Persons and Property*, Princeton.

—— (1977) *Society and Legal Change*, Edinburgh.

—— (1987) *Roman Slave Law*, Baltimore.

Weaver, P. (1990) 'Where have all the Junian Latins gone? Nomenclature and status in the Roman empire', *Chiron* 20, 275–305.

Westrup, C. (1939) *Introduction to Early Roman Law*, London and Copenhagen.

Wiedemann, T. E. J. (1985) 'The regularity of manumission at Rome', *CQ* 35, 162–75.

—— (1989) *Adults and Children in the Roman Empire*, London.

—— (1992) *Emperors and Gladiators*, London.

Winkler, J. (1989) *The Constraints of Desire: The Anthropology of Sex and Gender in Ancient Greece*, London and New York.

Wiseman T. P. (1971) *New Men in the Roman Senate 139 BC–AD 14*, Oxford.

—— (1985) *Catullus and his World*, Cambridge.

—— (1987) *Roman Studies*, Liverpool.

Wolf, J. G., and Crook, J. A. (1989) *Rechtsurkunden in Vulgarlatein aus den Jahren 37–39 n. Chr.*, Heidelberg.

INDEX